MORE DR. SEUSS AND PHILOSOPHY

MORE DR. SEUSS
AND PHILOSOPHY

Additional Hunches in Bunches

Edited by Jacob M. Held

ROWMAN & LITTLEFIELD
Lanham • Boulder • New York • London

Published by Rowman & Littlefield
A wholly owned subsidiary of The Rowman & Littlefield Publishing Group, Inc.
4501 Forbes Boulevard, Suite 200, Lanham, Maryland 20706
www.rowman.com

Unit A, Whitacre Mews, 26-34 Stannary Street, London SE11 4AB

Distributed by NATIONAL BOOK NETWORK

British Library Cataloguing in Publication Information Available

Library of Congress Cataloging-in-Publication Data

Names: Held, Jacob M., 1977– editor.
Title: More Dr. Seuss and philosophy : additional hunches in bunches / edited by Jacob M. Held.
Description: Lanham : Rowman & Littlefield, 2018. | Includes bibliographical references and index.
Identifiers: LCCN 2017051584 (print) | LCCN 2017060453 (ebook) | ISBN 9781538101346 (electronic) | ISBN 9781538101339 (pbk. : alk. paper)
Subjects: LCSH: Seuss, Dr.—Criticism and interpretation. | Philosophy in literature. | Children's
    stories, American—History and criticism.
Classification: LCC PS3513.E2 (ebook) | LCC PS3513.E2 Z784 2018 (print) | DDC 813/.52—dc23
LC record available at https://lccn.loc.gov/2017051584

♾ ™ The paper used in this publication meets the minimum requirements of
American National Standard for Information Sciences Permanence of Paper for
Printed Library Materials, ANSI/NISO Z39.48-1992.

Printed in the United States of America

This book is dedicated to my *favorite* child.

CONTENTS

PART III: THEM!

PART IV: US!

PREFACE

Contrary to appearances, this book is not a proper sequel to *Dr. Seuss and Philosophy: Oh, the Thinks You Can Think!* Rather, this book is an alternative vision of what that book might have been. When I first conceived *Dr. Seuss and Philosophy*, I had no home for it. Editors and presses I'd previously worked for were not interested. I shopped it around, sending proposals and emails to presses that I believed would be receptive. I found Jon Sisk and his colleagues at Rowman & Littlefield, and they agreed to gamble on the book. But they were clear: they were not interested in a series. The book was to be a one-time deal. So I put together a conservative project, an introduction to philosophy using the works of Dr. Seuss as a vehicle. It wouldn't be a random collection of essays that just happened to all discuss Dr. Seuss in some fashion; it would be intentionally structured as an introduction to main themes and topics in the history of philosophy. To make sure it was done well, I reached out to my small circle of trusted colleagues to find a full complement of authors. Where I couldn't find an author, I wrote the chapter. The book took shape and turned out quite well. I was pleased. But there were chapters and ideas that weren't written or developed for various reasons. But that first Seuss book was produced to be a general introduction to philosophy through Dr. Seuss.

There was another way it could have all gone: the book could have been a guidebook to living an examined, flourishing life, structured to intentionally walk the reader through philosophy with me, the editor, as a guide. As the years have worn on since the first book was published, more and more it's this version of the book I've wanted to see produced. Then circumstances started to line up. The first book was successful.[1] My publisher was interested in more books, even a series.[2] And we've had a successful, collaborative working relationship for several years. And then, finally, I got the email: "Would you be interested in doing a second Seuss book?" Yes, I would.

The first book was good, but I'd had an alternative idea all along, and it wasn't until recently that I felt comfortable with trying to pull it off. I've done enough academically, with truly brilliant and amazing people, to have fantastic authors willing to collaborate with me and help bring this alternative vision to life. So here's my alternative version of the Seuss book. Not a sequel, but rather a "could've been" that I was able to make a "finally is." A second chance to do it the other way.

More Dr. Seuss and Philosophy is intended to be a handbook for living well, one that uses Dr. Seuss's works as a common narrative or touchstone for readers. The book is intentionally structured to walk the reader through issues pertaining to living well as an individual, in relation to others, and as a member of society. It opens with chapters on the value of literature and imagination to focus the reader's attention on the fact that in reading Seuss you are already beginning your journey of self-discovery and considering issues fundamental to living a praiseworthy life. Some of these authors have an agenda—they are promoting a viewpoint, one echoed in Seuss even if not intentionally Seuss's—and the book has an agenda to promote a way of living: a reflective, engaged, humane life. I've intentionally invited and included each of these authors for the purpose of writing what they wrote. They're the best. This edited book is the result of many minds coming together for a common purpose, to present to you the best of philosophy in an accessible format as a handbook to life's journey. But your mountain is waiting, so get on your way!

EDITOR'S NOTE

Many of Dr. Seuss's works are not paginated, which can make citing them tricky. Luckily, the books are quite short, so if anyone wants to know on what page a reference occurs, they merely have to flip through until they find it. So, in order to make things simpler and to avoid vast amounts of endnotes, all references to Seuss's works will be parenthetical according to the key below. All works are published by Random House.

The 500 Hats of Bartholomew Cubbins (Hats)
And to Think That I Saw It on Mulberry Street (Mulberry)
Bartholomew and the Oobleck (Oobleck)
The Butter Battle Book (Butter)
The Cat in the Hat (Cat)
Did I Ever Tell You How Lucky You Are? (Lucky)
Fox in Socks (Fox)
"Gertrude McFuzz" in *Yertle the Turtle and Other Stories* (McFuzz)
Green Eggs and Ham (Eggs)
Happy Birthday to You! (Birthday)
"Horton and the Kwuggerbug" in *Horton and the Kwuggerbug and More Lost Stories* (Kwuggerbug)
Horton Hatches the Egg (Hatches)
Horton Hears a Who! (Horton)
How the Grinch Stole Christmas! (Grinch)
Hunches in Bunches (Hunches)
I Had Trouble in Getting to Solla Sollew (Trouble)
If I Ran the Circus (Circus)

If I Ran the Zoo (Zoo)
The Lorax (Lorax)
McElligot's Pool (Pool)
Oh, the Places You'll Go! (Places)
Oh, the Thinks You Can Think! (Thinks)
On Beyond Zebra! (Zebra)
One Fish, Two Fish, Red Fish, Blue Fish (Fish)
Scrambled Eggs Super! (Scrambled)
The Shape of Me and Other Stuff (Shape)
The Sleep Book (Sleep)
The Sneetches in *The Sneetches and Other Stories* (Sneetches)
Thidwick the Big-Hearted Moose (Thidwick)
"What Was I Scared Of?" in *The Sneetches and Other Stories* (Scared)
Yertle the Turtle in *Yertle the Turtle and Other Stories* (Yertle)
You're Only Old Once! (Old)
"The Zax" in *The Sneetches and Other Stories* (Zax)

Part I

Welcome!

Welcome! Hello! I'm so glad that you've come!
It's time for philosophy, rhyming, and fun!
You're just starting out with the opening pages,
Preparing to read the first two of our sages.

They'll talk about reason, truth, knowledge, and also
Our hopes and our dreams, all the places our minds go.
They'll talk about cats, hats, and jokes that are funny,
Why humor is needful when life gets too glummy.

On beyond evidence, logic, and fact
There's a world of "what ifs" far beyond that.
Philosophy isn't just all about proving
We also believe, hope, and trust to keep moving
Beyond where we are, toward a marvelous place,
Our dreams, which can't quite be located in space.
Our dreams, far beyond this world so mundane.
Our dreams, so essential to keep us all sane.

Philosophy offers a whole new perspective
A critical, thoughtful, reflective directive:
Think without limits, on beyond you!

Stay grounded. Remember, you're bound by what's true!
The world is quite vast, and you are quite small
So don't get discouraged, you can't know it all!
Do your best, make mistakes, you'll figure it out,
For thinking-type people there'll always be doubt.
Just remember that those who do matter, don't mind,
So long as in life you are thoughtful and kind!

I

ON BEYOND REASON

Dr. Seuss and the Romantic Imagination

Glenn Jellenik

If a man could pass through Paradise in a dream, and have a flower presented to him as a pledge that his soul had really been there, and if he found that flower in his hand when he awoke—Aye! and what then?
—Samuel Taylor Coleridge[1]

'Cause you never can tell
What goes on down below!
This pool *might* be bigger
Than you or I know!

—Dr. Seuss, *McElligot's Pool*

What makes humans so adaptable, so able to thrive in various environments? For evolutionary biologists, the answer is evident—to paraphrase Dr. Seuss, we have brains in our heads. Put simply, our large brains enable us to develop language, progressive technology, and abstract thought. Evolutionary historian Yuval Noah Harari uses that scientific premise to pivot toward a more philosophical argument about how, specifically, our big brains make us different than other species; according to Harari, we are "the only animal that can believe in things that exist purely in [our] own imagination, such as gods, states, money and human rights."[2] Our imagination positions us to thrive because it allows us to construct, communicate, and collectively accept a stream of enabling fictions. In short, we alone in the animal kingdom possess the capacity to live in and through imagination; we alone have the ability to transform the abstract into the real.

Of course, evolutionary biologists and historians are a little late to the party on this one. Since the Enlightenment, philosophers and poets have positioned the imagination as integral to our understanding and processing of knowledge and the world. Specifically, late eighteenth- and early nineteenth-century poets such as William Wordsworth, Samuel Taylor Coleridge, and Percy Bysshe Shelley developed an evolving philosophical theory of poetry that highlighted the constructive capacity of the imagination. Despite the fact that he began publishing his books more than one hundred years after the end of the Romantic period, Seuss functions as a philosophical ancestor of Romanticism's engagement with imagination. From his first book (*And to Think That I Saw It on Mulberry Street* [1937]) to his last (*Oh, the Places You'll Go!* [1991]), he demonstrates the powers of imagination and develops a progressive concept of its creative potential. As Seuss's work evolves, it pushes on beyond reason in order to sketch out an argument for imagination's capacity to productively construct reality.

THE KANTIAN (PROTO-ROMANTIC) IMAGINATION

Immanuel Kant's *Critique of Pure Reason* (1781) represents an early Romantic-period attempt to account for the ways in which human knowledge "may strive *independently of all experience*."[3] That is, in the midst of the systematic rise of science and reason, Kant shifts the foundations and limits of epistemology away from the British-Empiricist (namely, Hume) notions that rely on the empirical by dividing knowledge into two "stems": "*sensibility* and *understanding*. . . . Through the former, objects are given to us; through the latter, they are thought."[4] Thus, the stems of *sensibility* and *understanding* generally correspond to empirical knowledge (sensation), which we experience in the world, and conceptual knowledge (the positing and ordering of sensation), which exists in our mind a priori. From there, Kant extrapolates "pure" knowledge, which also exists in the mind—but rather than merely invert empiricism and exist as the result of *understanding*, "pure" knowledge is produced through a synthesis of *sensibility* and *understanding*, the combination of empirical and a priori knowledge. Importantly, that synthesis is enabled by imagination: "Synthesis in general . . . is the mere result of the power of imagination, a blind but indispensable function of the soul, without which we would have no knowledge whatsoever, but of which we are scarcely ever conscious."[5]

Kant posits imagination as the center of our thought-existence; it synthesizes/structures/constructs all knowledge. Yet he stops short of positioning it as a thing in and of itself. For Kant, synthesis is not *produced* directly by imagination; rather, it comes into being passively, as a sort of by-product, "the mere result of the power of imagination." And he further abstracts and muddies the process by modifying it as "blind" and a vague and unconscious "function of the soul." Thus, at the same time that Kant centers the concept of imagination in his system, he scarcely fleshes it out. We can see its vital product—synthesis—but on imagination itself, Kant remains fuzzy. It is essentially a mystery that explains the existence of mystery. According to Milos Rastovic, Kant avoids a clear explanation of imagination "because it is difficult for him . . . to explain synthesis by something as 'irrational' as the imagination."[6]

THE ROMANTIC IMAGINATION

Fortunately, the Romantic poets were scarcely concerned with issues of reason and epistemology and were thus far more comfortable with the irrationality of imagination. The rise of Romanticism (as a poetic construct) came on the heels of Kant's *Critique of Pure Reason*, and it too would center imagination in order to offer a response to the age's overreliance on reason. In *Lyrical Ballads* (1798), William Wordsworth attempted to fuse realism with imagination to construct a poetry that could fill in the considerable gaps left by scientific rationalism. "Expostulation and Reply" presents a rational character who upbraids the poet for spending his day idly dreaming rather than reading. The poet replies that, though he merely sits on a rock appearing idle, his mind is engaged in vital work:

> Nor less I deem that there are Powers
> Which of themselves our minds impress;
> That we can feed this mind of ours
> In a wise passiveness.[7]

In "The Tables Turned," the companion poem to "Expostulation and Reply," Wordsworth treats a further exchange on the same subject between the two men; however, this time it is the poet upbraiding his friend for his attempt to understand and process the world solely through intellect and reason, faculties Wordsworth considers inferior: "Our meddling intellect / Mis-shapes the beauteous forms of things:— / We murder to dissect."[8] The poem ends with a call for synthesizing the world through something beyond intellect.

> Enough of Science and of Art;
> Close up those barren leaves;
> Come forth, and bring with you a heart
> That watches and receives.[9]

Where Kant locates the imagination in the soul, Wordsworth houses it in the heart. Regardless of location, it has the same basic function—to comprehend the "beauteous form of things." Through this lens, Wordsworthian Romanticism functions as a counter-Enlightenment movement, pointing out the movement's failure to account for the considerable mystery that still exists in the world even after science and reason have their say. And Romanticism provides an answer: imagination (specifically, the poetic imagination) can bridge those rivers of uncertainty.

While Wordsworth offered theoretical sublimations of imagination in verse, Coleridge overtly expanded Kant's notions of imagination and carried them forward. Rather than vaguely describe imagination as a "function of the soul," Coleridge centers imagination as that which *produces* perceptions and concepts:

> The Imagination then I consider either as primary, or secondary. The primary Imagination I hold to be the living Power and prime Agent of all human Perception, and as a repetition in the finite mind of the eternal act of creation in the infinite I Am. The secondary I consider as an echo of the former, coexisting with the conscious will, yet still as identical with the primary in the kind of its agency, and differing only in degree, and in the mode of its operation. It dissolves, diffuses, dissipates, in order to recreate or where this process is rendered impossible, yet still at all events it struggles to idealize and to unify. It is essentially vital, even as all objects "as objects" are essentially fixed and dead.[10]

Coleridge replaces Kant's stems of knowledge with the primary and secondary imagination. The primary imagination parallels Kantian *sensibility*—it delivers the empirical world. But that empirical reality is static, "fixed and dead." By implication, "life" stems from the work of the secondary imagination, the "vital" imagination, which simultaneously functions as Kant's *understanding* and synthesizing imagination. The Coleridgian secondary imagination refers to our ability to transcend experience and reassemble perceptual elements to create new meaning.

The physical world—what we experience empirically—does not exist (at least not in any real and productive sense). What exists is the secondary imagination's ability to vitalize the "fixed and dead" empirical world through creativity and then unify it with our essential self. That is, the physical world does not really exist—only the metaphysical world, which is the unity between the primary and secondary imagination. Here Coleridge has fleshed out what the *Critique of Pure Reason* only suggests with regard to the function of imagination. For Kant, imagination is necessary, but its literal function remains vague. Not so for Coleridge. He centers imagination to construct what we now see as the Romantic Imagination. So what began with Kant's parsing of reason as a governing principle for processing and functioning in the world flowers fully with Romanticism.

Within the philosophy of Romanticism, the secondary imagination represents the creative or poetic imagination. It not only gives rise to the ideal but also functions to unify that ideal with our primary-imagination concept of empirical reality. That concept acknowledges and constructs a dual existence for us—the condition whereby we exist in a reality of primary and secondary imagination simultaneously. The possibility of such a dual consciousness paves the way for "the willing suspension of disbelief for the moment, which constitutes poetic faith."[11] Coleridge coined the term *willing suspension of disbelief* to describe the mental process required to productively read his *Rime of the Ancient Mariner*, a supernatural tale that seeks to cover emotional ground similar to Wordsworth's realist nature poetry.

For Coleridge, to willingly suspend disbelief is to reside in imagination. Romanticism's actualization of the Romantic Imagination resides in such moments of poetic faith: we all sleep, we all dream, and perhaps we all wonder about the linkages between the imaginary worlds our minds create and the physical world our bodies inhabit. For Coleridge, this balancing act between imagination and world was central to his poetry and philosophy. Within the Coleridge quote that serves here as an epigraph, the poet destabilizes our hold on certainty and engages with the possibilities of imagination. Yet the sentence's structure—the fact that it ends with a question—shows Coleridge's ambivalence about imagination's real capacity to structure our experiences. The wistful tone of that final question ("Aye! and what then?") suggests a deep optimistic desire to believe in the depth of those possibilities of imagination.

THE SEUSSIAN IMAGINATION: WAKING UP THE BRAIN CELLS

We find a similar dynamic in early Seuss, where stories of daydreaming young boys allow the author to rehearse the ways that imagination can transform mundane everydays into vibrant worlds of endless possibility. With his first book, *And to Think That I Saw It on Mulberry Street* (1937), Seuss creates a structure that he will revisit many times throughout his career. The book begins with young Marco on the last leg of his journey home from school. He knows two things—one, his father will ask him what he saw on the way home, and two, he saw nothing of interest. Marco longs for excitement and difference, but his daily routine is boring. His father's daily demand that he recount his dull experience only reaffirms the emptiness of the pattern. Marco's frustrations are twofold; he is frustrated by both the sameness of his small world and his father's demand that he report that sameness day after day.

Of course, the child develops an elegant workaround: his imagination. The brunt of *And to Think That I Saw It on Mulberry Street* is made up of Marco's imaginings, all sorts of fantastic inventions that effectively transform his drab walk into an amazing journey and his boring report to his father into a surprising poem. Through an act of imagination, Marco expands and enlivens his world. Dull Mulberry Street crackles and pulses with life, energy, and color. The long walk shortens, and his dreaded report becomes something he relishes. In short, Marco's actual daily activities are transformed by his imagination; his world becomes a bigger, fuller place.

Seuss repeatedly returns to this story structure. Each time, he considers and further develops our imagination's capacity to transform reality.

McElligot's Pool (1947) once again finds Marco contending with the boredom and limitations of his world. This time he is fishing at a small, polluted pool. When an adult informs him that the pool is empty and he's wasting his time, Marco answers by imagining a series of fantastic possibilities of the marine life that *might* exist beneath the surface of the tiny fishing hole. Marco's daydreams rehearse the same divide between imagination and reality as Coleridge's sleeping dream, as well as Wordsworth's "wise passiveness" in "Expostulation and Reply." When Marco imagines, he models a specific way of interacting with and constructing reality, of dexterously and deftly negotiating Life's Great Balancing Act between the banality of what-is and the possibility of what-if. Marco's negotiation has much in common with Coleridge's Romantic Imagination. He, like Coleridge, stops short of declaring his dream reality, but the optimism of the possibilities is front and center:

> *'Cause you never can tell*
> *What goes on down below!*
> This pool *might* be bigger
> Than you or I know! (Pool)

Marco's activation of imagination demands that we allow for the possibility of an expanded world. That is the move of the Romantic Imagination—it enacts the suppositional powers of the mind; once we allow for the Seuss/Coleridge "might be"/"what then?" we must also allow the possibility that the world is a brighter, bigger place than it appears on the surface. And allowing the possibility of an expanded world actually does expand the world.

THE EVER-EVOLVING SEUSSIAN IMAGINATION

Seuss repeated the structural formula of *And to Think That I Saw It on Mulberry Street* and *McElligot's Pool* in *If I Ran the Zoo* (1950), *Scrambled Eggs Super!* (1953) and *If I Ran the Circus* (1956). Each book offers a main character that represents a daydreamer faced with a boring reality. Rather than succumb to the banality of reality, however, these characters resort to spicing up their plain everyday lives with imagination. In the end, however, they return to the status quo—though we're all a little richer for the flights of fancy.

Yet within the identical macro-structure of these early exercises in imagination, Seuss develops an evolution with regard to the positioning and reception of such dreams. Each story represents a child using his imagination to extend the limited possibilities of his reality and transform his world into a more interesting and vibrant place, and each story employs a narrative that restores order by returning the child to his predaydream locale. However, the child's relationship with and attitude toward the power and possibility of his acts of imagination strengthens and develops across the texts. *And to Think That I Saw It on Mulberry Street* ends with Marco abashed by his father's potential reaction to his daydreaming. When faced with his father's daily request—"[T]ell me the sights / On the way home from school"—Marco capitulates to reality, abandoning his flight of fancy: "'Nothing,' I said, growing red as a beet, / 'But a plain horse and wagon on Mulberry Street'" (Mulberry). In refusing to reproduce the fantastic inventions that energized his trip home, the story calls back to his father's initial censure of imagination: "Stop telling such outlandish tales. / Stop turning minnows into whales" (Mulberry). What began as a demonstration of the power of imagination ends in containment, a story about reality and telling the truth.

In *McElligot's Pool*, the power of imagination increases: Marco's active imagination is no longer contained by an initial parental charge to describe the world accurately. There the boy's flight of fancy legitimately enlivens his time fishing, regardless of whether the fish he dreams of actually exist. And in the bookended illustrations, the farmer's initial, closed-eyed, condescending confidence that nothing exists beneath the hole's surface has been replaced by a final, wide-eyed, chin-stroking acknowledgment that there just *might* be something down there. Marco's expression in the illustrations undergoes a transformation, beginning as neutral and ending as knowing and optimistic. In the end, Marco is more confident for his act of imagination, and he appears to have given the adult something to consider.

If I Ran the Circus represents another step in the evolutionary capacity of the Seussian imagination. It mimics the structure of the earlier books: a bored young man, Morris McGurk, wanders alone around a vacant lot behind the local general store. To pass the time, he imagines cleaning up the lot and building a circus there. Of course, it won't be just any circus— it'll be the greatest circus with all sorts of fantastic animals, some real (a walrus, elephants, whales) but most imaginary (a drum-tummied snumm, a foon, a walloo, etc). Trapped in his mundane all-too-familiar setting, Morris uses his vivid imagination to create a fantastic world. On the final page, order is restored: Morris returns to his everyday reality. However, in this iteration, the boy's imagination has not merely dreamt a fantastic and exotic world; it has transformed the owner of the store and lot, old Mr. Sneelock, into a death-defying hero. Sneelock should function much like the farmer in *McElligot's Pool*—which is to say, as a myopic adult unable to see the potential for magic all around him. But in Morris's visions, the old shopkeeper is the star of the show. Just as Morris sees magic and possibility in the vacant lot, he sees something special in old Sneelock. Seuss dedicated the book to his father, "Big Ted of Springfield, the finest man I'll ever know" (Circus), suggesting that the story represents a son's recognition of his father's everyday heroism. To the literal-eyed world, Sneelock is nothing more than an old shopkeeper. But to Morris (and, by extension, to the reader), an act of imagination transforms him into a hero. And through Seuss's act of imagination, the reader can associate that heroism with the author's father. Thus, we get the nod to the possibility that the imagination can produce something that is not contained by the restoration of order.

IMAGINATION UNBOUND, OR MY ALPHABET STARTS WHERE YOUR ALPHABET ENDS

In fact, by the time *If I Ran the Circus* appeared, Seuss had already begun to experiment with untethering imagination from formulaic containment and shifting toward more open-ended possibilities. *On Beyond Zebra!* (1955) begins with a familiar set-up: an unnamed narrator who looks much like Marco (and Peter T. Hooper in *Scrambled Eggs Super!*) and his younger friend Conrad Cornelius o'Donald o'Dell stand in a school room. Conrad engages in the monotonous process of writing the alphabet on a blackboard and reciting corresponding animals: "The A is for Ape. And the B is for Bear . . ." The boy quickly reaches *Z* is for *Zebra* and declares anticlimactically, "Now I know everything *any*one knows" (Zebra), suggesting that, in the end, either knowledge is nothing more than the recitation of mundane facts or it does little other than make us all the same. But the narrator steps in and suggests that, for select individuals, for those who care to take the journey, the alphabet continues well beyond *Z*. He proceeds to introduce the boy to a series of letters that correspond to a series of fantastic animals and landscapes, which the two boys visit. On Mulberry Street or at McElligot's Pool, the presence of a rational adult at the end of the fantastic journey would restore order and code the flights of fancy as creative daydreams that temporarily enlivened mundane reality through imagination. They suggest the possibility of an expanded world, but we understand that reality still belongs to the adults, to reason and facts. But in *On Beyond Zebra!* the narrator takes the place of the authority figure. And in the end, he declares that the product of their activated imagination now exists in the world. Rather than being contained, the enabling change in his small friend, catalyzed by imagination, becomes a permanent one: "NOW the letters he uses are something to see! / Most people *still* stop at the Z . . . / *But not HE!*" (Zebra). The restoration of order fails to close the loop. On the journey, Conrad has been converted, to the extent that even though he and the narrator return to the schoolroom, their imaginations are no longer contained by the reality they find there. In fact, the schoolroom that they return to is transformed—the blackboard that Conrad writes on has now expanded exponentially to accommodate his new understanding of the world. Here, for the first time, Seuss alters/expands reality to correspond to an act of imagination.

This shift accords with a philosophical shift affected by Shelley toward the end of the Romantic period. As with his Romantic forefathers, Shelley equates imagination with poetry; however, his claims for both extend even further. In *A Defence of Poetry* (1821), Shelley uses Coleridge's treatment of reason and imagination as a starting point and pushes his exploration of imagination through Platonic idealism: "Reason is the enumeration of qualities already known; imagination is the perception of the value of those qualities, both separately and as a whole. Reason respects the differences, and imagination the similitudes of things. Reason is to imagination as the instrument to the agent, as the body to the spirit, as the shadow to the substance."[12] So Shelley begins with a Coleridgian concept of primary and secondary imagination, which he distinguishes as "reason" and "imagination." He seems to accord with Coleridge (and Wordsworth) when he makes the analogy: reason:imagination as instrument:agent. Once again, we see the idea that reason is a tool that can only be utilized by someone with imagination. Shelley then sublimates the analogy further: reason:imagination as body:spirit. Here he equates reason with base existence and imagination with essential existence. Again, this is well within the parameters set out by Coleridge. But then he makes a distinct turn toward Plato: reason:imagination as shadow:substance. For Shelley, the imagination becomes the REAL—or the *real* real. He theoretically transforms poetry's provocative question ("What if when you awoke you had a flower in your hand?") into poetry's provocative statement: "You will awake with a flower in your hand." For Shelley, reason functions as the shadow real, the mere perception of the real. Through that Platonic shifting of knowledge, Shelley posits imagination as actually structuring reality rather than vice versa. Imagination/poetry does not offer alternate realities; rather, it returns us to the real state of reality, which exists within us: "Poetry, in a general sense, may be defined to be 'the expression of the imagination': and poetry is connate with the origin of man."[13] Imagination exists inside of us as a fundamental essence, and poetry functions as a fundamental manifestation of that essence. But the poet's output does not merely express subjective consciousness; rather, it reflects an objective collective reality: "[Poetry] is less [the poets'] spirit than the spirit of the age . . . the mirrors of the gigantic shadows which futurity casts upon the present."[14] This represents a long stride forward from the marginal claims staked by Coleridge's dream poetry. Shelley's conclusion—"Poets are the unacknowledged legislators of the world"[15] —stakes a much larger claim for the power of imagination. That final metaphor pushes beyond the earlier expression of poetry-as-mirror. In its final line, *Defence* posits imagination as not mere reflections of reality through an internal glass—within Shelley's formulation, imagination constructs, structures, and governs reality.

Seuss's later work embodies and illustrates these ideas. In that later work, his books carry idealism to its logical conclusion—creating and rehearsing worlds composed entirely of imagination. In that way, he leads his young readers to a declarative construction of reality and fundamental self through imagination.

Oh, the Thinks You Can Think! (1977) and *Oh, the Places You'll Go!* (1991) are testaments to the centrality of imagination in Seuss's construction of the world. They are, in a sense, Seuss's answer to Coleridge's question, "Aye! and what then?" While both books resemble the author's early work with regard to the function of imagination, they depart completely from the initial structure outlined earlier. Whereas Seuss's initial engagements contained the power of imagination within a recognizable frame of the familiar, he sets his later work in worlds almost completely untethered from reality. Indeed, *Oh, the Thinks You Can Think!* develops a central argument that parallels Shelley's radical claims for imagination. The book suggests that we construct our world by thinking it into existence. The initial examples of this capacity are recognizable in form: "You can think about birds . . . yellow . . . blue . . . red . . . pink . . . a horse" (Thinks). At the same time, Seuss's illustrations are fantastic, suggesting that the world in which these things are thought into existence is newly invented. And the narrative quickly shifts to match the concepts with the visual flights of fancy. Seuss invents all sorts of things that can be thought ("a guff . . . snuvs . . . the rink rinker fink . . . a jaboo" [Thinks]), and he argues that through acts of imagination, we fundamentally alter and construct our world: "Think of black water / Think up a white sky / Think up a boat / Think of bloogs blowing by" (Thinks). In the end, *Oh, the Thinks You Can Think!* posits the world as a place that will be constructed through the mind, a place where the only limits of our experience are the limits of our imagination.

While *Oh, the Thinks You Can Think!* constructs its world through imagination, Seuss's final book, *Oh, the Places You'll Go!* instructs its reader how to find a place for one's own imagination in a world already constructed by the imaginations of others. Thus, the book advocates an individual idealism, but rather than act as escapism, Seussian idealism lays out the world as collectively constructed through ideas. Success, then, lies in the ability to navigate that world's obstacles through imagination.

In a way, the book is an expansion of Seuss's *Hunches in Bunches* (1982), in which an unnamed narrator, who looks exactly like Marco, struggles with his own conflicting ideas of what he should do one day. The ideas are represented as physical characters, called hunches, which attempt to manipulate him into certain activities, some dull (homework, chores, etc.) and some more stimulating (going outside and exploring). In the end, the narrator's complex and active imagination creates so many conflicting hunches that his world descends into chaos: "Wild hunches in big bunches / were scrapping all around me, / throwing crunchy hunchy punches" (Hunches). Here, the restoration of order comes not from a return to reality but rather from the acknowledgment that his imagination is multiple, not singular. In response to the multiplying hunches, the narrator imagines a series of selves that can debate the pros and cons of the warring hunches and ultimately succeeds in moving forward with his day. Where *Hunches in Bunches* presents a local problem—what will the narrator do on a given day?—*Oh, the Places You'll Go!* extends that question further to, what will you do with your future?

The book works through a series of existential obstacles that are thrown in the path of a young character trying to chart his future. As with *Oh, the Thinks You Can Think!*, the physical world of the book is a place largely untethered from reality, a series of fantastic landscapes that spring from the imagination of its author. But the crises/obstacles found along the way are familiar: not feeling *at home* at home, setbacks ("Bang-ups and Hang-ups"), stasis ("The Waiting Place"), solitude/loneliness, and fear and confusion. Each of these crises represents, in some sense, a failure of imagination. Specifically, the character repeatedly finds himself trapped in situations constructed by the imaginations of others. The solutions require him to appeal to and maintain contact with his own imagination in order to navigate those flawed landscapes. In the end, the book argues that one's ability to succeed in a world collectively constructed by the ideas of others will depend on one's own ability to *imagine* a place in that world.

As Coleridge's willing suspension of disbelief shows, any act of reading functions as an act of imagination; it involves the active mental experience and acceptance of another world—in Seuss's cases, a better world. That is the function of imagination: it allows us to construct the world as it could be and allows us to rehearse possibilities for ourselves in that world that don't yet exist in reality. And in doing that, all of these poets argue, we actually alter reality. Or, to put it in Seussian terms, imagination is how we get where we're going—it's how we move mountains, kid.

2

ARISTOTLE AND THE CAT ON
FUN THAT IS FUNNY

Dennis Knepp

Look at me!
Look at me!
Look at me NOW!
It is fun to have fun
But you have to know how.

—Dr. Seuss, *The Cat in the Hat*

Since life also includes relaxation, and in this we pass our time with some form of amusement, here also it seems possible to behave appropriately in meeting people, and to say and listen to the right things and in the right way.

—Aristotle[1]

Theodor Geisel's first big success as Dr. Seuss was *The Cat in the Hat*. He had published several books before, but the success of *The Cat in the Hat* is what immortalized him. Geisel himself told an interviewer, "It's the book I'm proudest of," and explained that it was written as a response to a call for better books for introductory readers.[2] Geisel deliberately limited himself to a list of three hundred words to make it accessible to the beginner. *The Cat in the Hat* was the first in the series of Beginner Books with the motto, "I can read it all by myself." It also presents an important lesson for children: that it is fun to have fun, but you have to know how. You will have a better life and people will like you if you know how to have fun. Jokes are a great way to help you endure hardships and make friends with others, and friends are also a great help in enduring hardships. Not that they should try the tricks of the Cat in the Hat. On the contrary, both the Cat and the fish in the pot present the extremes of *what not to do*, and the children in the story learn to navigate between them to find moderation and appropriateness using a model first described by Aristotle (384–322 BC) in his *Nichomachean Ethics*.

THE THINGS THAT WENT ON THERE THAT DAY

The Cat in the Hat opens with the kids stuck inside on a gloomy, rainy day. Their boredom is interrupted with a "BUMP!" on the front door, and then the titular Cat in the Hat barges into the house uninvited with this promise:

> I know it is wet
> And the sun is not sunny.
> But we can have
> Lots of good fun that is funny! (Cat)

The kids aren't sure about this because their mother is out of the house for the day. However, the fish in the pot is sure about this and loudly exclaims, "He should not be here when your mother is out!" (Cat). The Cat in the Hat reassures the kids that he knows lots of tricks and games that are fun and balances the naysaying fish in a pot on an umbrella to demonstrate. This is dangerous, as the fish in the pot says, but the Cat insists on balancing more and more items until it's too much and they all come crashing down.

Despite another scolding from the fish in the pot, the Cat in the Hat insists on showing "Another good game that I know!" (Cat). This game involves opening a box and letting loose Thing One and Thing Two, who proceed to knock over belongings in the house with antics like flying kites indoors. At this point, the fish in the pot sees that their mother is returning, and so the boy catches Thing One and Thing Two with a net and the Cat sadly removes them from the house with a description of the mess they left behind:

> And this mess is so big
> And so deep and so tall,

We can not pick it up.
There is no way at all! (Cat)

Luckily, in the penultimate scene, the Cat in the Hat returns with a many-handed machine that puts everything back in its proper place just in time before their mother comes in the front door. The book ends with the kids back in their seats as if nothing had happened, wondering whether they should tell their mother about the Cat in the Hat.

AN ANCIENT LESSON IN FUN THAT IS FUNNY

Theodor Geisel's writing of *The Cat in the Hat* mirrors elements of Aristotle's discussion of the virtuous life in his *Nicomachean Ethics*. Aristotle writes that a virtue is a habit—you have to practice the virtues to be any good at them. Aristotle is not a fan of the "rising to the occasion" theory of virtue. He's not a fan of the coward who overcomes his fears and rises to the occasion to be brave. Aristotle prefers the brave person who practices being brave, such as firefighters who practice putting out fires so that they are confident and skilled when a real fire happens. Similarly, the virtuously witty person must practice being witty. Geisel practiced as Dr. Seuss for years before the success of *The Cat in the Hat*. His first book was rejected by dozens of publishers, but he kept trying until it happened. But even then his first book wasn't a great success, and he kept trying and published many books before finally obtaining the success of *The Cat in the Hat*.

Aristotle also writes that virtue is a deliberate and enjoyable choice. You can't be coerced into virtue, you can't be virtuous by accident, and you can't hate being virtuous. Geisel was inspired to write *The Cat in the Hat* after reading a challenge for better writers to tackle early reading primers and bemoaning the paltry state of Dick and Jane books. Geisel chose to do it and enjoyed the challenge that the restricted vocabulary left him. The virtuous person chooses to do it "at the right times, about the right things, towards the right people, for the right end, and in the right way."[3] *The Cat in the Hat* was published at the right time when there was an audience of beginner readers, and about the right things that those readers would want to read about, and for the right end of encouraging young readers, and in the right way with the restricted vocabulary, rhyme scheme, and wacky visuals.

Aristotle wrote that virtue is found as a mean of moderation between two extremes. He uses an analogy with eating. Too much food is bad for your health, and too little food is bad for your health. The correct amount to eat is a mean between those two extremes: one should eat in moderation. This too much/too little/just right model is Aristotle's basic schema for each virtue. In regard to facing dangers, the foolhardy person does too much while the coward does too little. The virtuous, brave person knows moderation and when it is appropriate to rush into danger and when one should run away. In regard to giving money to those in need, the foolish person gives away all their money and becomes someone in need while the stingy person never gives money to anyone. The virtuous, generous person knows when it is appropriate to give and how much to give and to whom to give and so on. For Aristotle, the best life is the virtuous life of deliberately chosen and habitual moderation in all things.

Aristotle applies this mean-between-the-two-extremes moderation model to the virtue of wit—knowing how and when to joke. The buffoon goes too far and laughs inappropriately and harms others. The boor goes too far in the other extreme and frowns upon any frivolity. The witty person learns how and when to joke appropriately by being somewhere between the buffoon and the boor. *The Cat in the Hat* nicely illustrates this concept.

THE BUFFOON IN THE HAT

The Cat in the Hat goes too far in his tricks. It's true that we laugh at him, but it's also evident that we aren't supposed to be like him. He starts off with barging into the house uninvited, which itself is a no-no. He then claims to know "some new tricks" and "good tricks" (Cat), which itself seems odd and suggests that these are actually bad, old tricks. He introduces his first "game":

> Why, we can have
> Lots of good fun, if you wish,
> With a game that I call
> UP-UP-UP with a fish! (Cat)

This isn't a game. This "game" is nothing more than holding the fish in a pot up on top of an umbrella. This "game" is nothing more than putting other people in danger.

The Cat in the Hat then brags that he can hold more and more things up in the air, including a book and a cup, all while standing on one foot on a ball. But because he is able to do it, that's not enough, and the Cat adds more stuff: a cup, a cake, two books, the fish in the pot, a toy ship, and milk in a dish, all while now hopping on one leg on the ball. But because he is able to do this too, it is still not enough, and the Cat adds more: a little toy man in a toy ship, a red fan on his tail, and now the fish in the pot is balanced on a rake. All while hopping one-legged on a ball. And he promises even more.

It's a cliffhanger that encourages the beginning reader to turn the page and find out if the Cat can actually do it. We can see in the Cat's face in the illustration that he is really struggling, and, despite his boasting, he might not be able to keep it up. The boast with the ellipses encourages the young reader to turn the page to find out. And CRASH! The juggled objects fall to the ground all around the Cat. That's not good. The fish in the pot lists some of the damages:

> You sank our toy ship,
> Sank it deep in the cake.
> You shook up our house
> And you bent our new rake. (Cat)

The Cat could have tried holding up just a couple of things, but instead he kept adding more and more stuff until he went beyond his ability to hold it all up and everything crashed. The Cat's game damaged stuff and endangered others precisely because he went *too far* in his quest to make everyone laugh, failing to take into consideration who might get hurt.

THINGS GO TOO FAR

The Cat in the Hat really only has two games: holding up too much stuff until it all falls down and opening a box that contains Thing One and Thing Two. The Cat reassures us that FUN-IN-A-BOX is another "good game":

> These Things will not bite you.
> They want to have fun. (Cat)

Well, it's reassuring to know that these Things he keeps locked up in a box won't bite. But what do they do? Thing One and Thing Two basically run through the house breaking rules and breaking things.

> Then those Things ran about
> With big bumps, jumps and kicks
> And with hops and big thumps
> And all kinds of bad tricks. (Cat)

They don't act house trained; they act more like wild animals. Thing One and Thing Two are some of the least namelike names ever and signify that they are not persons who act like good people should. You are not to be a Thing; you are to be a person with a name. It's fun to laugh at their antics from the safe distance of reading about them, but you shouldn't be like them. Thing One and Thing Two fly kites in the house, run down the halls knocking over a vase and knocking pictures off walls, and even damage Mother's new gown and the head of her bed. They are going *way too far.*

Aristotle wrote, "Those who go to excess in raising laughs seem to be vulgar buffoons. They stop at nothing to raise a laugh, and care more about that than about saying what is seemly and avoiding pain to the victims of the joke."[4] And that's the problem: the "tricks" and "games" of the Cat in the Hat and of Thing One and Thing Two hurt other people and damage things. The Cat's juggling puts the fish in the pot in danger and bends the rake. Thing One and Thing Two destroy valuable things like Mother's new gown. The beginning reader can see this and understand that while it is funny to read at the distance of a book, their behavior is too extreme and dangerous to be brought into the real world. There must be a way to have fun that isn't harmful.

THE FISH IN THE POT IS A BOOR

The Cat in that Hat is the buffoon who is fun to laugh at but goes too far and needs to be stopped. The other side is the boor, the killjoy, the wet blanket: the fish in the pot who doesn't like having fun and doesn't like it when others have fun. Geisel calls him "my version of Cotton Mather," which means that he's an old-fashioned Puritan who's against music and art and laughter and is angered when others are having fun.[5] On the third page of *The Cat in the Hat* the fish is shown contentedly sleeping in the fishbowl. It grabs your attention because real fish don't look like that. Real fish swim in fishbowls. So the fish in the pot is not an ordinary fish, but rather a symbol of something else: of the frowning Puritan moralist. The fish in the pot would have preferred to spend the whole day sleeping in that fishbowl. The fish in the pot likes it to be quiet and boring. The fish in the pot likes it when nothing happens. Here's what the fish in the pot says about playing:

> But our fish said, "No! No!
> Make that cat go away!
> Tell that Cat in the Hat
> You do NOT want to play." (Cat)

Notice that the fish in the pot doesn't say that this is an inappropriate time or place for playing. No, the fish says something stronger: you do NOT want to play. Playing itself is bad. There should be no playing at any time. How awful! Here's what Aristotle writes about those who not only don't have fun but also are upset when others have fun: "Those who would never say anything themselves to raise a laugh, and even object when other people do it, seem to be boorish and stiff."[6]

Don't be boorish and stiff like the fish in the pot, because, as Aristotle writes, "The boor is useless when he meets people in these circumstances. For he contributes nothing himself, and objects to everything; but relaxation and amusement seem to be necessary in life."[7] Why does amusement seem necessary in life? Why not be a boor? Aristotle seems to provide some clues in his discussion about friendship, writing that "it is most necessary for our life. For no one would choose to live without friends even if he had all the other goods."[8]

The modern philosopher of jokes, Al Gini, explores the importance of making friendly connections in his recent book *The Importance of Being Funny: Why We Need More Jokes in Our Lives*. Gini writes that there are three main reasons for making jokes: for pleasure, for relationships, and for defense. Regarding the importance of jokes in building friendly relationships, Gini writes:

As Victor Borge suggested, jokes are "the shortest distance between two people." Jokes are an olive branch we extend to one another. Jokes attempt to be kind, to be convivial. Jokes are an attempt to mitigate hostility, reduce tension, demonstrate our shared humanity, and remind us of our commonality. Jokes can be an attempt to reach out and commiserate with others. Jokes are also an attempt to change the mood and the tone of an otherwise awkward or unpleasant situation. [9]

The fish in the pot can't do these things because the fish is a boor and frowns on making jokes. Thus the fish in the pot has difficulty getting close to others because it doesn't realize that jokes help us be successful with others. The witty person knows how to use jokes to make their world a better place by shortening that distance between two people.

ALWAYS PICK UP YOUR PLAYTHINGS

So the virtuously witty person should joke, but how to avoid the extreme of joking too much? The buffoon makes jokes that are harmful and drive others away. How can we be witty and not a buffoon? The Cat himself provides a clue. After making the huge mess in the house, the Cat brings in his deus ex machina—a machine that fixes everything—and cleans up the mess. The page is worth quoting in full:

> And THEN!
> Who was back in the house?
> Why, the cat!
> "Have no fear of this mess,"
> Said the Cat in the Hat.
> "I always pick up all my playthings
> And so . . .
> I will show you another
> Good trick that I know!" (Cat)

The lesson about play is the rule "I always pick up all my playthings." The other lines on this page are short with several rhymes, but the rule is set aside from the rest of the text as a longer prose line that doesn't rhyme with any other line. Geisel said in an interview that breaking up the pace and meter with a line of prose is one of his stylistic tricks. [10] I know from my own experience reading this aloud to children that the line "I always pick up all my playthings" gets a slower and more intoned reading.

The reader learns a valuable lesson: play all you want but pick up your playthings afterward. That means you can't break stuff because you can't unbreak it afterward. That means you can't endanger the lives of others because if you really hurt them, you won't be able to unhurt them afterward. By contrast, it's appropriately funny to make a house out of wooden blocks and then pretend to be a monster destroying it because it's easy to pick up your wooden blocks afterward. It's a good beginner's rule of appropriate play: make sure that everything can be cleaned up afterward, and don't do anything that is permanently damaging to yourself or to others. Aristotle writes that "a joke is a type of abuse" and that the "cultivated and civilized person, as a sort of law to himself," will use self-control to be funny without thoughtlessly harming others.[11]

WOULD YOU TELL?

But the Cat in the Hat does clean it up. He uses his many-handed machine to pick up the cake, the rake, the gown, the milk, the strings, the books, the dish, the fan, the cup, the ship, and even the fish in the pot. Mother returns on the last pages. Her face is not shown; only her hand and foot enter the door. She asks the central question of *The Cat in the Hat*: "Did you have any fun?" (Cat). If the book is a lesson in how to have "fun that is funny," and if the rule is "I always pick up all my playthings," then the kids were successful: they had fun that is funny and everything was picked up. Since they followed the rule of appropriate play, they should joyfully tell their mother about this strange cat who barged into the house and damaged their belongings and endangered the fish and let loose two wild things from a box that made it worse, and then, when they saw that she was coming home, the wild things were caught and the uninvited cat put everything back where it was as if nothing had ever happened using a big machine with lots of hands! But they can't admit to all that, can they?

> Should we tell her about it?
> Now, what SHOULD we do?
> Well . . .
> What would YOU do
> If your mother asked YOU? (Cat)

The implication seems to be, obviously, *NO! Don't tell Mother because you got away with it!*, which is a pretty subversive statement to leave for a beginner reader who might very well be reading that very book with their own parents or other adult authorities. Here's Geisel himself on *The Cat in the Hat* and subverting adult authority:

> "I'm subversive as hell!" Geisel replied. "I've always had a mistrust of adults. And one reason I dropped out of Oxford and the Sorbonne was that I thought they were taking life too damn seriously, concentrating too much on nonessentials. Hilaire Belloc, whose writings I liked a lot, was a radical. *Gulliver's Travels* was subversive, and both Swift and Voltaire influenced me. *The Cat in the Hat* is a revolt against authority, but it's ameliorated by the fact that the Cat cleans up everything at the end. It's revolutionary in that it goes as far as Kerensky and then stops. It doesn't go quite as far as Lenin." [12]

Theodor Geisel is able to raise issues of subversion and authority with a vocabulary of less than three hundred words and in a context that makes the beginning reader laugh. Why do that? Why do we continue to read *The Cat in the Hat* decades after its 1957 publication? Al Gini provides an answer.

Gini writes that jokes seem to serve three main purposes: pleasure, relationships, and defense. The pleasure of jokes is obvious, and the importance of relationships is discussed above. Regarding defense, Gini suggests that jokes can work as a way of dealing with hardships. The pleasure of a joke can help ease the pain of a bad situation. But jokes can do more: they can help illuminate difficult topics. By making jokes about scary issues we are trying to get a handle on a situation we don't really understand. Gini writes:

> Joking about illness, death, God, sex, or age is a way of defanging or domesticating something that essentially cannot be tamed, it is a way of being in charge of something that we really cannot control or completely understand. [13]

The Cat in the Hat makes a joke out of obedience to authority. By doing so, it creates a safe space in which the beginning reader can discuss important issues regarding obedience, authority, truth telling, and so on. As Aristotle reminds us, this is good practice. The real world contains situations in which it is legitimate to ask whether you should tell the truth, when to be subversive, and when to obey authority, and reading *The Cat in the Hat* provides the practice to do it "at the right times, about the right things, towards the right people, for the right end, and in the right way."[14]

Part II

You!

The first topic we'll cover is you—ain't that grand?
You and your welfare, your good, your life's plan.
It's you we begin with, for you are the one
Who has to be you until you are done.
From birth until death the one thing that remains
Is you, all your dreams, all your pleasures and pains.
So it's best to begin with you right at the start,
Learning to live's a most difficult art.

Starting with Greece, we'll talk about virtue,
Happiness, character, purpose, and so you
Can figure it out, why you're here, what to do,
As you work on that beautiful artwork called "You."

And on to the Romans, the Stoics are next,
Handing us tools to pass all of life's tests.
Reframe and accept, get your mind ready for
The bang-ups and hang-ups outside your front door.

Life can seem cruel, like meaningless pain,
So the French will come in and take part in the game.

Life is absurd, but that doesn't mean quit,
It means you must strive to put value in it.

And try as you will, each day that you're here,
There's a day you'll be gone, and it's always too near.
All things that can live are all things that must die,
Dealing with death is a fact of your life.

But at least in this life we don't go it alone,
We focused on you, but there's more people home.
People around you with whom you can bond,
Who share in your life, and of whom you'll grow fond.
Keep reading. For it's not just about you,
Others are going through all of this too!

3

ARISTOTLE AND EUDAIMONIA

Oh, the Virtues You'll Do!

Matthew Pierlott

Now in everything the pleasant or pleasure is most to be guarded against; for we do not judge it impartially.

—Aristotle (*Nico* II.ix)[1]

So be sure when you step. Step with care and great tact / and remember that Life's a Great Balancing Act.

—Dr. Seuss, *Oh, the Places You'll Go!*

Eudaimonia? What on Earth does that mean? No, it is not a territory within Solla Sollew or the island next to Sala-ma-Sond. Nor is it the prerequisite magical incantation for brewing up some oobleck. It is just a fancy-pants word for "the good life." Philosophers use this word mostly to conjure up, not oobleck, but ideas of the Greek philosopher Aristotle. In his two ethical works, the *Nicomachean Ethics* and the *Eudemian Ethics*, Aristotle gives us an account of the good life, and how we might get it.

The word *eudaimonia* is often translated as "happiness" or "flourishing."[2] Happiness is an easy translation, but very misleading. It's easy because it is so common to hold that we all want to be happy, and *eudaimonia*, as we shall see, indicates the life "we all want." But it is misleading since happiness often refers to a passing emotional state (i.e., feeling happy), and it is impossible to feel happy all of the time. *Eudaimonia*, by contrast, is not an emotional state, and it does seem to be an enduring state that we can achieve. So, "flourishing" is a better bet. If I am flourishing, and am living a flourishing life, things must be going well for me. And even if I have sad days, or bad days, I am probably deeply satisfied with my life. It's not just that I had a good breakfast (say, scrambled eggs super) or joined the high flyers and passed the whole gang to soon take the lead. These are simply good events within a life. Flourishing means that I can even meet with bad days and come out well. For example, suppose that a Grinch stole my town's Christmas. How wonderful it would be for me to belong to a community that would band together and still find joy in that moment of loss. Flourishing isn't just about having good days and avoiding bad days; it is about the secret to living well or, as the poet Rudyard Kipling put it, to be able to "meet with Triumph and Disaster / And treat those two imposters just the same."[3]

It might actually help to translate the term as "being blessed," in the sense of having had things go well. The roots of the word, *eu-* and *daimon*, actually mean "good" and "spirit," where spirits are understood as divine beings or forces, or guardians of sorts. So, achieving *eudaimonia* means being in a fortunate state, where the spirits are smiling upon you. It is pretty clear that Aristotle did not think of it in terms of real spiritual beings watching over you, but it helps us understand what we are talking about. *Eudaimonia* refers to the kind of life that all of us would wish for ourselves and anyone we cared about, a life that we might say seems "blessed."

THE HIGHER-ARCHY OF "IN-"S

Importantly, *eudaimonia* is not just *some*thing we all want; it is *every*thing we all want. To understand this, we need to see how Aristotle demonstrates that it is the *highest good*. It all starts with a simple recognition: everything we do aims at a goal (an "end"). This leads to a basic distinction between two "in-"s: *instrumental* value and *intrinsic* value. Sometimes we act because we know it will lead to something else; for example, we might dress up like Santa, but only because it will help us ruin Christmas. There is no joy, no value, in dressing up like Santa itself (at least for us grinches), but it does enable us to achieve something else that we think we will enjoy (like hearing all those little Who boys and girls cry in disappointment). This is instrumental value. In other words, the value that we find in the thing or activity is as a tool, an instrument, to get something else of value. But some things have a value in themselves. This is intrinsic value. It is kind of odd to ask why someone would want something of intrinsic value because it should be obvious. For example, imagine the Lorax asking the Truffula Trees why they want to be allowed to grow and flourish, or Sam-I-Am asking you why you would want to eat green eggs and ham when he knows how delicious they are. So, the intrinsic goods are the things we are after, and the instrumental goods are just useful to get us there.

With this basic distinction we can recognize a certain order of things, from lower- to higher-ranking goods. *First*, some things have no value in themselves but only have instrumental value. The best example, oddly, is money! (Can you imagine Sylvester McMonkey McBean discovering that all that money he made off the Sneetches had no value?!) Even though we talk about the value of money all the time, no one really wants money for itself . . . we want what money can get us. In fact, when it seems like someone lives for money, the rest of us can see this as a kind of sickness, or at least as a case of misplaced priorities. Money is purely instrumental, having value only through its ability to be exchanged for other things. Another example here would be a pain we endure to gain a greater pleasure. We don't really want the pain itself, and would other-wise avoid it . . . but we know that it helps lead to something good. For example, I sometimes (read: *rarely*) exercise, enduring the pains to win the gains. *Second*, some things have *both* intrinsic and instrumental value. For example, I enjoy eating food, and eating food can help me survive and stay healthy (although I would need to make better choices for that last one). I enjoy the activity itself, and I enjoy the results of the activity. *Finally*, there must be something that is sought for its own sake, and not for the sake of anything else. This would be the ultimate and highest good because all activity would ultimately point to this good. For Aristotle, this highest good is *eudaimonia*. The idea is that anything that has intrinsic value is obviously desired for its own sake, but it is also desired to contribute to an overall good life. For example, maybe I wouldn't want to be healthy if the life ahead of me would consist of me being tortured in a dungeon on a daily basis. Of course, being healthy is better than being sick, but I want my health *as part of* a good life.

We call this Aristotle's "hierarchy of ends." Every action we take is for a reason, and ultimately these reasons link up to the ultimate goal of the good life. Okay, so let's test this out: Why are you reading this book? Maybe you are doing it to pass time on a plane, or to explore a potential major in college, or to fulfill a weekly reading assignment in class, or to reconnect with your favorite children's author in an intellectually stimulating way. Whatever your answer, notice that we can ask why again. Why are you fulfilling your weekly reading, or why are you on the plane? That answer can be questioned again: "to get my degree," "because it is my job," "to visit my family," and so on. If you keep up that interrogation well beyond the point of annoyance, you should end up saying something like "Because I want to have a good life!" But once we reach *this* answer, it doesn't make any sense to ask why again. This is the highest good.

ON THE WAY TO SOLLA SOLLEW

So, exactly how does one get such a good life? Well, look around and you will probably find quite a few answers to that question. Celebrity gurus and corporate life coaches hawk their advice for the good life; social media circulates a constant barrage of profound quotes and simple life hacks; religious figures echo millennia-old ideas; politicians promise that all will be well if we just reelect them; and parents insist that their children study harder, go to college, and, whatever they do, "Don't major in philosophy!" What is clear is that there are lots of different opinions on the subject. Many are giving us their honest view, and some are selling us on a view that may or may not work for us. At times it feels that throughout our entire life, some Fix-It-Up Chappie or other is selling us a machine to stamp stars on our bellies. But we each have some vision of what a great life is supposed to be like, and we are trying to find the best path to get to that life. Like our good friend in search of Solla Sollew, we stumble through the challenges of life, hoping to arrive at some point. But we worry that, with all of the different opinions out there, maybe we aren't heading in the right direction, maybe we won't get there, or maybe the destination won't be as great as we thought it would be.

Aristotle was familiar with the feeling. He noted that it seemed that everyone could agree that we all wanted a good life, but we had very different ideas about what that actually involved. Some insisted that a life of pleasure or of wealth was the way to go; others insisted it was the life of honor; still others that it was the life of thought. But Aristotle wasn't content with letting such important matters rest on mere opinion.[4] He wanted objective answers to the question of the good life, so he started searching for the answer as diligently as a boy who wants to cook "scrambled eggs super" looks for rare eggs!

We might be tempted today to insist that each person gets to define for herself what makes for a good life. Maybe running a zoo would make you happy; maybe running a circus would. But Aristotle wanted to figure out what would make for a flourishing human life, regardless of the individual differences that make us unique. He was looking for a common vision of the human good. He wanted a universal answer because he knew that it would help us figure out the bigger question of how we should organize a society. As social beings, our happiness would be rooted in our social and political life. So Aristotle begins an examination of our common human nature.

PLEASE, WON'T YOU TELL US THE TALE OF OUR *TELOS*?

In order to understand human flourishing, we need to understand what makes a person excellent as a human. This requires us to understand what a human is *supposed to be*, so we can judge who does this very well and who doesn't. Aristotle assumes that humans are supposed to be some way because all the things in nature are directed toward some way of being. This is what we call a thing's *telos*, which roughly means its *goal* or *purpose*. Think of a Truffula Tree again. We know, as does the Lorax, what makes a Truffula Tree a good specimen of itself. We know when these trees are sick, dying, poisoned, malnourished, and more, and we know when they are tall, strong, with colorful and poofy soft tufts, as they should be. The *telos* of the tree is not merely a matter of choice or opinion; it is embedded in the very nature of what the tree *is*.

So how do we figure out what we are supposed to be, objectively, and not just leave it up to personal opinion and individual choice? To this question, Aristotle provides an insight. The excellence of a thing can be understood from how it naturally functions, and how it functions is based in its structure or form. Consider McBean's Star-On machine. We know when it is doing its job well because we know what it does: it puts stars on Sneetch bellies. We also know when something is not doing its job well, like the accommodations at the Zwieback Motel, where the "beds are like rocks and, as everyone knows, / The sheets are too short. They don't cover your toes" (Sleep). We know the purpose or function of Star-On machines and Zwieback Motel accommodations from their structure. We know the machine's function is to put stars on Sneetches because all of its parts are arranged to do just that. And we know the motel's beds and sheets are meant to provide a suitable place to sleep but fail to do so because of their structural defects. Now these are engineered objects, whose purpose is given to them by a designer. But natural objects have a *telos* related to their structure as well. Truffula Trees naturally bear fruit (that Bar-ba-loots enjoy), smell like sweet and fresh butterfly milk, and have silky soft tufts. If the Once-ler was a botanist instead of a Thneed manufacturer, maybe he would be able to explain how the tree thrives, what environmental influences support it, and what inner structures work to produce the soft, silky tufts or its delicious fruit. And if this is true of Truffulas, it's true of humans, too. Humans have a natural structure, and *this* tells us what the point of a human being is.

Fundamentally, humans are organized similarly to Truffulas and other plants. We take in specific materials from our environment, make them a part of our own body, and excrete specific materials back out into our environment. We can call this entire cycle a *nutritive* function.[5] So clearly one of the first things we can say about humans is that they are supposed to have healthy bodies, in which all of the parts function properly. Bodily health, then, is an intrinsic good, and it is also a component to the good life. Certainly we can endure aches and pains, injuries and times of sickness, but sustained disintegration of our bodily health always detracts from our quality of life. Now, much of my bodily functioning happens all on its own, without my trying to do anything, but, to the extent that I do have control over my health, I should be promoting good habits in my diet and exercise and making sure that my surroundings support my health (I wouldn't want to live on the Street of the Lifted Lorax, where the wind smells slow and sour, that's for sure).[6]

But humans are more than mere bodily functioning. We also have what Aristotle called an *animal* function. Animals, in his view, were capable of sensation and bodily motion. Animals took in information about the world through their sense organs and were able to navigate the world using that information. Along with that sensation, importantly, comes pleasure and pain. Every sensation is in some degree pleasurable or displeasurable. This animal functioning is also what gives rise to the emotions, which often are related to pleasure and pain. Very rudimentarily, we are afraid of things that might cause us pain (like pale green pants with nobody inside them!), we love things that cause pleasure (like green eggs and ham!), and we get angry with those that hurt or threaten us (like those Zooks and their badly buttered bread!). Because we have an animal soul, we are *supposed* to feel pleasure (and pain) and emotions, and a complete absence of these would not make for a good life. However, a life full of extreme emotional swings would not be best, either. And obviously, a life in which the greater proportion of experiences was marked by sustained pain and negative emotions would be no good. We could not call someone "blessed" who lived for decades in abuse and died full of anger.

Aristotle's insight into our structure reveals that we are still more than this, more than just sensation and emotion. What makes humans distinct, what makes us specifically *human* and not just some other animal, is our ability to reason, to use our intelligence. A Kweet has long legs to stand in the water, and a long beak so it can grab wog-eating trout out of the water. That's its thing, what makes it special. Our thing? Well, it's those brains in our head. And recognizing this is the key to Aristotle's ethics! If humans are *supposed* to use our reason, then becoming an excellent person involves developing our intelligence, our rational abilities, and using them in the course of our life!

THE GREAT BALANCING ACT OF EXCELLENCE

If it's your head full of brains that makes you human, then your virtue (that is, your excellence[7]) involves those brains. Aristotle tells us there are two types of human virtue: intellectual and moral. *Intellectual virtues* include the various skills of the mind and can be developed through training and education. But it is the account of *moral virtues* that has grabbed the attention of so many ethicists. Moral virtues are the result of your human rationality regulating your animal appetites, the desires for pleasure and the emotional responses to pleasure and pain. In other words, it's our ability to control our behavior by intelligently responding to our feelings and desires that can allow us to thrive and be successful.

We learn from Aristotle that moral virtues are good *habits* we acquire over time as we define our own character through our choices. Telling the truth *once* when you were afraid of the consequences does not make you an honest person, but *habitually* favoring the truth in the face of potential pains or losses of pleasure would. Every day, our choices contribute to shaping how and whether we master our inclinations. Like the young boy on Mulberry Street, we must decide how much we let our imagination run wild, and we must decide at the moment of action whether we tell a fabulous story or report the truth. We must choose whether we let our initial impression of distaste at green eggs determine our willingness to try them. And each time we choose, we refine our character a bit and slowly establish habits. Those habits might be good, and they might be bad. Stubbornness in the face of new experiences (green eggs?) is a bad habit, or a *vice*. Mastering our inclinations to make the best choices will develop good habits.

At this point Aristotle reveals what has become known as the "doctrine of the mean."[8] Typically, this doctrine is explained rather simply (and misleadingly):[9] every virtue is situated between two extremes, a vice of excessiveness and a vice of deficiency. For example, if you give away too little, you are selfish, cheap, stingy, or a Grinch; if you give away too much, you are wasteful, or irresponsible, or a pushover (I'm looking at you, Thidwick!). To be generous, you must give away the right amount. Simple enough, right? The problem emerges only if we take this simple account as all there is to Aristotle's doctrine, or, worse, if we think he is simply saying that we need to balance everything out: "Give sometimes, but not all the time, and then you are okay."

Aristotle's full account of the doctrine of the mean (or the "intermediate") doesn't present a virtue as merely striking a balance between two alternative extremes. Aristotle tells us that moral virtue

> is concerned with passions and actions, and in these there is excess, defect, and the intermediate. For instance, both fear and confidence and appetite and anger and pity and in general pleasure and pain may be felt both too much and too little, and in both cases not well; but to feel them *at the right times, with reference to the right objects, towards the right people, with the right motive, and in the right way*, is what is both intermediate and best, and this is characteristic of virtue. (*Nico* II.vi, emphasis added)

What we actually see here is a complex view of the many ways in which we can fall short of excellent behavior.

Let us take the narrator of "What Was I Scared Of?" The narrator informs us that he or she is not very afraid of things, which seems plausible. After all, the narrator walks around at night in dark forests, goes grocery shopping at night, goes fishing on lakes at night, and frequents dark and gloomy Snide-fields. But the narrator *was* afraid of the pale green pants, floating with nobody inside them. It seems reasonable to be afraid of floating pants when your experience tells you that such things are strange. Of course, we know by the end of the story that the fear was unwarranted. But the fear of the pale green pants was not initially excessive. Indeed, it grew as more experiences suggested the pale green pants were aggressively stalking our narrator. Here we see a character who is not overly afraid, nor unable to feel fear when it seems appropriate. Even at the climax, our narrator has enough sense about him or her to see the reciprocated fear in the pants and to try to calm them. Nonetheless, we know that the fear in this one instance is based on ignorance. Our narrator seems close to virtuous, to being courageous, but just falls short a bit in this story, letting a small fear born of ignorance develop into a great fear.

So the doctrine of the mean means more than some simple moderation but requires a "Great Balancing Act," for which one must "be dexterous and deft" (Places). Aristotle deepens his account by showing that acquiring virtuous habits actually realigns one's inclinations. It's not just that we have a fear and act in the face of it but also that we change our relationship to that fear to overcome it:

> We must take as a sign of states of character the pleasure or pain that ensues on acts; for the man who abstains from bodily pleasures and delights in this very fact is temperate, while the man who is annoyed at it is self-indulgent, and he who stands his ground against things that are terrible and delights in this or at least is not pained is brave, while the man who is pained is a coward. (*Nico* II.iii)

A virtuous person acts for the sake of the noble, and her inclinations change as a result of it.

Let's think about one of the most loved Seussian characters: Horton. This faithful elephant generously agrees to sit on Lazy Mayzie's egg and endures seasons of bad weather, the mocking of fellow elephants, and the threat of hunters. Through it all he chooses to remain faithful to his vow, overcoming his own desires and fears.

He held his head high
And he threw out his chest
And he looked at the hunters
As much as to say:
"Shoot if you must
But I *won't* run away!
I meant what I said
And I said what I meant . . .
An elephant's faithful
One hundred per cent!" (Hatches)

Of course, Horton is not feeling happy throughout much of what he endures, but in the end all things work out for him. In "Horton and the Kwuggerbug," Horton strikes a deal to share Beezlenuts with the Kwuggerbug, who manipulates Horton to endure danger and struggle and tricks him by giving Horton the shells of the Beezlenuts as Horton's half. Throughout, again, Horton stays true to his principles, reminding himself that "a deal is a deal" (Kwuggerbug). Horton displays bravery facing crocodiles and perseverance climbing mountains. Horton has certainly overcome his animal nature and developed many moral virtues.

If Horton fails to achieve *eudaimonia*, it is only because he has a knack for entering into arrangements with quite awful characters. Beyond this root of his troubles, Horton shows an amazing development of his own inner character. If I were as virtuous as Horton, my desires and emotions would realign to my rational nature, as Horton's do. If I were excellent, I would not miss the "sacrifices" I make for others when I recognize those sacrifices as being just and noble. If I do in fact miss them, my thoughts and feelings are still rather caught up on those would-be pleasures, too much for my actions to be considered truly virtuous. This realignment is not something I can achieve easily or quickly. It is an accomplishment of maturity. But the seeds are sown all along from the earliest days of my life. [10]

98 AND 3/4 PERCENT GUARANTEED

So, where exactly does all of this leave us? Well, remember that we were trying to ask what would make our lives good, objectively. And we discovered that to flourish as humans, we had to do what humans are supposed to do well. And what we are supposed to do is use our "head full of brains and shoes full of feet" (Places) to make deliberate choices that regulate our emotions and desires so that we make smart decisions. And if we make these smart decisions, we will slowly develop into a reliably virtuous person, which will help us flourish and live that good life!

What Aristotle ultimately means by all of this is that we will become happy if we live a philosophical life. By developing our wisdom and our skill in choosing the best paths, we will become "too smart to go down any not-so-good street(s)" (Places). We won't be as dependent on material goods to make us *feel* happy. Nor will we be as dependent on the superficial opinions of others, preoccupied with keeping up a reputation. We will not just want to be popular or famous but will only want the best people to recognize the good qualities in us (and even here, we will be glad when it happens but not bent out of shape if it doesn't). Of course, Aristotle recognizes that the good life requires more than the self-mastery of virtue. Traumatic events, deep misfortunes, and the like will certainly problematize calling that life "blessed." But developing virtue greatly reduces the power external situations have over defining the quality of one's life.

Ultimately, developing virtues is an important component of living a flourishing life. For Aristotle, the virtuous life is an active life, engaging with one's society and refining oneself along the way. Seuss, like Aristotle, warns us that we don't want to get trapped in the Waiting Place, waiting for some event or some external circumstance to bring us happiness. As if *eudaimonia* came from a store! As if *eudaimonia* weren't a little bit more! Realigning my desires and emotions so that I habitually act in noble ways will provide the strength of character to weather hard times and to be immune to what less virtuous people would consider misfortune. After Bang-ups and Hang-ups, I'll be quicker to get out of a Lurch and to Un-slump myself. I will also attract virtuous people to me, and so surround myself with others whose friendships strengthen and ennoble me. They will help me push on, even though my sneakers may leak. These folks will help me find where the Boom Bands are playing!

So, if we spend some time considering Aristotle's perspective, we will find that the path to flourishing isn't as difficult to find as it first appeared. It's a long road, and we might meet with misfortune, but the journey itself seems worthwhile. And the steps we must take are fairly clear. We start by examining our own desires and emotions and subjecting them to rational scrutiny. Then we slowly and deliberately start acting in ways to create habits that reflect the things we *know* to be valuable. With some luck and determination, we will build up a strong character and the rewarding life that flows from it. So . . . be your name Buxbaum or Bixby or Bray, reflect on your life and get on your way!

4

DID I EVER TELL YOU HOW STOIC YOU ARE?

Benjamin Rider

I'm off to the City of Solla Sollew
On the banks of the beautiful River Wah-Hoo,
Where they never have troubles! At least, very few.
>—Dr. Seuss, *I Had Trouble in Getting to Solla Sollew*

Difficulties show the true man. Therefore, in case of any difficulty, consider that God, like a gymnastic trainer, has pitted you against a rough antagonist. . . . No man, in my opinion, has a more profitable difficulty on his hands than you have, provided you will but use it, as an athletic champion uses his antagonist.
>—Epictetus, *Discourses* I.24[1]

Life can be hectic and stressful, full of setbacks, disappointments, and frustration. It so rarely goes the way we want or hope. Religions, self-help gurus, and advertisers take advantage of our hope that someday, somehow, we can get to a place where we have no troubles (or at least very few). Perhaps it will be when we land that perfect job with financial security, buy the luxurious car we always wanted, or find a special person to share our life. Or maybe true contentment is found not in this life, but only in the next. Try these life hacks, buy the right things, perform the proper rituals (so you're told), and you too can live trouble-free! But are such promises believable? Or are they as unattainable as the wondrous Solla Sollew, locked away and defended by a Key-Slapping Slippard? What can we do about life's troubles?

The Greek and Roman philosophers of the Stoic tradition offer insightful meditations on these problems, as well as hard-nosed advice on how to live well when the world does not conform to our expectations. They don't claim to eliminate hardship. Nor do they promise trouble-free life. Instead, they offer strategies for dealing with problems head-on, a set of attitudes, practices, and habits of thought that enable you to live with the world *as it is* in the most effective and healthy way you can. It's not the only philosophy to offer this kind of advice, but it does, in my view, offer an eloquent and compelling vision of a good and meaningful human life that will appeal to many people.

WHAT IS STOICISM?

Stoicism was founded around 300 BCE by Zeno of Citium, a native of Cyprus who moved to Athens as a young man.[2] Stoicism flourished for centuries in the Greek and Roman world, influencing the development of early Christianity as well as subsequent Western philosophy. Much of the material that survives today from the ancient Stoic tradition comes from the writings of three Roman Stoics: Seneca (ca. 4 BCE–65 CE), an aristocratic advisor to Emperor Nero; Epictetus (ca. 50–135 CE), a freed slave who became a famous Stoic teacher; and Marcus Aurelius (121–180 CE), the Roman emperor.[3]

Stoicism is a *eudaimonist* philosophy, which, as the previous chapter explained, means it centers on the question of *eudaimonia*—happiness, flourishing, a well-lived human life. Stoic authors debated and wrote copiously on all areas of inquiry—logic, psychology, science, political philosophy—but for them these subjects derive their importance from the fundamental problem of human life: What does it mean to live an *excellent human life*, and what practical steps can we take to progress toward that goal?

The Stoics' answer sounds simpler than it is: We must live "in accordance with nature," both our human nature as rational and social beings and the broader Nature of the world we inhabit together.[4] Seneca eloquently explains the goal of a Stoic life in one of his essays:

> The life that is happy is in harmony with its own nature. This can only come about when the mind is in a healthy state and in permanent

possession of its own sanity, robust and vigorous, capable of the noblest endurance, responsive to circumstances . . . ready to make use of the gifts of fortune without being enslaved to them. You understand, even if I do not spell it out, that, once those things that irk or alarm us have been driven out, the result is lasting tranquility and freedom; and in place of pleasures that were paltry and ephemeral, there comes into being an overwhelming sense of joy, steady and invulnerable, a peace and concord of the soul, and sublimity that is also humane. For cruelty always arises from weakness.[5]

Humans are *rational* beings, capable, as no other animal is, of understanding and conforming ourselves consciously to the world in which we live. We can view ourselves as part of a larger community and act with reason and forethought to respond well and appropriately to the situations that arise. Those who deny, abandon, or fail to cultivate their distinctively human capacities, who refuse to respond calmly and thoughtfully to the circumstances the world throws at them, not only live frustrated, angry, and anxious lives but also fail to achieve much in the way of effective positive action. The Stoics offer a better way.

In this chapter, I focus on three interconnected Stoic disciplines: acceptance (understanding and accepting the world for what it is); reframing (changing your perspective or interpretation of events to overcome irrational and unhealthy attitudes, habits of thought, and emotions); and sociality or philanthropy (playing our part in our broader communities with integrity to create a better, more just world).[6] These disciplines aren't really separate—changing your perspective will let you see things more accurately, seeing more accurately enables you to understand your connections and duties to others, and so on. Still, it is helpful to focus on each separately, so that we can build a full picture of the Stoic mindset.

IT'S A TROUBLESOME WORLD: STOIC ACCEPTANCE

Now, I never had ever had
Troubles before.
So I said to myself,
"I don't want any more.
If I watch out for rocks
With my eyes straight ahead,

I'll keep out of trouble
Forever," I said. (Trouble)

When most people think of being "stoic," they think about *acceptance*: A "stoic" person accepts things without grumbling or getting emotional. To live well—"in accordance with nature"—you must understand both *your own* nature as a rational, social, finite, and mortal being and the nature of the world that you live in, the way it works, the kinds of things that happen. And as a first step, you must accept those inevitable realities. As Epictetus says in his *Handbook* for Stoic living, "Don't demand that things happen as you wish, but wish that they happen as they do happen, and you will get on well."[7] Failure to adjust to reality is a big reason people are miserable, frustrated, and upset so much of the time.

The hero of *I Had Trouble in Getting to Solla Sollew* learns this lesson the hard way. At first, he had been "real happy and carefree and young . . . nothing, not anything ever went wrong" (Trouble). But he was careless and, not looking where he was going, he stubbed his big toe on a rock. And so his "troubles" began.

The Stoics wrote perceptively about human development.[8] Young children, they explained, are instinctive beings, much like nonhuman animals in how they perceive and react to things. They follow instincts for self-preservation, grasping for what keeps them alive and whole, avoiding what hurts or threatens them. But soon they discover that not all of their desires are automatically filled—the world does not always give you what you want. A child wants cookies for dinner, but her parents say she must eat broccoli. Her beliefs about how things *should* be run smack into the unyielding rocks of how they *are*, and she feels frustration.

Frustrated desires and thwarted expectations are bad enough, but, as our hero soon discovers, "there are troubles / of more than one kind. / Some come from ahead / And some come from behind" (Trouble). Our bodies get hurt and sick; our possessions are broken or stolen; people we care about let us down or die. Sometimes it feels like we are "completely surrounded by trouble" (Trouble)!

So what do we do? Are we condemned to suffer? Our hero meets a "chap" riding a "One-Wheeler Wubble" who offers to take him to Solla Sollew, "where they *never* have troubles! At least, very few" (Trouble). He promises a quick fix. But contrary to the chap's assurances, the journey is neither short nor easy, and fears and challenges multiply. First, the camel pulling the Wubble gets sick. Then the bus doesn't arrive. A storm blows in, and the house our hero uses for shelter is washed away by a flood. He is saved from that danger only to be conscripted by an army, and then he is almost torn apart by vicious Poozers. He escapes into a tunnel with "billions of birds" engaged in strange and mysterious business. Only his dream of Solla Sollew—"sleeping on billowy billows / Of soft silk and satin marshmallow stuffed pillows" (Trouble)—keeps him pressing forward, until, finally, he arrives.

As it turns out, though, Solla Sollew has *one* small trouble—its gates are locked and no one can get in! As the Doorman explains,

> "There is only one door into Solla Sollew
> And we have a Key-Slapping Slippard. We do! . . .
> That's why we're stuck
> And why no one gets in and the town's gone to pot.
> It's a terrible state of affairs, is it not!" (Trouble)

The Doorman offers to take him to find "Boola Boo Ball / On the banks of the beautiful River Woo-Wall, / Where they never have troubles! *No troubles at all!*" (Trouble). This time, however, our hero makes a different choice:

> Then I started back home
> To the Valley of Vung.
> I know I'll have troubles.
> I'll, maybe, get stung.
> I'll always have troubles.
> I'll, maybe, get bit
> By that Green-Headed Quail
> On the place where I sit. (Trouble)

Turning aside from quick-fix solutions and fruitless quests, the hero realizes and accepts that he—like everyone else—will *always* have troubles. It's built into the way the world works, and anyone who promises otherwise—like the Wubble chap or the Doorman—is either self-deluded or trying to con you. Yet so often we deny reality and refuse to accept things as they are. In so doing, we replay the childhood dynamic of the toddler throwing a tantrum when she doesn't get cookies for dinner.

Epictetus's comments on this immaturity are scathing:

> If you wish your children, and your wife, and your friends to live forever, you are stupid; for you wish to control things which you cannot, you wish for things that belong to others to be your own. So likewise, if you wish your servant to be without fault, you are a fool; for you wish vice not to be vice, but something else.[9]

No matter how much you might wish for your family and friends to live forever, it is not going to happen. Nor is it reasonable to expect people around you always to act perfectly. They are going to be rude and thoughtless; they are going to drive while talking on their phones, forget appointments, and snap at each other when hungry. Being human, you'll mess up too! We're finite, vulnerable beings, and we need to accept that.

Epictetus has a helpful proposal for how we can think through these issues. In the first passage of his *Handbook*, he explains:

> Some things are in our control and others not. Things in our control are opinion, pursuit, desire, aversion, and, in a word, whatever are our own actions. Things not in our control are body, property, reputation, command, and, in one word, whatever are not our own actions.[10]

This idea is sometimes called Epictetus's "Dichotomy of Control." It warns us against two opposite but equally dangerous mistakes: both the expectation that we can control too much and the fatalism of thinking that we don't control anything about how our lives go.

On the one hand, much of what we deal with in life is not up to us. Sometimes it's obvious: I can't control the weather, earthquakes or drought, or the laws of nature. But, as Epictetus points out, we often overestimate our control over other, more central parts of our lives. For example, while I can take *care* of my body—exercise, eat healthy foods—I can't pick what kind of body I have or its genetic predispositions. I can't stop it from getting sick. And I can't stop accidents or other people from damaging or even destroying it. People who hope to control whatever happens to their bodies or how they look set themselves up for fruitless obsession and disappointment.

The journey to Solla Sollew demonstrates the limits of control. Through much of the story our hero is the victim of circumstances. The Wubble chap tells him where to pull; General Genghis Khan Schmitz conscripts him into his army; he's pushed around and banged by busy birds. Moreover, as so often happens, his determination to avoid difficulty drags him deeper in! As Epictetus puts it, "A man's master is he who is able to confer or remove whatever that man seeks or shuns. Whoever then would be free, let him wish nothing, let him decline nothing, which depends on others; else he must necessarily be a slave."[11]

All we *directly* control, Epictetus explains, are our own beliefs, desires, and choices, the attitudes we take about situations. But this doesn't mean hopeless resignation. Instead, Stoicism empowers the individual to take charge of their life and what it will be—you alone choose *how* you will respond and deal with what life gives you. This is what the hero of Solla Sollew finally recognizes. He cannot run from the world, because, if anything, running just makes things worse. Instead, he chooses to take it head on and to use what life gives him to build his own happiness in the world he has.

Epictetus has many great metaphors to explain this state of mind. In one passage, he compares living life with the way a skillful player approaches a game:

> Model yourself on card players. The chips don't matter, and the cards don't matter; how can I know what the deal will be? But making careful and skillful use of the deal—that's where my responsibility begins. . . . Where will I find good and bad? In me, in my choices. [12]

We are dealt our cards, and we must play them as skillfully as we can. Some get favorable hands—loving parents, a rich education, financial support—and some the opposite. Once you have your "hand," though, it is up to you to choose what you do with it. A "successful" life in an external sense is not guaranteed, nor is it the point. For the Stoics, a person lives well if they act with justice, wisdom, and skill, even if their more conventional projects end in failure.

You may wish you lived in Solla Sollew, with no rocks, no sick camels, no storms, no wars, and no jostling birds. But that isn't going to happen, and once we recognize and accept the limits of our control—focusing on our *own* attitudes and choices and leaving the rest—we can deal with it in a calmer and more effective way. It is not always easy to see where the limits fall, and it is just as unreasonable to accept passively what we might change as it is to fight against inevitabilities. It takes wisdom, gained through years of thoughtful life experience, to develop a keen understanding of the boundaries.

EVERYONE IS DUCKIE: REFRAMING

> That's why I say, "Duckie!
> Don't grumble! Don't stew!
> Some critters are much-much,
> oh, ever so much-much,
> so muchly much-much more unlucky than you!" (Lucky)

While we can't change what happens, we can change our *attitude* about it. The Stoics argued, rightly I believe, that the way we respond to events, and the emotions that we feel, result from the interpretations that we place on what we experience. Change the way you interpret or *frame* what has happened, and you can change your response.

When I perceive an external event (for example, another driver swerves toward me on the freeway and almost causes an accident), my initial reaction is reflexive, a kind of bodily response (my pulse rises, muscles tighten, face becomes flushed). But then my mind *constructs* or *interprets* the event and its significance, as I make choices about how to frame the event in my mind. If I choose to construct the event in the wrong way (this person is an idiot, he acted very badly, I need to teach him a lesson), I will react in an emotional, counterproductive, and possibly dangerous way (honking the horn, yelling, tailgating the other driver). The way I react—with disturbing emotions (like rage, anxiety, or despair) as opposed to a more rational response (calm cheerfulness, friendliness, and determination)—depends on my interpretation. If we can *reframe* the event, we can respond in a more rational and productive way.

The ending of *Solla Sollew* provides a great example of how reframing works. For most of the book, the hero runs away, trying not to face troubles at all. But finally, he adopts a new perspective:

> I've bought a big bat.
> I'm all ready, you see.
> Now my troubles are going
> To have troubles with *me!* (Trouble)

Now he accepts that troubles are unavoidable and decides to take them head on. He sees that troubles are part of his path to happiness. [13]

In a powerful passage from the *Discourses*, Epictetus suggests a way to reframe difficulty:

> What do you think that Hercules would have been if there had not been such a lion, and hydra, and stag, and boar, and certain unjust and bestial men, whom Hercules used to drive away and clear out? And what would he have been doing if there had been nothing of the kind? Is it not plain that he would have wrapped himself up and have slept? . . . He would not have been a Hercules, when he was dreaming away all his life in such luxury and ease. . . . Come then, do you also having observed these things look to the faculties which you have, and when you have looked at them, say: "Bring now, O Zeus, any difficulty that Thou pleasest, for I have means given to me by Thee and powers for honoring myself through the things which happen."[14]

Hercules became a hero *because* of the trouble he faced; his labors forged him into his best self. Each experience can be a challenge to improve. So the Valley of Vung has rocks—all the better to develop your strength, endurance, and ability to climb!

Suppose that someone you love dies. It's considered one of the worst things that can happen, perhaps even a catastrophe from which you will never recover. Epictetus suggests a different way to think about the loss, so that you can move forward in life:

> Under no circumstance say "I have lost something," only "I have returned it." Did a child of yours die? No, it was returned. Your wife died? No, *she* was returned. "My land was confiscated." No, it too was returned.
>
> "But the person who took it was a thief."
>
> Why concern yourself with the means by which the original giver effects its return? As long as he entrusts it to you, look after it as something yours to enjoy only for a time—the way a traveler regards a hotel.[15]

In another passage, Epictetus compares difficulties to a heavy container that you must carry:

> Every circumstance comes with two handles, with one of which you can hold it, while with the other conditions are insupportable. If your brother mistreats you, don't try to come to grips with it by dwelling on the wrong he's done (because that approach makes it unbearable);

remind yourself that he's your brother, that you two grew up together; then you'll find that you can bear it. [16]

In any situation, you have a choice about how to "come to grips with it." Any problem appears intractable if you think about it the wrong way— the person on whom my whole happiness depends is gone; my brother has betrayed me! You'll see no way forward if you frame things that way. But, as Epictetus perceptively observes, there are other "handles." Shift your perspective—my child has been given back; he is my brother, with whom I shared my formative years—and you'll be able to move forward without the incapacitating emotional baggage.

Another Stoic method for shaking free of inhibiting thoughts and emotions is to step back and view your situation from a broader perspective. Dr. Seuss playfully explores this idea in *Did I Ever Tell You How Lucky You Are?* The main character meets an old man—a Sage, in Stoic terms— sitting on a cactus in an empty desert:

> He sat on a terrible prickly place.
> But he sang with a sweet smile on his face:
> When you think things are bad,
> when you feel sour and blue,
> when you start to get mad . . .
> you should do what *I* do!
> Just tell yourself, Duckie,
> you're really quite lucky!
> Some people are much more . . .
> oh, ever so much more . . .
> oh, muchly much-much more
> unlucky than you! (Lucky)

The Cactus Sage then describes all of the terrible things people suffer— however bad you have it, he says, at least you aren't these guys!

Epictetus uses a similar technique:

> We can familiarize ourselves with the will of nature by calling to mind our common experiences. When a friend breaks a glass, we are quick to say, "Oh, bad luck." It's only reasonable, then, that when a glass of your own breaks, you accept it in the same patient spirit. Moving on to graver things: when somebody's wife or child dies, to a man we all routinely say, "Well, that's part of life." But if one of our own family

is involved, then right away it's "Poor, poor me!" We would do better to remember how we react when a similar loss afflicts others. [17]

This passage sounds harsh, but sometimes honest advice is hard to hear. It is easy to get caught up in a dreadful moment, shut into our own narrow perspective and selfish desires. The emotions overwhelm us, and we cannot see past the grief and hurt right in front of us; thus we inflate the tragedy of what has happened so that we no longer think clearly about it. Seeing our problems in the context of broader patterns and common experiences of human life can make them more manageable. What's happened to me has happened to others. Other people have suffered this; I am not alone. They recovered and moved forward, and so can I!

The problems humans face are akin, and we are more resilient than we know, if only we give ourselves the chance. Like others working long hours just to keep up with bills, Ali Sard "has to mow grass in his uncle's back yard" for the "piffulous pay of two Dooklas a day. / And Ali can't *live* on such piffulous pay!" (Lucky). Some struggle with chronic illness; similarly, "the Crumple-horn, Web-footed, Green-bearded Schlottz" has a tail that "is entailed with un-solvable knots" (Lucky). Your job might seem pointless and repetitive, but "poor Mr. Potter . . . has to cross *t*'s / and he has to dot *i*'s / in an I-and-T factory / out in Van Nuys!" (Lucky). Everyone feels lonely sometimes; so does "Gucky Gown, / who lives by himself / ninety miles out of town, / in the Ruins of Ronk" (Lucky). Each of the wacky characters and situations Duckie learns about represents a common human experience. We know these things happen—some will happen to us! But, the Stoics insist, we can handle them.

CREATING A REAL SOLLA SOLLEW: STOIC SOCIALITY

Everything that you see, everything human and divine is one. We are all limbs of one all-encompassing body. Nature brought us into existence as creatures related to one another, forming us from the same elements for the same ends. She instilled in us reciprocal affection and made us innately sociable. . . . That line of poetry should ever be in our hearts and on our lips: "I am human and I count nothing human as foreign to me." [18]

When you zoom out and see how lucky you are, the most important lesson to learn is that we are not alone—we have each other. Humans are not isolated calculating machines; we are *social* beings, and we grow and flourish as members of communities that provide our lives meaning. As Epictetus explains, "As human beings, we are born to be faithful to one another, and . . . whoever denies this denies their humanity."[19] Epictetus confronts a man who was caught cheating on his wife—he's become less than human, like a wasp that stings and poisons everyone around him.[20] In another passage he talks to a father who ran away when his daughter was deathly ill. What kind of fatherly affection did that show?[21] He selfishly prioritized his own comfort (he couldn't bear seeing her suffer) over his role as a father and his daughter's need to have him there.

Our relationships and social roles, Epictetus explains, show us how to act. You are a son or daughter, a brother or sister, a friend, a spouse, a parent, a coworker. These roles call for certain feelings and actions. Turn away from human relationships, abandon the honesty, loyalty, patience, and support they require, and we surrender our humanity. We become no more than beasts, driven by fear, jealousy, and hatred to tear apart those who should be closest and most important to us.[22]

These close relationships are oddly missing from most of Dr. Seuss's stories. The hero of *Solla Sollew* has no family or friends in the Valley of Vung. Duckie gets advice from the Cactus Sage, but we don't hear about his parents, siblings, or neighbors. Each ends his story wiser but evidently still alone to face life's challenges. (Seuss stories like *Oh, the Places You'll Go!*, the Horton stories, and the Bartholomew Cubbins stories are similar—a lone protagonist faces adversity, without any friends or much support mentioned.)

The hero of *Solla Sollew* has a bat, but will he spend his whole life fighting Quail and Skritzes, trying to beat his problems into submission? Recognizing that troubles will not go away and reframing them as challenges to be overcome is a good start, but he'll find an effective solution only if he recognizes and develops connections to *others* with whom he can work to build a better world.

The same goes for Duckie. By the end of the book, he has perspective. He sees that his own problems are similar to and less severe than problems faced by others. But smug self-satisfaction cannot be the end of it. One cannot flourish as a human while sitting on a cactus in the middle of nowhere. Human nature demands we reach out to each other, share our labors, help each other solve puzzles, and ease each other's loneliness and isolation. Thinking about what others are going through should not merely make you feel better about yourself; it should also evoke compassion and a sense of shared humanity.[23]

Our most important identity, according to the Stoics, is as a *citizen of the universe.* Epictetus puts it this way:

> Who are you? In the first place, a human being, which is to say, a being possessed of no greater faculties than free choice . . . and reason: They set you apart from wild animals; they set you apart from sheep. By virtue of these two faculties you are a member of the universe with full citizen rights; you are born not to serve but to govern. . . . Now, what does the title "citizen" mean? In this role, a person never acts in his own interest or thinks of himself alone, but, like a hand or foot that had sense and realized its place in the natural order, all its actions and desires aim at nothing except contributing to the common good.[24]

Epictetus says, "you are born not to serve *but to govern*"—that's why we're different from wild beasts and domesticated animals. This fact creates both an opportunity—the freedom to make our own choices—and a responsibility. Though each person's area of influence is limited, we each contribute, in our small ways, to creating the world in which we live. The responsibility for creating a healthy, flourishing community falls upon each of us. Solla Sollew may be locked away, but perhaps, through embracing our shared humanity, we can create a Solla Sollew we can live in together![25]

When bad things happen, we're tempted to despair, to hide, to turn our frustration and anger against others, to fight each other for scraps of security or indulgent pleasure. Epictetus and the Stoics refused to give in to this shortsighted and immature egoism and nihilism. In fact, most of us don't know how lucky we are to live with joy and beauty, where each of us has, in our ability to reflect and reason and choose, a fragment of the divine, and with that the ability to appreciate and *participate* in the unfolding of the world.[26] To paraphrase the poet Terence, whom Seneca quoted in the passage above: You are human; let nothing human be foreign to you.

5

ONE MUST IMAGINE DR. SEUSS HAPPY

Existential Freedom and the Search for Meaning in
Happy Birthday to You! and *I Had Trouble in Getting to*
Solla Sollew

Elizabeth Butterfield

Open your mouth and sound off at the sky!
Shout loud at the top of your voice, "I AM I!
ME!
I am I!
And I may not know why
But I know that I like it.
Three cheers! I AM I!"

—Dr. Seuss, *Happy Birthday to You!*

As for us, whatever the case may be, we believe in freedom. . . .
Freedom is the source from which all significations and all values
spring. It is the original condition of all justification of existence. The
man who seeks to justify his life must want freedom itself absolutely
and above everything else.

—Simone de Beauvoir, *The Ethics of Ambiguity*[1]

Have you ever paused to wonder, who am I? Why am I here? What is
my purpose? And where should I even begin to look for the answers? At
some point, these perennial questions of human existence seem to arise in
almost everyone's life. Perhaps it is a common experience that we all
share—part of what we might call "the human condition."

What does it mean to call these questions "perennial"? We can think of their perpetual, cyclical return, like flowers that return to blossom every year, in two ways. First, take the question "Why am I here?" Let's say that someone, maybe the ancient Greek philosopher Aristotle, tells us that he has found the answer—he believes he can tell us *why* we exist, and what our true purpose is. Well, that is all well and good, but it's not like his particular answer will solve the question satisfactorily for all humans in all times. Human beings who are curious continue to pose these questions themselves, throughout history and generations.

Second, there is a way these questions about existence are perennial even in our own individual lives. It may be that at some point in my life, I come to feel as if I have a really good answer to this question, and that answer satisfies me and gives me a sense of direction. But the way life often works is that as time moves forward, things change, and I change, and there is no guarantee that this answer will continue to ring true. And so these perennial questions of human existence reemerge again and again for us throughout a lifetime, as that daffodil that arises to greet us anew each spring.

Human beings tend to be the sorts of creatures who crave answers and a sense of purpose, who desire to find truth and certainty and understanding. This is at the heart of our curiosity, and at the heart of our journey in philosophy. But as a group of philosophers called "Existentialists" noticed, the answers to these big questions tend to be slippery—they come and go, they change and shift, and we can't really seem to rely on them in any permanent way. The answers are not always obvious or easily found. In fact, some of these philosophers suggest that finding truly permanent or objectively "true" answers to these questions is impossible. Perhaps the answers are beyond our reach, or don't actually exist at all.

If this is the case—that it is a fundamental characteristic of our shared human condition to spend our lives really invested in finding answers to these big questions, but with satisfying answers always beyond our reach—what are we supposed to *do* with that? Given these circumstances, what could it mean to live *well*?

That wise philosopher Dr. Seuss explored this question in *Happy Birthday to You!* In this work, as we visit Katroo and celebrate the amazing fact that we were born at all, we also find the questions "What does it mean to be you?" and "What is it that makes being a human being so special anyway?"

If only we could do as they do in Katroo . . . but, of course, real life is not all parties and celebrations. It feels safe to say that another part of our shared human condition is that at some point the going gets tough, and this is what we find in *I Had Trouble in Getting to Solla Sollew*. When we're partying in Katroo, exploring the deeper questions of existence might seem like an entertaining pastime. But when you find yourself being attacked by a Skritz and a Skrink, and you have "*so* many troubles, I just couldn't think!" (Trouble), these questions inevitably take on more urgency. We might find ourselves asking: Where can we turn for answers? Is there any escape from suffering? And again, how can we live *well*?

I won't promise you that in reading this chapter you'll find any satisfactory answers. In fact, I feel pretty safe wagering that you won't. But, as Bertrand Russell wrote, "Philosophy is to be studied, not for the sake of any definite answers to its questions, since no definite answers can, as a rule, be known to be true, but rather for the sake of the questions themselves."[2]

So let's spend some time hanging out with one of the coolest groups of philosophers: the existentialists. The existentialists weren't really an organized school of thought as much as a loose collection of intellectuals who enjoyed having passionate conversations about these big questions. While existentialism has its roots in the work of nineteenth-century thinkers like Søren Kierkegaard (1813–1855) and Friedrich Nietzsche (1844–1900), I'm going to focus on three twentieth-century French thinkers: Jean-Paul Sartre (1905–1980), Simone de Beauvoir (1908–1986), and Albert Camus (1913–1960). While many of the philosophers labeled as existentialists disagree with each other—and some object to the label altogether—one thing that many of them have in common is a rejection of the more abstract concerns of the tradition of Western philosophy. Instead, many of them were motivated by a desire to *do philosophy* in a way that is relevant to our lived experiences. They tried to take philosophy out of the metaphysical clouds and put questions like "Who am I? Why am I here? How should I live?" at the forefront of philosophical concern.

IF WE DIDN'T HAVE BIRTHDAYS, YOU WOULDN'T BE YOU. IF YOU'D NEVER BEEN BORN, WELL THEN WHAT WOULD YOU DO? (BIRTHDAY)

In *Happy Birthday to You!* we visit the land of Katroo, where "they sure know how to say happy birthday to you!" (Birthday). It's a celebration of just how special it is that you exist, that you were born at all. We are told that on your birthday, the day begins with a visit from the Great Birthday Bird, who is in charge of the day's festivities. On this day, you get to eat whatever you want. There are no rules. You don't have to be tidy or neat. You can eat with your feet. You can travel on a railway with boats built just for you. You can visit the birthday flower jungle, where who-bubs will clip the best sniffing flowers just for you. You can go swimming in mountaintop tubs built just for you. You get presents: the best pet of all, a time-telling fish. And the day ends with a big birthday bash at the birthday pal-alace, with music and singing, and the biggest cake ever, with friends from all over Katroo. "When it ends, you're much happier, richer and fatter. And the Bird flies you home on a very soft platter." And "all of it, all of it, all is for you" (Birthday).

But in the midst of all this celebration Dr. Seuss throws in some pretty deep thoughts. Your "day of all days" is meant to celebrate the amazing fact that you were born at all, and just how special you are. But what, he asks, if you had never been born at all?

> If we didn't have birthdays, you wouldn't be you.
> If you'd never been born, well then what would you do?
> If you'd never been born, well then what would you be?
> You *might* be a fish! Or a toad in a tree! . . .
> Or worse than all that. . . . Why, you might be a WASN'T! (Birthday)

This line of questioning about what it means to be human, as opposed to, say, a tree, is reminiscent of Jean-Paul Sartre's book *Being and Nothingness*. In this text, as Sartre sets out to describe exactly what it is that makes us special, he contrasts two different types of being, or ways of existing. The first he calls pure being-in-itself. This is the type of existence that we find in material objects or plants that don't possess what we would recognize as consciousness or freedom. Sartre gives us the examples of a stone, or a cauliflower. These things are fully determined or dependent on other things. The stone can't spontaneously or freely decide to roll down the hill and plop into the stream. Its movement, and its whole existence, depends on factors outside of itself. And (as far as we know) the stone has no conscious awareness of these experiences. It is not troubled by the fact that it is rolling down the hill, and it doesn't have to struggle over how to respond to the fact that it has now fallen into the stream. It just is.

At the other extreme, we have what Sartre calls pure being-for-itself. This would be the sort of existence that is completely free and independent, like we might find in the Christian idea of God. God does not depend on others, and his existence is not determined by others. He is fully free, all-powerful, and self-causing. This is the realm of pure freedom.

According to Sartre, humans occupy a special position because as long as we are alive and conscious, we dwell in an ambiguous middle space, experiencing *both* types of being. On the one hand, I am made of being-in-itself in the sense that I have a body that is not ultimately within my control. I have physical needs—for example, I cannot freely choose to no longer need to breathe. My body is subject to gravity, to time, to aging. I am vulnerable to injury and sickness.[3] In these and many other ways, my existence is dependent on other things. Sartre refers to this as the "facticity" of my being—the facts of my existence. My facticity includes things like where and when I was born, my height, the language I grew up speaking, and other similar factors. All of these things shape and determine who I become.

But as long as I am a living, conscious human being, and I am not, as Dr. Seuss says, a fish or a toad in a tree, then I am always also being-for-itself, which means that within this situation I am also always free. Sartre refers to this as my "transcendence," because as long as I am alive and conscious I am free to transcend or rise above my given circumstances. Now exactly what kind of freedom are we talking about? In *Being and Nothingness*, Sartre isn't so concerned with political freedoms or practical freedoms. It is the freedom of mind to choose how we will understand and interpret what we are experiencing. It is also a freedom to assign value, in the sense of getting to decide what we will care about. We are free to choose how we will respond to our experiences, and that includes our emotional responses.

It might seem pretty normal to hear someone say, "When you ate my slice of birthday cake, you made me really mad!" But Sartre would disagree. This simple statement ignores our freedom, and doesn't accurately take responsibility for the role we play in our own choice of responses to our lives. My little brother may have eaten the cake I was looking forward to all day. That is the fact of the situation. But I also get to choose how I am going to interpret what happened, and how I will respond. If I respond with anger, that is a product of my own free choice.

Sartre argues that even in situations in which we seem completely determined, we retain our fundamental human freedom. Consider, for example, someone who is imprisoned, chained to a wall, who has lost all practical freedom, control over movement, and so on. As long as this person remains alive and conscious, he or she is still free in the sense of having the freedom of consciousness to think about the situation and to decide how to understand it, interpret it, and respond. As long as we are alive and conscious, we are always both free and determined at the same time. Sartre may overstate his case, as he is prone to do, when he writes, "Man is nothing else but that which he makes of himself. That is the first principle of existentialism."[4] We might rephrase this to say, "A man can always make something out of what is made of him."[5] And this is fundamental to what it means to be human.

YOU HAVE TO BE BORN, OR YOU DON'T GET A PRESENT

> If you'd never been born, then you might be an ISN'T!
> An Isn't has no fun at all. No he disn't.
> He never has birthdays, and that isn't pleasant.
> You have to be born, or you don't get a present. (Birthday)

So while we are celebrating your birthday in Katroo, and celebrating what an amazing thing it is that you were ever born, one of the best things about the day is that you get a present! Now we might think of this in terms of gifts, like a time-telling fish. But, to take this more literally, if you were never born, you would never get to dwell in this moment, in this *present*. And this is another common theme that we find running through the works of many existentialist philosophers—the fact that, as human beings, we are bound by time. And, even more important, as time is passing, we constantly have choices to make.

This takes us right back to the perennial questions of human existence. What are we going to do with our time? How are we going to make the most of this present? Sartre has shown us that freedom is central to our existence—but now, what are we actually going to DO with it? Sartre's emphasis on freedom might at first seem exhilarating, liberating, exciting. We can do anything! We are free! But it can also be intimidating, because along with freedom comes responsibility. And how we ought to choose is not always so obvious.

In "Existentialism Is a Humanism," Sartre—who is an atheist—explains that if God existed, we could believe that when God created human beings, he created them with a specific purpose in mind. He would have made us with a human nature, a built-in pattern to follow. And so when we face these perennial questions of human existence, it would be possible to seek true, complete answers to these questions. God made me for a purpose. God gives me a reason for existing. How should I choose? I should choose according to God's plan.

But Sartre argues that in the absence of God, there is no such thing as an essential human nature. There is no objectively true preset pattern for us to follow. What we have, rather, are human beings, thrown into existence, free, conscious, scrambling to figure out what we are doing. According to Sartre, it is human beings who come up with ideas like "values" and "purposes," and we use these ideas to try to make sense of our existence. But they possess no greater meaning. If something appears meaningful to us, it is because we freely choose to interpret it as meaningful—we are the ones who assign it meaning. Dwelling at the intersection of freedom and determinism, it is up to us to make something out of our situation.

THE TROUBLE BEGINS

Back in Katroo, the idea that I may not have all the answers was not so troubling. With carefree hearts we were able to "sound off at the sky." "ME! I am I! And I may not know why, but I know that I like it. *Three cheers!* I AM I!" (Birthday). But life is not always a party. Unfortunately, not every day can be our day of all days.

This takes us to *I Had Trouble in Getting to Solla Sollew*. The opening illustration on the front cover introduces us to the main character, who is stuck in a maze that has no obvious beginning or end. It's not clear what the goal is, or which way he should go. We find him wide-eyed, with his mouth turned down in a frown. His arms and legs are turned out in different directions like he's not sure which way to step next. This poor kid is all mixed up. How did he end up in this mess? Well, he begins by telling us that once upon a time, he started out happy, and that nothing ever seemed to go wrong, but then "one day I was walking along / And I guess I got careless. I guess I got gawking / At daisies and not looking where I was walking" (Trouble).

At first our friend's troubles start small. He stubs his toe on a rock; then he falls and sprains the bone in the tip of his tail. He had never had any troubles before, and he doesn't want any more, so his first response is to think that maybe, if he can just be more careful and look out for rocks, "'With my eyes straight ahead, I'll keep out of trouble forever,' I said. . . . But watching ahead. . . . Well, it just didn't work" (Trouble). Next his tail is bitten by a quilligan quail, "And I learned there are troubles of more than one kind. Some come from ahead and some come from behind" (Trouble). Once again, he determines to be careful. But once again, this resolution fails to keep him from trouble, as he's then attacked from above and below by stinging Skritz and Skrink.

As our friend begins to learn, being careful isn't enough to keep us from having troubles, and it can't ever be enough. If we think back to what Sartre tells us about the human condition, we see that we are contingent, dependent creatures who are vulnerable. We might have freedom of consciousness, but this consciousness is carried around in a material body in a material world. And this material body needs some food and water and air, and it is aging, and it is prone to sickness. We are creatures to whom anything can happen. One of the most important facts of human existence is that the situation is NOT totally within my control.

Just when our friend is coming to realize that being careful will not be enough to protect him from trouble, he meets someone who promises him an answer—an escape:

> There I was,
> All completely surrounded by trouble,
> When a chap rumbled up in a One-Wheeler Wubble.
> "Young fellow," he said, "what has happened to you
> Has happened to me and to other folks, too.
> So I'll tell you what I have decided to do . . .

I'm off to the City of Solla Sollew . . .
Where they *never* have troubles! At least, very few." (Trouble)

The Wubble chap promises him a means of escaping his vulnerability. At first this sounds like an excellent opportunity. We can understand what our friend might be thinking: "Look, here is someone who is wiser than I. He knows how it feels to have troubles, but he also has an answer to the problem. I'll trust him and follow." Surely we can all sympathize with this desire.

Another common theme among existentialist philosophers is our experience of anxiety. Whereas at first glance, Sartre's emphasis on our freedom may have seemed really exhilarating, as time goes on we also discover that freedom can be difficult. In the face of the open-endedness of our own possibilities, and lacking clear answers to our big questions, we experience anxiety. This is why Sartre writes what at first may seem puzzling: "Man is condemned to be free."[6] Our freedom is a life sentence of responsibility that is inescapable. So, when the troubles come along, I have choices to make about how I am going to respond. But in the absence of a clear set of instructions, it can be really tempting to look outside of ourselves for direction, as our troubled friend does when he meets the Wubble chap.

SERIOUSLY IN PURSUIT OF SOLLA SOLLEW

Another existentialist philosopher, Simone de Beauvoir, makes some really helpful observations about our tendency to want to flee our own freedom (and our responsibility) in her book *The Ethics of Ambiguity*. Beauvoir explains that when we are children, we naturally believe that the answers and values we are given by our adult authority figures are objectively true. But at some point in adolescence, we come to realize that no one actually has the answers—that humans are the creators of meaning and value, and that all of those adults were just making it up, as we ourselves must also do.

Beauvoir explains that this is a crucial turning point in our existence. What matters is how we choose to respond to this insight. We can choose to be honest with ourselves about our own freedom, which requires taking responsibility for making our own decisions, as well as honestly dealing with the consequences of our choices. Or, if the anxiety of ambiguity and not knowing gets to be too much, we might fall into another pattern: we might look outside of ourselves for an objective truth to ground our existence, to give us a sense of purpose. Both Beauvoir and Sartre see this as a form of dishonesty with the self and as a flight from responsibility.

Beauvoir gives many examples of this sort of flight, but one that is particularly poignant is that of the "serious man." The serious man is someone who looks outside himself for an ultimate answer and finds one that he chooses to dedicate himself to. It could be a religious purpose, a political party, or perhaps a social identity like "father." Whatever it is, the serious man takes this ultimate truth and holds tightly to it, using it to provide him with a definite sense of identity and, more important, a well-defined set of specific instructions about what he should value and how he should live. This replaces the open-endedness of possibility, and the groundlessness of lacking objective answers, with a clear sense of iden-tity and purpose. It temporarily numbs his natural anxiety.

As our troubled friend follows the Wubble chap on the path to Solla Sollew, he encounters unimaginable troubles along the way. The road gets rocky and tricky, and our friend starts to feel icky. The camel gets sick, and soon our friend finds himself pulling the camel along (and the Wubble chap too). The chap bosses him around while our friend does all the work. We get a sense that the chap might be taking advantage of our friend's anxiety.

Soon he must part ways with the chap and the camel, but, believing in the promise of Solla Sollew, our troubled friend continues on. But things just keep getting worse. He journeys to the Happy Way Bus Route, only to find that the bus can't go and he'll have to keep walking. After another one hundred miles, it starts to rain, so he takes shelter in a rodent-infested house that is cold as ice, and while he is sleeping and dreaming of Solla Sollew, a flood washes the house away. He floats twelve days in the floodwaters but is finally rescued, only to find that he's been fished out of the water by a general in the middle of a war, and he is forced to join the army. Now he's a private first class, with a shooter and one bean. As they retreat from the enemy, our friend jumps into a vent hole that leads to a "frightful black tunnel." He spends three days in the crowded and claustrophobic tunnel, starving, damp, and injured. The text and the drawings bring to mind images of World War I trench warfare or daring dark escapes in World War II. We see the darker side of Dr. Seuss. This is usually when my own children ask me to stop reading the book and go back to *Happy Birthday*.

But it is worth remarking that up until this point, our friend keeps going. He's tired, cold, wet, in danger, living through traumatic experiences that push the very limits of what a person can handle—but because of his faith in the promise of Solla Sollew, he is motivated to keep going. Looking outside of himself for grounding, a guarantee, he founds his whole being on this hope of getting to Solla Sollew. The goal gives his life what feels like an objective meaning. He's a serious man with a serious purpose. We have to acknowledge that, in many ways, what an existentialist might see here as an "escape" can actually be a source of incredible strength and comfort. It sustains our friend through seriously hard times. It enables him to patiently endure his present suffering, because, in the end, he trusts he will reach the Promised Land.

Unfortunately, as our troubled friend will soon learn, this attempt to ground his existence in what Beauvoir calls "an external absolute" is futile. Beauvoir explains that the serious man's attempt to find purpose outside of himself will fail because these objectively true answers don't exist—there are only human beings, who freely create meaning and values and use them to interpret their experiences in the world.

After three traumatic days in the crowded underground tunnel, our friend sticks his head out of a tiny trap door, and lo and behold, he sees blue sky. "There it was! With its glittering towers in the air! I'd made it! I'd done it! At last I was there! And I knew that I'd left all my troubles behind" (Trouble).

Our friend has reached his destination! The kind Doorman welcomes him to Solla Sollew, "where we never have troubles. At least very few" (Trouble). But the Doorman goes on to explain that there's just one little problem: Apparently, there is only one door into Solla Sollew, and the keyhole in that door is inhabited by a "Key-Slapping Slippard" who always slaps the key right out of the keyhole. The Doorman explains that this means, "No one gets in and the town's gone to pot. It's a terrible state of affairs, is it not!" So the Doorman himself has decided to leave for "the city of Boola Boo Ball, on the banks of the beautiful River Woo-Wall, where they never have troubles! *No troubles at all!*" As he leaves, the Doorman offers our friend a promise he has heard before: "'Come on along with me,' he said as he ran, 'And you'll never have *any* more troubles, young man!'" (Trouble).

Unimaginable. Inconceivable. How could this be? After everything he has endured . . . all the suffering that seemed to be worthwhile because it was supposed to serve the purpose of reaching the Promised Land. How could there be troubles here too? What is our friend going to do?

INTERLUDE: SISYPHUS IN SOLLA SOLLEW

Let's take a deep breath and pause for a moment to consider the situation of Sisyphus. Sisyphus is a character from ancient Greek mythology who deceived the gods and cheated death. So when they finally got him to the underworld for good, the gods decided that no typical run-of-the-mill punishment would do. No, no, for Sisyphus they had to come up with something clever, suited to the trickster he was.

Sisyphus was sentenced to an eternity of hard labor—he must roll an enormous boulder to the top of a mountain, only to watch it roll back down again, and to begin the task once more. Here we need some suspension of disbelief—this is the ancient Greek underworld, after all. Sisyphus cannot simply walk away or stop pushing the boulder. He has no control over that part of his situation. He is doomed to repeat the infinite cycle.

Now wherein lies the clever torture in this punishment? It is not simply the physical struggle. The gods could have come up with any sort of task for that. No, what makes this punishment especially cruel is its *futility*. It is that Sisyphus has to struggle, only to watch all of his work come to nothing. This plays on our human craving for meaning and purpose—we want all of our work and struggles and experiences to *mean* something. We want to achieve some sort of answer or permanence or legacy. We want things to matter!

The parallels to our troubled friend in his search for Solla Sollew are painfully clear. He worked so hard for his dream. He was willing to sacrifice and to suffer for the promise of a better future. That promise helped him to make sense of all of his struggles. But once he arrives, it must seem as if all of his struggles were for nothing. Heartbreaking! Soul crushing! What will he do?

The existentialist author Albert Camus uses the story of Sisyphus as a metaphor for our own human predicament. In his essay "The Myth of Sisyphus," Camus describes the situation of a "modern man" caught up in routine: "Rising, streetcar, four hours in the office or the factory, meal, streetcar, four hours of work, meal, sleep, and Monday Tuesday Wednesday Thursday Friday and Saturday according to the same rhythm."[7] Like Sisyphus, we wear ourselves out, but to what end? Camus writes that at some point in everyone's life, "it happens that the stage sets collapse,"[8] and we look deeper into our situation and begin to ask: What does it all mean? What am I living for?

Camus again draws attention to the fact that we humans are the sorts of beings who crave meaning. But as an atheist, he shares with Sartre and Beauvoir the belief that while it is a fundamental part of our human condition to pose these big perennial questions of human existence, the final answers can never actually be found. Camus writes that nothing in life has objective meaning—even though our lives seem to be defined by the need for it—and he calls this absurd.

But of course, as an existentialist, Camus's main concern is not to simply say "life is absurd"—he is much more interested in the next question, which is: What are we going to *do* about it? How should we *live*?

In the face of the absurdity of existence, we could give in to despair and let absurdity crush us. But Camus says that would be the wrong response. Instead, he suggests that "one must imagine Sisyphus happy."[9] Sisyphus may have no practical freedom left—he cannot simply walk away from his situation. And, likewise, we cannot simply walk away from the absurdity of existence—this is the reality of the situation we find ourselves in. But even in this situation, Sisyphus retains the freedom to interpret his experience. He gets to choose what he will think of it, how he will value it. Camus suggests that if Sisyphus were to fall into despair and to see himself as a victim, then the gods would win—Sisyphus's punishment would truly be torture. But what if Sisyphus could find a way to make the situation his own? What if, for example, he found a way to entertain himself along the way? "Hey, let's see if I can get the boulder up faster this time than the last!" Or "Wow, look at the cool colors on the boulder as the light reflects off of it as I roll it along." Or "Let me whistle a tune to the rhythm of the work." With a change in attitude, freely choosing to make something of his situation, Sisyphus can give it a different value and once again outsmart the gods. He may be pushing the boulder, but now, as Camus writes, "his rock is his thing."[10] And it is no longer torture.

Camus suggests that, like Sisyphus, we have the power to be "the absurd hero." Instead of giving in to the meaninglessness of existence, or feeling sorry for ourselves, we can take responsibility for freely creating *our own* meaning and value. Take that, absurdity! I'm going to make my life have meaning anyway! I'm going to make my rock my thing!

MY TROUBLES ARE GOING TO HAVE TROUBLES WITH ME!

So we return to our troubled friend. He has reached Solla Sollew only to find that the Promised Land has gone to pot. He finds that the "absolute" that had given his struggle meaning and purpose doesn't actually exist. And now he is faced with the question: Will he move on to the next offer of an absolute, and follow the Doorman to Boola Boo Ball?

> I'd have no more troubles . . .
> That's what the man said.
> So I started to go.
> But I didn't.
> Instead . . .
> I started back home
> To the Valley of Vung.
> I know I'll have troubles. . . .
> I'll always have troubles. . . .
> But I've bought a big bat.
> I'm all ready, you see.
> Now my troubles are going
> To have troubles with *me*! (Trouble)

At the beginning of the tale, our friend was troubled by trouble, and he was searching for an escape from his vulnerability. As we are so often tempted to do, he looked outside of himself for the answers and found someone more than happy to oblige and to promise him an absolute, an escape. But, eventually, our friend comes to realize that there are no perfect answers, no escape routes in life. He comes to reconcile himself to the reality of his situation: that he is vulnerable and dependent. The difference now is that instead of letting himself be defined by the situation, he is taking matters into his own hands. He is embracing his freedom, and taking responsibility for creating his own meaning.

As the existentialists remind us, even when we don't seem to have any good options for escaping our troubles, even when all the chips are down, we still have the freedom to choose how we are going to interpret what we are experiencing, and how we will respond. We get to choose our attitude in response to the situation. We could flee, we could complain, or we could celebrate it. To a very great extent, and much more than we often want to admit, we have the opportunity to create ourselves, as well as the world we live in, through the choices we make.

It is a fundamental part of being human to pose these perennial questions of human existence. But in a world in which we can never find complete answers, how can we live well? The existentialists, and our friends from Seuss, might tell us: embrace the chance to create the answers for yourself. Step up and *give* your life meaning. Make it meaningful for you, while also knowing that the answers you come up with today are not permanent. Your answers will grow and change as you grow and change. So as they say in Katroo:

> Shout loud, I am lucky to be what I am!
> Thank goodness I am not just a clam or a ham
> Or a dusty old jar of sour gooseberry jam!
> I am what I am! That's a great thing to be!
> If I say so myself, HAPPY BIRTHDAY TO ME!

With an attitude of thankfulness for this absurd life, we can see it as a lucky opportunity to do something amazing, to make something out of it! We must imagine Seuss-yphus happy.

6

YOUR ENDING IS WAITING

Seuss and Socrates on Death and Aging

Robert Main and Matthew Pierlott

It's not about what it is, it's about what it can become.

—Dr. Seuss, *The Lorax*

For in that sleep of death what dreams may come.

—Shakespeare, *Hamlet*

Just when one thinks life makes sense, something happens that challenges everything: a child first learns she will someday die, a typical day is interrupted by a brush with death, or an aged man endures a Pill Drill in Room Six Sixty-Three. Yes, there are plenty of Hang-ups and Bang-ups that can happen to "You."

Oh, the Places You'll Go! was the last book Dr. Seuss published while alive, a year before his death at age eighty-seven. It tells the story of what "you" will do and encounter on life's journey. In this way it functions as a sort of final message to children (of all ages) from someone nearing the end of his life. Seuss had also recently published his first book for "obsolete children," *You're Only Old Once!*, which details the experiences of a much older "you" encountering the health concerns and "care" that come with aging. Seuss said that, "in the interest of commerce," he gave the book "a happy ending. The other ending," he said, "is unacceptable."[1] However, even without this shadow cast by the author's biography, everyone knows how the stories in these two books will end—in fact, must end—even if it remains unspoken. Of all the places you'll go, only one is assured, and though we all end up at this same place, it is uniquely personal and subjective for each of us. All our journeys end in (or, better, are interrupted by) death. As a story about life's journey and the obstacles one faces, the first book is necessarily also a story of death. Death lurks behind the narrative as an absence, in much the same way it lurks behind our daily lives. This is more evident in the second book, whose protagonist is subject to the slow deterioration of his body due to age.

The contemplation of death is a dark thought, of course, scarier even than Clark from *One Fish, Two Fish, Red Fish, Blue Fish* or Foo Foo the Snoo from *I Can Read with My Eyes Shut!* But Seuss himself warns us that we will encounter thoughts like these, particularly in the "lonely" parts of life: "I'm afraid that *some* times / you'll play lonely games too. / Games you can't win / 'cause you'll play against you" (Places). Life itself might be viewed as a game one plays against oneself. Growing as a person requires constantly trying to transcend or surpass the limitations we were born with, limitations that will inevitably lead to failure at times. Foremost among these limitations, and a chief concern for all our philosophical, religious, and artistic endeavors, is our mortality: How can we live our lives knowing that we will die?

The most absurd truth about life is this: the only thing every living thing will do, and must do, is die. At some point (most likely unknown to you), you will die. Everyone you've ever known, heard of, loved, hated, or ignored will also die. Cheery thought, no? Death is a part of life, and it seems that we are hardwired to find some meaning in it, in much the same way that one cannot escape seeing pictures and forms in the random (meaningless) patterns of a Rorschach inkblot. It's this need to understand the meaning and place of everything that enables Dr. Seuss to transform nonsense and gibberish words (as well as entirely new letters from *On Beyond Zebra!*) into stories capable of entertaining generations in the way that only the most meaningful stories do.

PHILOSOPHY AS A PREPARATION FOR DEATH

Facing our mortality has been a preoccupation of a variety of thinkers and philosophical schools for millennia. In the previous chapters, we have already had a taste of Aristotelian ethics, Stoicism, and existentialism. Aristotle urged us to examine what would make for a good life over the whole of our time. The Stoics understood the inevitability of death and our vulnerability to fate as a reason to discipline our own will. The existentialists challenged us to recognize our freedom to choose and make meaning, and to embrace our existence authentically. As we have seen in the previous chapter, a contemporary of Seuss, French philosopher Albert Camus (pronounced "Kam-oo"), points out the absurdity of life and death as well as a way of responding to it. He does so by way of a story of his own, borrowed from Greek mythology (also about a mountain and a "you"), with the appropriately Seussian name, Sisyphus. The gods intend to punish Sisyphus—but if he can approach his task, his boulder and mountain, as anything *other* than a punishment, he has effectively robbed the gods of their power over him and freed himself. As Camus says, "A fate is not a punishment."[2] Sisyphus may not be able to change his condition, but he can change what it means to him. "It is during that return, that pause, that Sisyphus interests me. . . . At each of those moments when he leaves the heights and gradually sinks toward the lairs of the gods, he is superior to his fate. He is stronger than his rock."[3] We all face the same fate: death. So, how can we make meaning out of the fact that we will all die?

Each of these strains of thought (Aristotelean, Stoic, and existentialist) can be traced back to the Athenian patron of Western philosophy—Socrates. It is through Socrates's most famous student, Plato, who depicts Socrates in many of his dialogues, that we get a glimpse of the patron's concern for a life worth living, as well as his existentialist and Stoic tendencies. We also see the clear link he makes between philosophy and death. Plato's *Apology*, among other dialogues, represents Socrates asserting his authenticity, questioning earnestly how he should live while refusing to live as convention would dictate, even though it means he will face his death. As he defends himself in court against the accusation of corrupting the youth and disrespecting the gods, we find him resolute that living a worthwhile life should not be abandoned merely to survive in conformity. Plato's *Crito* depicts a man rationally accepting his fate in good Stoic fashion. He refuses to escape prison with his friends, who have bribed the guards, citing the principles of the law and of his own life as necessitating his acceptance of his death sentence.

But it is in the celebrated dialogue, *Phaedo*, that Plato portrays the final conversation of Socrates's life. Socrates now waits in prison to drink the hemlock poison. His friends assemble to witness his passing. Oddly, it is not Socrates who is in need of consoling, but rather those who are not facing death that day. Plato tells us that, while his friends and students went from laughing to weeping and back again, Socrates "put his feet on the ground and remained in that position during the rest of the conversation" (61d),[4] showing stability as he nears his final moment. Amazingly, as he attends to his distraught companions, Socrates reveals that philosophy is itself a preparation for death:

> I am afraid that other people do not realize that the one aim of those who practice philosophy in the proper manner is to practice for dying and death. . . . They are not aware of the way true philosophers are nearly dead, nor of the way they deserve to be, nor of the sort of death they deserve. (64a–c)

Philosophers deserve death?! Why would Socrates say this? Is it because philosophers, like Zooks, eat their bread with the butter side down? Did they refuse to take off their hat to King Derwin of Didd, like Bartholomew Cubbins?

Like Seuss, Socrates played with words, turning upside down the expectations of his listeners. Socrates defined death as "separation of the soul from the body" (64c), at least for his interlocutors in this dialogue. Socrates develops a kind of dualism in *Phaedo*, opposing the body and the soul like a North-Going Zax and a South-Going Zax coming foot to foot, face to face in the prairie of Prax. The soul, in its search for truth, is headed toward the Just, the Beautiful, and the Good. The body, in its drive for pleasures, is headed for food, drink, sex, creature comforts, and so on. These pleasures bind us to the pursuit of them and are coupled with inevitable pains that follow upon them. The true philosopher, then, wishes to be free of them, just as Socrates was freed from his bonds before drinking the hemlock. These desires, Socrates tells us, are the cause of many bad things in life:

> The body keeps us busy in a thousand ways because of its need for nurture. . . . It fills us with wants, desires, fears, all sorts of illusions and much nonsense. . . . Only the body and its desires cause war, civil discord, and battles, for all wars are due to the desire to acquire wealth, and it is to the body and the care of it, to which we are enslaved, which compel us to acquire wealth. (66b–d)

Bodily desires preoccupy our attention, bodily emotions confuse our thinking, and bodily sensations mislead us into illusion. Philosophers despise the distraction from their pursuit of the truth and readily reject the suffering that follows in the wake of our pursuit of pleasure. Both *intellectually* and *morally*, the body is simply in the way. So, philosophy becomes a method of slowly detaching from the bodily cravings that corrupt our living well, and death ends up being a final victory, a relief.

YOU'RE ONLY DEAD ONCE

This view of death is at odds with our typical contemporary understanding. Death is not to be sought after. We try to avoid it, like it is a pair of pants with nobody inside them! But just like that Seussian narrative, perhaps we need not be as afraid of death as we typically are. Generally, we make one of two assumptions: (1) death is an end to being, a transition to nonexistence, or (2) death is a change of being, a transition from what we are now to what we end up being (i.e., we become what we really are or are supposed to be). This gloss of the two alternatives grossly simplifies things, but the wide variety of views about death should boil down to one or the other. Socrates offers these two possibilities to us in *Apology*, as he reasons why "those of us who believe death to be an evil are certainty mistaken" (40b–c). He tells us that "death is a blessing, for it is one of two things: either the dead are nothing and have no perception of anything, or it is, as we are told, a change and relocating for the soul from here to another place" (40c–d).

Exploring the first possibility, Socrates argues that if death is like a dreamless sleep, a kind of nonexistence, then it would be a relief, and we would not be aware of our own state so there would be no pain, no sense of loss, no worries. Dreamless sleep is often cherished, he tells us. Seuss backs Socrates up on this assertion: in *I Am NOT Going to Get Up Today!* the boy insists that today is better spent in bed sleeping, and we all can relate to that! If death is like a day asleep in bed, we simply would not have anything to fear about death. This view is taken up by the ancient materialist Epicurus of Samos, who said, "Death, therefore, the most awful of evils, is nothing to us, seeing that, when we are, death is not come, and when death is come, we are not."[5] What could be so bad about that?

It would seem the worst thing about death is not the state of being dead, but the dread it produces in us while we are alive. The idea that death introduces a state of nonbeing, which itself is somehow bad, has deep roots in our psychology. Being itself is understood as a good thing, and so by consequence nonbeing is considered evil. We don't want to not exist! Seuss himself echoes this idea in *Happy Birthday to You!*

> If you'd never been born, well then what would you be? You might be a fish! Or a toad in a tree! You might be a doorknob! Or three baked potatoes! You might be a bag full of hard green tomatoes. Or worse than all that. . . . Why, you might be a WASN'T! A Wasn't has no fun at all. No, he doesn't. A Wasn't just isn't. He just isn't present. But you. . . . You ARE YOU! And, now isn't that pleasant! (Birthday)

It is clear from this logic that nonexistence is worse than being any old object you can think of. There is no fun in nonexistence. If death is a return to a nonexistence like before we were born, then we miss out on all of the good things of existence. All of this comes from the perspective of a living being aware of the pleasures to be had in living. When we contemplate our death, we think of all the things we will miss. Psychologists Daniel Kahneman and Amos Tversky have documented the powerful influence of loss aversion,[6] a bias toward keeping what we have, so that we generally would prefer not to risk losing some possession even with a good chance of greater reward. This can explain why our awareness of what we will miss weighs heavily on us as we contemplate our nonexistence.

But Epicurus would quickly point out to us that the fear of death itself produces great pain and anxiety to the living, and the wise would rid themselves of such troubles. We all have experienced in ourselves or others the wasted energies on fearing things that may or may not come. Imagine spending your final months worried about what you will miss after you pass and thereby failing to spend your final months enjoying what is present to you. If you could train yourself to be at peace with your death, you could meet your final months with grace and find joy. This is in part what Plato meant when he had Socrates define philosophy as practicing for death.

In many ways, Seuss highlights this appreciation for living life well in the face of getting closer to death in *You're Only Old Once!* The trials and tribulations of confronting the "medical industrial complex" are set out plainly before us in the text. As we age, it is much more likely that our various bodily parts will encounter difficulties working properly. Our societal fear of death and desire to prolong life, all of that desire for continued pleasurable existence, has erected great health care institutions, with an array of procedures and technologies to diagnose and treat everything from heart disease to restless leg syndrome, and maybe even Spleen Readjustment and Muffler Repair. "You" will be whisked around by Oglers, who poke and prod to see how all your parts are faring, subjected to tests and quizzes to determine what needs to be fixed, and often make you wait and wait and wait until they are ready for the next test.

Of course, modern medicine has brought us wonderful results, and it would be foolish to criticize it too much given how many conditions that were once a death sentence are now routinely treated without much fanfare at all. Nonetheless, as we age, we might find that the time we spend going to and fro, between doctors' offices, labs, hospitals, clinics and pharmacies, and the variety of pills and bills to which we are subject, begins to undermine our appreciation for modern medicine's marvels. Indeed, in some cases, quality-of-life concerns may even outweigh the medical imperative to treat a condition, such as when the chemotherapy and radiation will create so much suffering but offer little hope to extend one's time on Earth. Sometimes trying to stave off death only prolongs a suffering existence, and the Epicurean resolve would help us tremendously to meet our final days with a better attitude. We should not worry about what the sleep of death will be like, and so we should not waste away our final days in a vain attempt to avoid it.

Recalling the two possibilities that death could bring, according to Socrates, the other possibility to explore is that death is a transition to another kind of being, that there is some kind of afterlife. Sages and saints, prophets and poets in every culture have provided diverse visions of what is to come in the great, undiscovered country. Sometimes it is described like "Boola Boo Ball, On the banks of the beautiful River Woo-Wall, Where they never have troubles! *No troubles at all!*" (Trouble). For Socrates, the poets describe the afterlife as a continuation of the spirit in Hades, where one could meet all of the great heroes. A good person had no reason to fear death, if the poets were right, since this afterlife would be rewarding. Many sects of the Abrahamic religions (Judaism, Christianity, and Islam) share some vision or another of a heaven or paradise, in which God rewards the faithful. Many Buddhist sects teach that one's karma will influence what one experiences after bodily death and how one is reborn (even though breaking the cycle of death and rebirth is offered as the ultimate goal). Plato even has Socrates play with the idea of karmic reincarnation in *Phaedo* (81c–84b) as part of his narrative about the possible afterlife. Generally speaking, the conventional religious narratives about what to expect in an afterlife hold a promise of a good state, provided we meet whatever conditions there are for being considered "good" in this life.

The assumption behind these perspectives is that one's morality is causally related to one's postmortem experience. Obviously, it is logically possible that an afterlife is looming filled with quite awful experiences, and nothing we do will help us avoid it, such that our morality in this life is irrelevant to our eventual status. In a similar way, our morality might be causally related to the afterlife in a more inverted way than convention teaches: the good will suffer and the evil will find joy. These logical possibilities may have no practical relevance to those of us committed to a tradition that provides a certain perspective on the afterlife. It is interesting to think about, but there is not much in the conventions of our cultures that would motivate us to entertain the ideas much beyond that. If we have reason to think there is an afterlife, then either our current life helps set our trajectory or it doesn't. If it doesn't, then there is nothing we can do, so we might as well not worry about it at all. If it does, then there is no reason to think it is otherwise than as convention would have it—that is, that our goodness now is rewarded later. To that extent, then, we are left with Socrates's reasoning: we just need to live a good moral life (however that is defined).

This is an optimistic attitude toward an afterlife, one that has faith that the cosmos has some basic moral alignment. It is a fundamental hope that speaks to us all. We see it in the way the Whos down in Whoville respond to the Grinch's sour plot. We see it in Horton's eventual vindication, when the egg hatches an elephant-bird, or when the Kwuggerbug gets sneezed off the mountain. We see it when the Sneetches learn to get along in the end. Indeed, the great philosopher Immanuel Kant argued (controversially) that our common power of moral reasoning requires that we are committed to the idea that, in *some* way, we all will be rewarded (or punished) according to our moral worth, in this life or in the next. Whether or not we could ever show that the universe actually is morally just, we are implicitly committed to the idea that happiness will be ultimately tied to moral worth in our rational actions and practices. So, there is nothing to worry about, as long as we are good here and now.

THE MEANING OF DEATH

So, in either case, if death is nothing or simply a change, we are to conclude that there is nothing to worry about. We are in for a really long nap, or a really great party in Fotta-fa-Zee, where we all feel fine for eternity. Yet, for all the bravado of these philosophic attitudes toward death—that is, that it shouldn't concern us—most of us will find little comfort in these arguments. Outside of the abstract, death is always experienced in a concretely unique and personal way. Some logical argument about how we all should uniformly respond to death will touch these experiences only a little. Is there really a uniform way that parents experience the death of a child? Does losing your elderly mother as an adult compare easily to losing her as a child? What if an acquaintance of yours as a teen commits suicide? Is this similar to learning that a distant great-uncle passed away in his sleep? And what about the threats of death that loom large but may not actually come? A troubling diagnosis. A terrible car accident. Almost being on the flight that went down. We each will see "close calls" or "dodge a bullet" ourselves. It is doubtful that Epicurus's or Socrates's arguments will do much to prepare us for many of these potential outcomes.

Obviously, we all will experience the actual or potential death of someone else in some way, but it will always be a very specific event, and our personal relationship to that event and that person is not easily categorized. And undoubtedly our experiences of the death of others (and the close calls) will shape our own perspective on death and our way of confronting our own mortality. It is easy to say that when we die we won't exist to worry about what we are missing. But while we live we recognize the potential meanings of our own death. It is not merely the egocentric desire to exist that worries us; we can be concerned with the others we will leave behind, knowing how death has already affected people in our lives. And we can worry about how others have left us behind.

Consider the Lorax. He speaks for the trees, and recognizes that the loss of the Truffula trees will cause suffering for Swomee-Swans, Bar-ba-loots, and Humming-Fish. His concern about death is connected to real-life consequences of the loss of life, and it is not easily assuaged by a consideration that Bar-ba-loots won't exist to feel their suffering once they are gone. In the same vein, a father may try to muster the strength to persist against an illness because he wishes to support his child for as long as he can, or a lover may mourn the heartache she will leave in the heart of her lover when she passes.

Given these considerations, philosophy is a preparation for death only to the extent that it enables us to meet the challenges posed by facing an impending death. Have we forged healthy relationships with the important people in our lives? Have we helped our loved ones build resilience and peace of mind so that they can navigate the challenge of our mortality with us? Have we reflected clearly enough on our own priorities so that we live out our time well and can leave the world without feeling too much was left unsaid or undone?

The study of philosophy can help us reflect on what really matters in our lives so that we navigate the real-life concerns around the impending death of ourselves and of others in our lives. The logic of Socrates or Epicurus can stir us to reflect on our fears and reconsider our assumptions about death, which can be helpful. Also helpful, though, would be the attention to our choices and the consequences that we explored in the previous chapters on *eudaimonia*, on Stoic exercises of acceptance and reframing, and on an existentialist examination of our authentic response to the human condition. Perhaps most helpful of all? Enjoying the silliness, the creativity, and the simple, clear insight of Seuss in his many wonderful stories. After all, experiencing the joy that shines through us when we read Seuss for ourselves and share Seuss with others is at least one fine way to spend some of those moments we have left. Perhaps you are sitting in the Golden Years Clinic on Century Square, wondering why you are there, and wishing you were in Fotta-fa-Zee. . . . Pick up a Seuss book and smile a bit. It is at least better than chatting with Norval the Fish, wouldn't you say?

7

DR. SEUSS AND ARISTOTLE ON THE MOST IMPORTANT FRIENDSHIP OF ALL

Sharon Kaye

Step with care and great tact, and remember that Life's a Great Balancing Act.

—Dr. Seuss

It is best to rise from life as from a banquet, neither thirsty nor drunken.

—Aristotle

Both Dr. Seuss and the ancient Greek philosopher Aristotle (384–322 BC) had a best friend named Theophrastus. Dr. Seuss died at the age of eighty-seven in 1991. His last words were directed to his stepdaughter, asking her to take care of Theophrastus.[1] We don't know Aristotle's last words, but we know that he left his school, the Lyceum, and his entire library to Theophrastus, a constant companion and collaborator throughout his life.

Who was Dr. Seuss's Theophrastus? Well . . . um . . . he was a stuffed dog. A gift from his mother, the fat brown pug sat in Dr. Seuss's study, supervising his ingenious drawings since he was a boy.

Dr. Seuss's attachment to a stuffed dog struck me as sweet until I began studying his last and (in my view) greatest work, *Oh, the Places You'll Go!* Started in 1989, when he already knew the cancer that would kill him was spreading, this book was Dr. Seuss's final message to the world. As I studied this message, I found it more and more disturbing . . . until its true meaning hit me like a tweetle beetle paddle.

WHAT IS THIS BOOK ABOUT?

Oh, the Places You'll Go! is the story of a boy setting out on his life's journey—wearing what looks like yellow pajamas. The narrator wants to tell him about the highs and lows he will encounter, emphasizing the importance of making good choices along the way.

> You have brains in your head.
> You have feet in your shoes.
> You can steer yourself in any direction you choose. (Places)

Here the resonance with Aristotle is positively striking. Aristotle wrote a work called *Nicomachean Ethics*, named for his only son, Nicomachus. Like *Oh, the Places You'll Go!*, it is a guide to the good life. Though it is without illustrations and its language is a bit more sophisticated, its message is the same:

> But whatever deeds arise in accord with the virtues are not done justly or moderately if they are merely in a certain state, but only if he who does those deeds is in a certain state as well: first, if he acts knowingly; second, if he acts by choosing and by choosing the actions in question for their own sake; and, third, if he acts while being in a steady and unwavering state. [2]

Dr. Seuss never had any children of his own. "You make 'em, I'll entertain 'em," he always said. Yet his message to the unnamed boy in *Oh, the Places You'll Go!* is more than entertainment. He assures the boy that good decision making will take him "straight out of town" to the "opener air," where he'll "start happening."

> Wherever you fly, you'll be best of the best.
> Wherever you go, you will top all the rest. (Places)

The life of a mind-maker-upper is no cakewalk. Faced with not-so-good streets, Bang-ups, Hang-ups, and Slumps, he must persevere with courage and fortitude.

> Simple it's not, I'm afraid you will find,
> for a mind-maker-upper to make up his mind. (Places)

Plowing through the Waiting Place, the Hakken Kraks, and things that will scare you right out of your pants, our young man finally makes it to bright places where the Boom Bands are playing.

> And will you succeed?
> Yes! You will, indeed!
> (98 and 3/4 percent guaranteed.) (Places)

The book is often given as a graduation gift because our hero overcomes all challenges and in the end MOVES MOUNTAINS! Sounds great, right? Wrong.

WHAT'S WRONG WITH THIS BOOK?

From start to finish our hero is alone. Completely alone. Well, okay, there are plenty of helpful elephants to be found. But it is plainly evident that the boy *has no friends*.

> I'm afraid sometimes you'll play lonely games too,
> games you can't win because you'll play against you. (Places)

Where are this boy's friends? Surely the most important message to give to a graduate is the importance of friendship! How hard would it have been for Dr. Seuss to sketch in a Sally or a Sneetch or a Thing for this boy to commiserate with? Not hard at all! This is no accidental omission. On the contrary, Dr. Seuss is making a deliberate point about the friendlessness of life's journey:

> All Alone!
> Whether you like it or not,
> Alone will be something
> You'll be quite a lot. (Places)

So then I began to wonder, was Dr. Seuss some kind of friendless psychopath, who could only relate to a stuffed dog?

But further research quashed that hypothesis like a Bofa on a Yottle! Dr. Seuss had lots of friends. Good friends. And two lovely marriages as well. (The first one ended in tragedy, but this was due to his wife's long illness.) In this respect, it seems Dr. Seuss was again much like Aristotle, whose last will and testament proves that he was surrounded by many loved ones to the very end, despite having to leave the Lyceum due to illness and persecution.

The point of departure between these two men, however, is that Aristotle does not neglect to discuss friendship. In fact, after surveying all the goods one might achieve in life—wealth, health, fame, beauty, talent, knowledge, friendship—Aristotle argues that friendship is the most important good of all. He writes, "Without friends no one would choose to live, though he had all other goods."[3] Aristotle devotes all of books VIII and IX of the *Nichomachean Ethics* to an extended discussion of the nature of friendship with an aim to proving that it is the key to the good life.

WHY IS FRIENDSHIP SO IMPORTANT?

Aristotle explains there are three kinds of friendship. First is the Friendship of Utility. Here Aristotle is referring to a relationship based on some kind of exchange. For example, Dr. Seuss's *Fox in Socks* depicts a Friendship of Utility between Sue and Joe Crow.

> Who sews crow's clothes?
> Sue sews crow's clothes.
> Slow Joe Crow
> Sews whose clothes?
> Sue's clothes. (Fox)

The accompanying picture shows a rather prissy young lady and an actual crow—an exceptionally large one—sewing clothes for each other. It is a strange pair. They would not be likely to hang out once the sewing is done. Their relationship exists for the sake of the exchange of services.

We have many friendships like this in our lives. Consider the teacher-student relationship. The teacher provides the student with credits toward his or her degree; the student pays tuition, which provides the teacher with a salary. It is more than an acquaintance; yet it is only minimally a friendship. It is mutual use.

Second is the Friendship of Pleasure. Here Aristotle is referring to a relationship based on common interest in some kind of activity. For example, Dr. Seuss's *One Fish, Two Fish, Red Fish, Blue Fish* depicts a

Friendship of Pleasure between Mr. Gump and a handful of unnamed children who get together to ride a camel-like creature.

> We know a man
> called Mr. Gump.
> Mr. Gump has a seven hump Wump.
> So . . .
> If you like to go Bump! Bump!
> Just jump on the hump of the Wump of a Gump. (Fish)

Mr. Gump, sporting mustache and top hat, is clearly a very serious Wump-rider. It is difficult to picture him hanging out with these children for any reason other than Wump-riding.

Wump-riding being rather rare, we might be more likely to have experienced a Friendship of Pleasure through extracurricular sports or hobbies. We love people who enjoy the same activities we enjoy, and we enjoy doing those activities with them. But our love is directed first toward the activity and then toward the people.

In this way, the Friendship of Pleasure is like the Friendship of Utility, where the primary interest lies in the good or service being exchanged. These two kinds of friendship are common and important. But because the people involved are not primarily focusing on each other, neither is the highest kind of friendship.

The third and highest form of friendship Aristotle calls the Friendship of Virtue. Here he is referring to a relationship in which the people involved regard each other as valuable in themselves. They may sometimes have something to exchange or an activity to share, but they are content to hang out together without any such excuse.

Dr. Seuss's works provide a number of possible examples of the Friendship of Virtue. My personal favorite comes from an obscure little book called *The Shape of Me and Other Stuff*. It features a boy named George and his unnamed female friend—let's call her Sally. They spend the entire book hanging around, noticing how things are shaped.

> You know. . . . It makes a fellow think.
> The shape of you, the shape of me
> the shape of everything I see
> a bug . . . a balloon, a bed, a bike
> No shapes are ever quite alike. (Shape)

George and Sally imagine what it would be like to be shaped like something else. The book ends with them celebrating their own shapes.

Someone might object that George and Sally's relationship could be characterized as a Friendship of Utility. After all, they are exchanging ideas. Likewise, someone might object that their relationship is a Friendship of Pleasure. After all, they seem completely engrossed in the activity of noticing how things are shaped.

Aristotle would be happy to grant that both utility and pleasure are involved in George and Sally's relationship. I believe he would insist, however, that more is at stake. George and Sally are thinking about the world together. Aristotle sets intellectual activity apart from the practical activities featured in the other two forms of friendship. He writes, "Man is the only animal capable of reasoning, though many others possess the faculty of memory and instruction in common with him."[4] Intellectual activity is unique to humans, but it is a very difficult thing to do alone.

Friendship is important because, at its best, it promotes just hanging around and thinking about stuff. Aristotle goes so far as to assert that it is crucial to accomplishing our purpose in life.

WHAT IS OUR PURPOSE IN LIFE?

Aristotle and his best friend Theophrastus spent a lot of time hanging around, noticing the shapes of things. Their studies formed the foundations of science as we know it today. For example, by observing what makes animals similar to and different from each other, they invented the species-genus system of classification.

While used in real-world biology today, this system can also be used in the wubbulous world of Dr. Seuss. For example, all those nupboards in the cupboard, while varying slightly in size and color, are clearly more closely related to one another than any of them is related to the wocket in my pocket.

Aristotle wanted to understand everything in nature, and to understand human beings as an integral part of the natural world. He believed prior attempts at a comprehensive science had failed to ask the right questions. To set us on the right track, he proposed the Doctrine of the Four Causes. Truly understanding anything means answering not one but four questions about it:

1. *What* is it made of? (the "material cause")
2. *Who* brought it into existence? (the "efficient cause")
3. *What* is its purpose? (the "final cause")
4. *How* does it accomplish this purpose? (the "formal cause")

Setting aside the progress this doctrine sparked in science generally, it provided revolutionary insights when applied to the human being. A human being is a thing made of flesh and blood, brought into existence by a mother and a father. But what is its purpose?

Being an empiricist, Aristotle went out and observed us. Suppose, for example, you spot a man in a blue suit driving a broken-down horse and wagon down Mulberry Street. You might conduct the following conversation with him:

You: Where are you going?

Him: To the market.

You: Why?

Him: To sell my three little trees.

You: Why?

Him: To make some money.

You: Why?

Him: So I can get married.

You: Why?

Him: So I can have a family.

You: Why?

Him: So I can live happily ever after.

Now, if you were to further ask this proud little mustached man why he wants to live happily ever after, he might look at you as though you'd just coughed up Uncle Ubb's umbrella and his underwear.

Him: Why do I want to be happy? Why does anyone want to be happy? We all just do!

And he would be right. Happiness is what all humans are after. We are the only ones on the planet with brains big enough to conceive of happiness, and once we conceive of it, it becomes the ultimate goal lying behind every single little thing we do.

But how to achieve it? Now, that's a quick-trick-chick-stack and a quick-trick-clock-stack all in one! Aristotle had no doubt it would be a matter of our special talent: intellectual activity. Intellectual activity applied for the purpose of achieving happiness he called *virtue*.

HOW DOES VIRTUE WORK?

Not just any kind of thinking is liable to lead to happiness. After all, human beings can think about all kinds of thinks.

> Oh, the Thinks you can think!
> If you're willing to try
> Think invisible ink! Or a gink with a stink!
> Or a stair to the sky. (Thinks)

Being a scientist through and through, Aristotle was sure that the right kind of thinking would have something to do with proper measurement. Suppose, for example, that you are confronted by a beautiful shlopp with a cherry on top. What should the thinking person do?

On the one hand, you could gobble the whole thing up and ask for another. But this would be too much. You would likely get sick or grow as fat as a Zizzer-Zazzer-Zuzz. On the other hand, you could turn up your nose and walk away like a Grinch whose heart is two sizes too small. But this would be too little. Too much denying yourself will make you shrivel up and grow sour from not enough fun.

When it comes to schlopp, the thinking person would have just the right amount—neither deficiency nor excess, but rather the middle point in between. Upon careful consideration, Aristotle came to the conclusion that the same can be said about all the choices we mind-maker-uppers face. Confronting a choice thoughtfully, a mind-maker-upper will consider what would be too much and what would be too little, and then do the thing that lies in the middle. Summing up his discovery, Aristotle wrote that virtue "is a state concerned with choice, lying in a mean, relative to us, this being determined by reason."[5] Aristotle's discovery came to be known as the Doctrine of the Golden mean: moderation in all things is the key to human happiness.

Dr. Seuss no doubt had occasion to read Aristotle as a student at Dartmouth and Oxford. Yet we will never know whether he realized that he was echoing the ancient Greek philosopher when, at the climax of *Oh, the Places You'll Go!*, he wrote, "Step with care and great tact, and remember that Life's a Great Balancing Act." In the picture for this page, Dr. Seuss has drawn our yellow-capped hero navigating a path through the multitude of strange birds that one inevitably encounters throughout life.

It might be objected that moderation is nothing but another name for mediocrity, and all the people whom we really admire were extremists in one way or another. Dr. Seuss and Aristotle themselves were both famous authors.

> Fame! You'll be famous as famous can be,
> with the whole wide world watching you win on TV. (Places)

Truly great people don't go halfway when it comes to their passions.

Aristotle is careful to point out, however, that he never intended his Golden Mean to be a mathematical quantity that applies universally across the board. Milo the wrestler may eat twice as much meat as the rest of us. This doesn't make him a glutton. He needs more meat than the rest of us in order to be a good wrestler. He has found the right amount for him, given what he does best.

So, while the Golden Mean at first appears to provide a very specific recommendation for the good life, it actually requires a great deal of personal adaptation in application for elation around the nation (sorry—temporary rhyming-control failure).

But this is why Aristotle stresses the importance of friendship. Even when you know what virtue is, why it's important, and how it works, you still have to determine each and every day what it implies for you. You need help from those who know you best to figure this out and then support you in actually carrying out the implication. "Friendship is essentially a partnership," Aristotle wrote. "Perfect friendship is the friendship of human beings who are good, and alike in excellence; for these wish well alike to each other qua good, and they are good in themselves."[6]

When thinking of perfect friendship, one can't help picturing the good citizens of Whoville, gathered together in joyous song, despite the fact every last scrap of Christmas had been stolen from them. Aristotle explicitly applied his account of friendship to the political level, insisting that only virtuously friendly citizens can make democracy work.

But Whoville brings us back to our original problem. Notice that all the examples of friendship we have discussed from Dr. Seuss come from works other than *Oh, the Places You'll Go!* Why, oh why, would Dr. Seuss leave this crucial ingredient out of his final work?

OR DID HE?

Reading more carefully, I realized he didn't.

It was Aristotle, once again, who aroused my suspicions. One of Aristotle's most famous quotes is "Love is a single soul dwelling in two bodies."[7] He extends this image to friendship when he writes, "A friend is a second self, so that our consciousness of a friend's existence . . . makes us more fully conscious of our own existence."[8] Here Aristotle is talking not about the broader community but about the few intimate confidants with whom we spend the most time: best friends. Loving a best friend is like loving yourself. This insight made my head ring like the Royal Bell (without oobleck)!

Friendship with others presupposes friendship with yourself. So self-love is logically prior to other-love. We can see why this is when we look closely at Aristotle's formula for a best friend. "My best friend," he writes, "is the person who, in wishing me well, wishes it for my sake."[9] Our best friends don't wish us well to get something from us or to advance their own happiness in any way. They wish us well even if they do not stand to gain anything from it at all.

Aristotle's best-friend love meets such a high standard that we may pause to wonder whether any human being is capable of it.

But we have proof that we *are* capable of it.

Whom do we love so perfectly? Ourselves, of course. One may even argue that self-love is a function of our most basic survival instinct. How would our species ever have come to dominate the planet if we did not have an instinctual urge to take care of ourselves, benefit ourselves, even fight for ourselves, with every ounce of energy we have?

While selfishness may be necessary to our species, our ability to extend our selfishness beyond ourselves is what makes us noble. When I identify with you, I'm ready to take care of you, benefit you, even fight for you—to the death. Human beings have proved it to be true again and again. The friend in the mirror becomes the friend beyond the mirror. [10]

And this is the same movement we see in *Oh, the Places You'll Go!*: A narrator, the voice of a man with a lifetime of experience under his belt, looks back at himself as he began his journey. His poignant description of the heights of victory ("with banner flip-flapping") and the depths of despair ("your sneakers may leak") suggests that his entire life is passing before his very eyes. Dr. Seuss is communing with his past self, as if reaching through time to give himself the support he needed to become the person he is.

If you have never tried communing with your past or future self, I highly recommend trying it as soon as possible! I make my students do it every semester at the end of the course when we write letters to ourselves. I hand out university letterhead stationary and ask them to write a permanent address on the envelope (or, failing that, the alumni office). I instruct them to begin the letter "Dear *your name here*"; I give them some suggestions about what to write—their hopes and dreams, their resolutions and promises to themselves. I vow that I will not open the letters but will store them in my file cabinet for ten years, after which time I will put them in the mail.

Yes! I have been doing this for more than ten years. Yes! I have started sending out batches of ten-year-old letters. And yes! Many of them have found their owners and had an amazing impact. These letters work in the opposite direction from *Oh, the Places You'll Go!*; yet there is a similar effect. You get a sense of the whole of yourself over time, and how the things you do now are made possible by the things you did before, and how they in turn make possible things you will do in the future.

If Dr. Seuss had ended *Oh, the Places You'll Go!* by addressing himself by name, we would have to blush, realizing that we have invaded a sacred privacy. It would be like opening one of my student's letters! But he doesn't address himself. He addresses us all:

Be your name Buxbaum or Bixby or Bray
or Mordecai Ali Van Allen O'Shea,
You're off to Great Places!
Today is your day! (Places)

In his role as omniscient narrator, Dr. Seuss knows that we all need to send the message of the book to ourselves. He invites us to look back and look forward and rise to the challenge of being our own best friends.

I conclude that *Oh, the Places You'll Go!* is about the most important friendship of all: your friendship with yourself. The interplay between the boy (young Dr. Seuss) and the narrator (old Dr. Seuss) is the philosophical genius of this book. Prerequisite for any other friendship, it is the secret of the good life.

What are the chances that two of the most important authors in the history of Western civilization happened to have a best friend named Theophrastus? Maybe it was not a coincidence, and Dr. Seuss knew all along that he was following in Aristotle's footsteps. The members of Aristotle's school were called the Peripatetics (from the Greek words for "walking around") because they walked around while they hung out doing philosophy. Dr. Seuss knew that brainy and footsy was the way to be.

Part III

Them!

If it's not about you, it must be about "They,"
All of the others you see in your day.

You can't go around as if you're the best,
Thinking you're special, ignoring the rest.
For others have needs, others need care,
Treating yourself as the best is not fair.

You must be concerned with the welfare of others,
Feel for your brothers, and sisters, and mother.
Care for them all. Whether like you or not.
We're all a bit different, but we're all that we've got.

And some are quite different, we might call them "Other."
But even an "other" is somebody's brother!
Don't be a bigot to Yooks or to Zooks.
People are people regardless of looks.
So on beyond you, there are people of worth
All shapes and sizes are found on this Earth.
Find value where possible, and always care,
We're all a bit different to others out there.

8

IT SHOULD BE LIKE THAT!

Egoism, Philanthropy, and a Virtuous Elephant

Jacob M. Held

Everyone makes himself the center of the world, and refers everything to himself.

—Arthur Schopenhauer[1]

I *can't* put it down. And I *won't*! After all. A person's a person. No matter how small.

—Dr. Seuss, *Horton Hears a Who!*

Horton the elephant is a good elephant. He's faithful, 100 percent. He says what he means and means what he says. He saves the Whos. He hatches Mayzie's egg. He's faithful, honest, devoted, and caring, and he has integrity. Horton's stories are morality tales, fables about character, virtue, and decency. Horton is a moral exemplar. He exemplifies courage and loyalty. He bravely protects the Whos, experiencing great suffering as he does so. He endures great hardship as he hatches the egg. There is much to be esteemed in Horton, and there is much we can learn from him.

The lesson in Horton is not a simple ethical rule or code; it's a lesson about perspective and disposition, about how we ought to face the world and the kind of person we should be as we do so. Horton doesn't choose to be the patron of the Whos; he doesn't choose to be abandoned on the egg. Horton is forced into his predicaments. He's forced to make choices, to act, in an indifferent and often hostile world. The world he faces is unfair; it is harsh and unforgiving. The people he is surrounded by are petty, selfish, and cruel. But how does Horton respond? Does he scream, "The world's unfair!"? No. He helps the Whos. Does he lament how poorly Mayzie acted and that he doesn't deserve to be stuck on the egg, that she's selfish and doesn't deserve his help? No. He sits and he hatches an elephant-bird. Does he repay cruelty with hatred or violence? Does he despair and fall into depression, or, worse, resentment? No. Horton responds with compassion. Who else would save the Whos? Who else would hatch the egg? In an "unfair" and harsh world full of shirkers and ne'er-do-wells, Horton is kind; Horton helps! This is the lesson we can learn from Horton, a lesson also articulated by nineteenth-century German pessimist Arthur Schopenhauer (1788–1860).

THE JUNGLE IS SUNK IN EVIL

Although Horton makes his appearance in several places in Dr. Seuss's work, I'm going to focus on *Horton Hears a Who!* and *Horton Hatches the Egg*. These two portraits of Horton depict well what kind of world Horton is up against, and why his response is so admirable. Let's begin with *Horton Hears a Who!*

We are all familiar with the basic story. At least we should be. Horton, who's happily splashing in a pool in the Jungle of Nool, hears a small noise, the Whos. They are tiny, a whole town in fact no larger than a speck of dust. But he can hear them, and he decides to move them to safety. It's really no skin off his back, and otherwise they are sure to be trampled. "I'll just have to save them. Because, after all, [a] person's a person, no matter how small," Horton reasons. Eventually, he encounters a sour kangaroo and her child, as well as the many other denizens of the jungle. They can't hear the Whos. They think Horton is being silly. But more important, they're not interested in hearing the Whos. To do so would inconvenience them. To hear, and thereby recognize the existence of, the Whos would require that they acknowledge the world to be larger than they had previously thought, occupied by beings whose interests may conflict with their own or otherwise cause them an inconvenience. Better to ignore the possibility, and if Horton insists, well, they'll deal with him then. Horton does persist, and all the other animals, from the troublesome Wickersham brothers to Vlad Vladikoff, do all they can, expending a great deal of energy, to get rid of the Whos. They threaten

Horton, tie him up, and are about to boil the Whos in Beezlenut oil when at last they are heard. The jungle's occupants can no longer deny their existence, not in good faith, and so the Whos are saved. All's well that ends well—at least for now. But there is an important lesson here.

Horton, although spared at the end, has caught a glimpse of the dark hearts of his jungle neighbors. They were ready to commit genocide. The Jungle of Nool is no paradise. It is a den of iniquity populated by Wickersham brothers ready to perpetrate unspeakable evils when it serves their interests, and the mob is behind them. The nature of Horton's compatriots is dark, it is easily tainted, and they are all too ready to commit atrocities given the right circumstances and motivation. This should sound familiar, for it speaks to a weakness in humanity: the blind drive of the ego, of selfishness, that is willing to put one's own interests above the welfare and, at times, even the existence of others. Schopenhauer notes, "Egoism is colossal; it towers above the world; for if every individual were given the choice between his own destruction and that of the rest of the world, I need not say how the decision would go in the vast majority of cases."[2] Horton is clearly an exception to the rule. And if this episode isn't enough to illustrate the point, Horton has another adventure in *Horton Hatches the Egg*.

Horton Hatches the Egg is not as popular as his encounter with the Whos, but it is just as rich and tells us more about human nature than perhaps we want to admit. In *Horton Hatches the Egg*, Horton does a simple favor for Mayzie, a lazy[3] bird. She's been sitting on her nest and needs a bit of a break. She asks Horton to sit on her egg for her. That is a strange request—an elephant hatching an egg. But he agrees. He figures out the physics of the situation and perches himself right atop the nest. But Mayzie, like oh so many, is human, all too human, even if a bird, and her ego gets the better of her. Off in Palm Beach, she's "having *such* fun, such a wonderful rest, [she] decided she'd NEVER go back to her nest!" (Hatches). She's enjoying herself, and that's what matters most—her happiness. Why should she sacrifice or be put out, especially for a measly egg? She abandons her egg with Horton because it's just too inconvenient to actually be a parent, to care for something that's not herself. She has things of her own to do.[4]

So Horton sits and sits. He endures snow and sleet, along with jibes and jokes from his neighbors. "His friends gathered round and they shouted with glee . . . they taunted. They teased him. . . . They laughed and they laughed. Then they all ran away. And Horton was lonely" (Hatches). Horton would prefer not to be on the egg, either. But what option does he truly have? So he endures. He even faces the threat of death when hunters arrive. Ultimately, he's spared only to be tied up, caged, and shipped off to be sold to the circus. Fortunately, it all ends well—eventually. Mayzie stumbles upon Horton when the circus comes near Palm Beach, recognizes him, and, as the egg begins to hatch, puts in her claim: "'But it's MINE!' screamed the bird, when she heard the egg crack. (The work was all done. Now she wanted it back.) 'It's MY egg!'" But when the egg hatches, it's an elephant-bird: "IT HAD EARS AND A TAIL AND A TRUNK. . . . IT'S AN ELEPHANT-BIRD!! And it should be, it *should* be, it SHOULD be like that! Because Horton was faithful! He sat and he sat!" (Hatches). And everyone's happy (except Mayzie).

So what does Horton learn here? He learns once again that people will fail you. People are driven by their egos, their own selfishness, and so they will harm you and take advantage of you when it's to their benefit. If Horton became jaded, he might respond the way Schopenhauer cautions against: "To many a man, particularly in moments of melancholy and depression, the world may appear to be from the aesthetic standpoint a cabinet of caricatures, from the intellectual, a madhouse, and from the moral, a den of sharks and swindlers. If such a dejected mood becomes permanent, misanthropy is the result."[5] Perhaps Horton will just learn that people suck. Avoid them when possible, and use extreme caution if contact is necessary. Who'd fault Horton if he did respond this way? He's had a tough go of it. Horton should be sour. Horton should be a misanthrope. He's had no experiences that would lead him to believe people are at root good. Everything he's seen speaks to their selfishness. The Jungle of Nool is a harsh place, full of danger and cruelty, with vile, base creatures taking advantage of each other. But Horton doesn't become a misanthrope. He doesn't hate people, even though he knows, from experience, from his life, that they are more often than not rotten. He doesn't focus on the negative. Nor does he naively focus on the positive and ignore the negative. How could he? You can't ignore being bound, enslaved, taunted, and so on. Nor does Horton resort to selfishness himself. He doesn't abandon the egg when Mayzie fails to return. He doesn't abandon the Whos even though it'd be easier than defending them. Nor does he turn to resentment or anger. No. Horton cares for the egg. Because who else would? He cares for the Whos. If he doesn't, who will?

Horton chooses virtue. Schopenhauer claimed that the first lesson any teacher of ethics should begin from is this: "The world is sunk in evil, and men are not what they ought to be; do not let that lead you astray, and see that you are better."[6] Horton is better; he is motivated by compassion.

AND ANIMALS ARE NOT WHAT THEY SHOULD BE

The denizens of Nool, the other animals with whom Horton must live, are not what they should be. They are selfish. They look out for their own interests, often at the expense of others. They exemplify egoism. Schopenhauer claims, "The chief and fundamental incentive in man as in the animal is *egoism*, that is, the craving for existence and well-being."[7] The animals demonstrate this. The sour kangaroo is not deaf; she chooses not to hear. Perhaps a louder yell is all that is needed, but it's necessary to break through her willingness to ignore others' interests at the possible expense of her own. Caring costs something. Caring isn't free. You have to invest your time, your energy, and maybe your resources in another being, and that means not you. So she's deaf to the Whos because she can only hear her own interests. It is against this drive, this blind or deaf self-interest that we must contend. Schopenhauer states, "*Egoism* is . . . the first and principal, although not the only force with which the *moral incentive* has to contend."[8] And we must fight against this drive because that's all it is—a basic, base, animalistic drive. But we are greater than our selfish interests, and we are not defined by our own selfish wants and desires. We are members of a community. We are one among many, and others matter. Schopenhauer notes that self-interest destroys the moral worth of any action, and it is the other's benefit without any reference to one's own good that gives an action its real moral worth.[9] "The absence of all egoistic motivation is, therefore, the *criterion of an action of moral worth*."[10]

In excluding egoistic actions from actions of moral worth, Schopenhauer implies that self-interest is not a moral interest, but perhaps merely a fact, like the self-preservation of an animal. An animal saving its own life is not a moral act, but instinct, and egoism in humans, although of a higher degree than that of animals, stems from the same source—self-preservation—and thus isn't a moral position; it is just a fact of our animal nature. So it appears an orientation toward the other, an ability to see the other as oneself, to recognize them as the same as ourselves is the beginning of an ethical disposition. Horton *sees* the Whos, even if he only hears them. He has recognized them as beings worthy of value, as beings like himself. He thus forms an empathetic bond with them, and thereby recognizes their value as clearly as he recognizes his own. And so Horton acts according to the foundation of Schopenhauer's moral philosophy: "Injure no one; on the contrary, help everyone as much as you can."[11]

Whether it's the sour kangaroo or Mayzie the lazy bird, Horton has learned that animals are prone to act selfishly over and against the interests or welfare of others. This egoistic bent motivates their disregard of the interests of others, like the Whos. It leads to them abandoning their duties, their eggs, their children. But it's not the simple consequences that make egoism so problematic, it's that it is fundamentally contrary to our social nature. Although we may have an innate drive to egoism, we are also, by nature, social beings. We need other people in order to be fully realized individuals. "Man is not the solipsistic egoist that the moral sceptics presupposed but is, as Aristotle insists, a political animal: a being that lives and thrives in communities and for whom the good of others furnishes a reason for action just as does his own."[12] Schopenhauer notes our base instinct, our animal drive to egoism, but he also asks that we be better, that we be the humans we ought to be: social beings who seek the benefit of their fellows as if it were their own. We ought to orient ourselves toward the other such that "that other man . . . becom[es] *the ultimate object* of my will in the same way as I myself otherwise am, and hence through my directly desiring *his* weal and not *his* woe just as immediately as I ordinarily do only *my own*."[13] This is compassion, and compassion begins with empathy.

HORTON DOES NOT LET IT LEAD HIM ASTRAY

Empathy, or fellow feeling, is mysterious. Consider Horton. Why does he save the Whos? It's hard to really know his motivation, but one thing is certain: he does it because of the kind of elephant he is. He doesn't recall his lessons in Philosophy 101, recite the categorical imperative or Kantian ethics, or resort to a utilitarian calculus about the greatest happiness for the greatest number. He simply hears the Whos and recognizes that they are like him—they have interests, loves, hopes, and dreams. He is affectively connected to them and so driven to protect them as he'd protect himself. He has formed an empathetic bond with the Whos. He connects to them.

Why does Horton hatch the egg? He might recite the formula that elephants are faithful 100 percent. But it's not blind loyalty or the duty to keep a promise that motivates him. How easy would it have been for him to rationalize breaking his promise to Mayzie? How easy would it have been for him to discount the value of one measly egg? He could've resorted to utilitarian calculations or discounted the egg as not deserving respect. He could've rationalized his selfishness or disregard of the egg in infinite ways. Ethics journals and books are full of theories that allow one to pick and choose who does and does not matter under the guise of rational discourse. But that's not how Horton thinks, *because that's not who Horton is!* He sees the egg as a potential bird, as a child in the making, and so he bonds with it; he forms a connection to it, caring for the egg as if it were his own. And this is important. Its interests are treated as if they were his own, because to a great extent they actually are. Horton is faithful, and loyalty is important: "Loyalty acknowledges the critical place of sociality in our identity and protects our settled identity from the erosions of short-term advantage."[14] Horton wouldn't be Horton if he weren't loyal, if he weren't faithful. This is integrity, truth to one's deep character, one's self. He is loyal, and faithful, he cares for others and fundamentally orients himself to their welfare, to their good. His identity is tied to his connection with others, as it should be, given his nature—as we all should be, given our natures as social animals.

The interests of others are our own interests, for we're all of a kind. To be is to be in relationship to others, like it or not. This understanding of the nature of personhood is presented by another nineteenth-century German philosopher, J. G. Fichte (1762–1814): "The human being . . . becomes a human being only among human beings; and since the human being can be nothing other than a human being and would not exist at all if it were not this—it follows that, *if there are to be human beings at all, there must be more than one.* . . . Thus the concept of the human being is not the concept of an individual—for an individual human being is unthinkable—but rather the concept of a species."[15] This is the problem with the sour kangaroo and Mayzie. They try to act in isolation and exploit others, only thinking of themselves. However, in so doing they undercut their true natures as social beings, and they harm themselves while harming others. The sour kangaroo, the Wickersham brothers, and Mayzie are not what they ought to be. But Horton does not let that lead him astray. He does not become resentful, angry, or misanthropic. He sees that he is better, by being disposed to others as he ought to be, as compassionate.

AND SEE THAT YOU, LIKE HORTON, ARE BETTER!

From all that Horton has seen he knows that people are not what they should be. They are often petty, selfish, arrogant, cruel, and in general, problems. Whenever things go wrong it's always people that are at the center. So it might seem, as noted above, that his best option is to avoid people when possible and use caution when engagement is necessary. But that's too limiting. That will surely lead to a sad and lonely existence. Somehow, Horton has to recognize that people are not what they should be, that the world is often disappointing, but also see to it that he is better—that in the face of a harsh world, he will be the elephant he ought to be. And as with Horton, so it is with us. We can't simply lament that people are lacking, or hide away and stew in our pessimism, or else we will become the misanthropes that Schopenhauer warns us against. Horton can't hide his head in the sand; he can't hide under a bush. He has to live in Nool among the rest of the animals, while admitting and accepting that chances are things aren't going to get any better and his neighbors will always be troublesome. He has to learn how to live among them, without becoming one of them, without letting their failings drive him to depression, despair, or hatred. He has to see that he is better because he is the only thing he can control.

There is a Stoicism about Schopenhauer and Horton. They recognize people won't become better. You can't hinge your hope on that or you'll be disappointed time and time again. You don't control others, you can't change them. Your choice, what is in your power, is how to respond. Schopenhauer tells us to respond with the virtue of philanthropy, kindness, *caritas*.

As noted above, Schopenhauer builds his moral philosophy on a simple principle: "Injure no one; on the contrary, help everyone as much as you can."[16] Implicit in this view is a rejection of egoism. We can't live in this world as if it's all about us. Other people matter. So we must begin by hurting no one. If the jungle is as dark and dreary as it appears to be, then the least we can do is not contribute to it. We can simply not make it any worse. This is simple, and for Schopenhauer this is justice. We should avoid being burdens on other people as far as we can, and seek that in our actions we don't actively cause them harm or discomfort. At a minimum, don't make matters worse. This is no problem for Horton. Nor should it be very difficult for any of us. But there's more to life than just not being troublesome. We should also orient ourselves to others in a way that makes their lives better. We can do more than simply not cause pain; we can alleviate suffering when and where it is possible.

Although philosophy often likes to pretend at having answers, at analytic solutions to deep human conundrums, in ethics, as in most areas of life, that's not the case. There's no simple equation for how much one should help and when. To try to systematize ethical behavior is to ignore the fundamentally messy nature of human existence. So it's better to talk about dispositions rather than equations or rules. It's better to talk about character than calculations. So Schopenhauer favors a character-based approach to the problem of human suffering and ethics. Schopenhauer is a virtue theorist.[17] He maintains that certain dispositions exemplify human excellence and ought to be fostered. He begins with the simple statement noted above: Injure no one; in fact, help as much as is possible. The first demand, do no harm, is met with the virtue of justice. Justice demands people be treated equally, with equal concern, and so we are to harm no one; no one person's good should come at the expense of another. But more interesting for our present discussion is the demand that we ought to help as much as is possible. This is Schopenhauer's virtue of philanthropy.

Philanthropy, for Schopenhauer, is the virtue of loving kindness; a disposition in us to take the other's weal or woe as the motive for our action, and this virtue is manifest in acts of compassion, in sacrifice, and *caritas*. When discussing philanthropy, Schopenhauer often mentions compassion. In opposition to compassion, he notes, cruelty is the most offensive thing to humanity. Schopenhauer states, "Nothing shocks our moral feelings so deeply as cruelty does. We can forgive every other crime, but not cruelty."[18] Schopenhauer notes specifically horrific real-life examples, such as a mother who murdered her five-year-old son by pouring boiling oil down his throat.[19] And how cruel for the denizens of Nool to threaten to boil the Whos in a vat of Beezlenut oil! We can forgive those who do wrong, but cruelty is inhuman, a perversion of our nature. The gravest evils, the worst horrors, are the result of calculations, disregarding others, or treating people as things.[20] The only check against this tendency is empathy—to begin from caring for others as ourselves, seeing their good as our good, their pain as our pain. Horton has great empathy, but he also works at it. He sets compassion as his goal, and then he strives to act accordingly. As he does so it becomes easier, it becomes habit, until he simply is compassionate. His identity is such that he can't not help; he can't envision himself not sitting on the nest or rescuing the Whos. He has developed the character he ought to have by behaving routinely as if he already had it. And now it is simply *who he is*.

Horton exemplifies *caritas*. Horton cares for the egg. He cares for the Whos. Even at the risk of great sacrifice he gives of himself to help others in need. The egg and the Whos didn't ask to be threatened or vulnerable; they couldn't help but be vulnerable to a harsh or indifferent world. But Horton found himself in a position to assist. He was the only one willing and able, so what else could he have done? He could've been indifferent; he could've walked away. But what would that say about him, his character? So he recognizes the value of the other; he values their pain and their good as if they were his own, and he commits to helping. He sees the world for what it is, and he makes it better. He knows he can't stop all suffering or pain in the world, or even in the jungle. No one can, and we'd be fools to try, or to even wish for it. The elephant-bird is going to have a rough go of it no matter what. It'll surely have some emotional issues from having been abandoned by its mother. And the Whos are going to face a lot more troubles as they continue to live in a threatening world. They may still get crushed. They can't be inoculated from the world: "Life itself is a sea full of rocks and whirlpools that man avoids with the greatest caution and care, although he knows that, even when he succeeds with all his efforts and ingenuity in struggling through, at every step he comes nearer to the greatest, and total, the inevitable and irredeemable shipwreck, indeed even steers right into it, namely death."[21] The Whos will inevitably succumb. As will the elephant-bird, and even Horton someday. But he can do something rather than nothing; he can help where he can, when he can. And what more can we ask?

The world is, unfortunately, full of Mayzies. Surely you know one, or several. If you don't, you might be her. The world is full of people who think only for themselves, or who fail too often to think of others. People who act without forethought and become burdensome to those that planned ahead. The world is full of bumbling, stumbling, selfish humans. That's just how it is, and how it will always be. But don't let that lead you astray. You can't hate humans for being human. What else could they be? Don't resent them for being flawed, and don't despair of it or let it drive you to resentment, or worse, misanthropy. People are what they are. They are what they have been trained or allowed to become. And too often that is not the best, the brightest, the most exemplary. But we can't hide away. We're part of the species, like it or not; we're part of the human family. You can't change that fact, nor can you change other people. Horton couldn't make the world a place safe for the Whos, nor could he through argument or persuasion convince the others to care for them alongside him or convince Mayzie to be a responsible mother. Instead, Horton simply was better, as we must aspire to be. Horton is a moral exemplar. He's an inspirational picture of how we ought to be, of a disposition we ought to inculcate in ourselves, about how we ought to relate to others and the world, regardless of how they relate to us.

BE BETTER, 100 PERCENT!

Both of the Horton stories we've been discussing, *Horton Hears a Who!* and *Horton Hatches the Egg*, end well. The Whos are saved, and the whole jungle comes around to Horton's way of thinking and promises to protect the Whos. The egg hatches and it's an elephant-bird, as it "should be." These are nice, happy endings where the world becomes what it ought to be. It's nice to tell children this. It's nice to give them happy endings. Hope is nice, in small doses. Hope is important, for it often inspires acts of faith that otherwise wouldn't be possible. We can hope for the best, act as if it were possible, and often achieve what otherwise wouldn't have been thinkable. But let's not delude ourselves. More often than not kangaroos don't come around. They persist in their errors. They persist in selfishness. And the world is rarely (if ever) as it "should be." What people get isn't commensurate with what they are owed. The good suffer and the evil prosper. The wicked often go unpunished, and the only thing the beneficent, hardworking, trustworthy people get is more work, more burdens placed on them by the Mayzies of the world. The world is not a Dr. Seuss story. Remembering this can be disheartening, but it's important. And that's when Horton is most needed, that's when we need to remember his stories. We can't be led astray. We need to see that we are better. We've got a simple choice, compassion or egoism. We can care for ourselves and others, or we can be a part of the problem; we can add to the suffering of the world.

Although the world is sunk in evil, we are to see that we are better; that we are compassionate in the face of suffering, that we care even though the world is indifferent and others petty or cruel. The suffering of the world can't be defeated; evil can't be eliminated. But in our small sphere we can make it a little bit better for our fellow sufferers. In the grand scheme of things, like the Whos, we are small. We are inhabitants of an inconsequential speck of dust in a vast and endless universe. And we can't count on a benevolent elephant to make it all better. But we can learn from one. We are insignificant, except to each other. A person's a person, no matter how small, so be compassionate, 100 percent.

9

FEELING AS, FEELING FOR, SEEING WHAT'S RIGHT, AND SO MUCH MORE

Empathy, Concern, and Moral Growth in Dr. Seuss

Jennifer L. McMahon

Our experience is, without fiction, too confined and too parochial. Literature extends it, making us reflect and feel about what might otherwise be too distant for feeling.

—Martha Nussbaum, *Love's Knowledge*

Unless someone like you cares a whole awful lot, nothing is going to get better. It's not.

—Dr. Seuss, *The Lorax*

Humans have been telling stories for all of our recorded history. Historical records are one type of story we tell. Children's stories are another. For as long as we have been telling stories, we have been using them to teach. Though most people would accept the notion that stories can instruct, philosophers have debated this issue for centuries.

Recently, there has been a renaissance of philosophic and popular interest in the heuristic function of fiction, interest buoyed by new empirical research, particularly from the neurosciences, that provides compelling evidence that reading literature has a variety of benefits. Perhaps the most celebrated is literature's capacity to assist us in understanding others by arousing empathy, a response that may influence prosocial behavior and promote moral development.[1]

EMPATHY AND UNDERSTANDING

> I never heard such whimpering
> And I began to see
> That I was just as strange to them
> As they were strange to me!

> —"What Was I Scared Of?"

The wave of interest in the benefits of literature has garnered critical attention. While there seems to be consensus that empathy is valuable, and typically involves mirror neurons, recent studies provide evidence that empathy should not be reduced to that system.[2] Other studies suggest that empathy's capacity to promote prosocial action and thereby foster moral development might not be as strong as originally assumed.[3] In addition, though studies generally support the assertion that literature can help us learn things through the arousal of empathy, several emphasize that further study is needed before reliable conclusions can be drawn regarding literature's general impact and whether its influence is typically positive.[4]

One domain of literature that has received little attention, and yet would seem to be of critical interest, is children's literature. After all, if research suggests that the effects of literature are significant, then it stands to reason that attention should be paid to the impact it exerts on individuals in their formative stages.[5] Parents, caregivers, and educators have long relied upon children's literature as a teaching tool. Perhaps no children's author is as beloved as Dr. Seuss in that regard. His tales delight readers while at the same time providing important life lessons, often moral in nature. This chapter examines the way in which four of Seuss's stories instruct their readers by employing varied means to arouse empathy, widen readers' spheres of concern, and perhaps increase the likelihood of prosocial behavior and heightened moral awareness.

Recent research regarding literature and empathic response suggests that literature is more likely to elicit empathy if it provides a detailed narrative that is memorable, encourages imaginative immersion, and utilizes divergent, multisensory mechanisms to arouse audience response.[6] Several studies differentiate between pictorial cues and abstract linguistic ones, arguing that it is critical to distinguish these cues because they engage different neural systems. Recent research also suggests that empathic response can be manipulated, even blocked, by the presence or absence of certain narrative features. They indicate that the likelihood of a prosocial reaction to empathic response can be diminished if empathy produces high levels of personal distress and heightened if the narrative fosters not only empathy but also concern.[7] Seuss's stories "What Was I Scared Of?"; *How the Grinch Stole Christmas!*; *The Sneetches*; and *The Lorax* all serve to illustrate these new findings regarding the impact fiction can have.

"What Was I Scared Of?" is an endearing tale of a small, bearlike creature who encounters an ominous Other while walking in the woods. Through the narrative, our little hero discovers that the individual who inspires his terror is not a genuine threat but, indeed, "just as scared" as he is. Over the course of the story, our protagonist is transformed, coming to see the Other not as a threatening object but as a like-feeling subject. Importantly, this transformation is occasioned by empathy and narrative features that reinforce it and supplement the reader's understanding of the situation.

The story begins with our protagonist in an anxious situation trying to bootstrap his self-confidence. He enters a dark forest. Despite the disconcerting color scheme and ominous shadows, he declares that he sees "nothing scary." Perhaps mostly for his own benefit, he asserts, "For I have never been afraid of anything, not very." Our hero's constitution is put to the test shortly thereafter when he sees a pair of "pale green pants." These pants aren't sitting innocuously in a heap or fluttering benignly on a clothesline. They have "nobody inside them"; yet they are walking. Seuss introduces the audience to the source of his protagonist's fear, illustrates that fear as it emerges and increases, and, in doing so, he compels a little of the audience's own.[8]

Seuss carefully crafts his narrative to build suspense by eliciting increasing levels of anxiety on the part of the reader. This anxiety emerges for two main reasons. First, it occurs as a result of the reader's concern, or *feeling for* the protagonist, a small and vulnerable-looking creature who inspires strong levels of sympathetic distress. It also results from the fact that the creature elicits powerful feelings of empathy, or *feeling as*, as readers simulate the unease he displays. In a sequence of increasingly disturbing encounters, the protagonist's fear of the pants escalates. In the first frame, he sees the pants walking and faces them. In the next, they are running after him, and he flees with fear evident in his expression. In the third encounter, our hero narrowly escapes being run over by the pants as they pedal by him on a bicycle. Alarm is apparent on his face, reinforcing the reader's impression of the severity of the situation. Seuss ratchets up the tension further with his language and the quality of his illustrations. Initially, the protagonist describes the pants as "empty" and says he doesn't "care" for them. However, as the scenes progress, the pants become more threatening; they are described as "spooky" and our protagonist as "scare[d]!" This pattern of escalation is echoed in the illustrations. The frame narrows successively, bringing the reader closer to the threat that the protagonist experiences and more able to appreciate the heightened emotion evident in his facial expressions and gestures. Moreover, both the bear and the pants adopt more dynamic poses as the narrative continues, a feature that increases the reader's sense of energy and cues empathy even more decisively. The pants chase the bear over Roover River and through the woods, with our hero finally hiding in a brickel bush until hunger draws him out and into the climactic scene of the narrative. Reaching into a snide bush for sustenance, the amiable little creature finds not a succulent snide berry but his nemesis: the pale green pants. His exclamation makes the profound level of his fear evident. Cast in the form of a direct appeal, it commands emotional engagement on the part of the reader: "I yelled for help. I screamed. I shrieked. / I howled. I yowled. I cried, / 'Oh save me from these pale green pants / With nobody inside!'" (Scared).

Much to the protagonist's and the reader's surprise, Seuss upends expectation by having the pants, not the protagonist, collapse in fear. The illustration pattern shifts immediately as well. The pants move to the foreground, becoming both the bear's and the reader's focal point as they are brought low by their own terror. In a decisive shift in language and image, Seuss prompts a classic reversal and a shift in empathic identification. Now the pants become the focus of compassionate concern and the target of empathic response. Literary features, most clearly the actions of the protagonist, prime the reader's empathic response to the pants. He sits down and puts his arm around them. His speech reinforces the action, guiding the reader to a different emotional engagement with the pants; he describes the pants now as "poor" instead of "dreadful" and adopts a congenial relation to the pants instead of an antagonistic one. In the last scene, Seuss depicts the protagonist and the pants interacting positively. The reader now responds empathically to both figures, not just the initial protagonist. Thus, the text not only illustrates the transfiguration of its protagonist relative to the Other but also transfigures the reader, widening the sphere of empathic response and the scope of compassionate concern to include the character initially perceived as dangerous and strange. Interestingly, the two main characters literally mirror one another's stance in the closing illustration. In both their positions and their speech, they reinforce the reader's understanding, at various perceptual levels, that the previously objectified pants now occupy the same ontological position of sympathetic subject.

EMPATHY AND EXPANDED SPHERES OF CONCERN

> And the minute his heart didn't feel quite so tight
> He whizzed with his load through the bright morning light.
> —*How the Grinch Stole Christmas!*

Seuss achieves a similar transfiguration in his beloved classic, *How the Grinch Stole Christmas!* Here, the metamorphosis that takes place is more substantial than that observed in "What Was I Scared Of?" Readers witness the transfiguration of a reviled villain into a sympathetic protagonist. Seuss sets the stage for this transformation by casting the villain in the lead role, a position that fosters reader identification. However, rather than portray his main character in sympathetic terms, Seuss makes the Grinch's malign demeanor evident. Seuss depicts him in an unfriendly pose and with a sour expression. He tells readers that the Grinch hates Christmas and explains that the most likely reason is that his heart is "two sizes too small." Rather than use literary features to reinforce empathic response, Seuss ingeniously sets his character in a position that should arouse it, but he confounds that response by portraying him in terms that discourage empathic identification. As recent studies show, empathy is highly subject to "in-group bias."[9] As a result, individuals are more likely to display empathy toward those they "perceive as closer or more similar to [them]."[10] Conversely, individuals can experience an "almost complete blockage of empathic responses"[11] relative to those who seem different or threatening. By portraying the Grinch not only as a physical and ideological outlier but also as a clear and present danger, Seuss primes his reader to be unsympathetic to the Grinch, despite their tendency to identify with him as the main character, and to instead empathize with the Whos, whom the Grinch subsequently dupes.

This pattern is reinforced as the narrative continues. Not only is the Grinch described as hating nice things like singing, but he is also described as hating the Whos, who, unlike the Grinch, are characterized in positive terms. Whereas they feast and play and sing, he frowns, and snarls, and sneers. A caricature of Dickens's Ebenezer Scrooge, Seuss moves his plot forward with the Grinch's plan to rob the Whos of the joy of the holiday season. Donning the guise of Saint Nick, he sets upon the unsuspecting Whos.

As the "Santy Claus" ruse takes shape, Seuss echoes the language and rhythmic patterns of Clement Clarke Moore's "A Visit from St. Nicholas,"[12] but he reverses the actions of its main character. His anti-Santa empties stockings rather than fills them and steals presents rather than leaves them. His efforts are imperiled only once, when his deceptions are nearly discovered by Cindy-Lou Who. However, before she can discern the devilish nature of his action, she is subject to deception herself. The slick old deceiver lies to the girl and gets her back to bed. The Grinch's deception galvanizes readers' disdain for him. While the fact he is dressed in a bright red Santa Claus suit commands visual attention, his violation of our positive associations with Santa Claus undercuts the potential for a positive response. Readers loathe the Grinch even more acutely because he is dressed as Santa.

Ultimately, the Grinch's trip to the peak of Mount Crumpit brings both him and readers to the literal and figurative climax of the narrative and its critical pivot point. Here the Grinch experiences his transformative epiphany, an epiphany that changes not only the Grinch but also readers' emotional relation to him.

At the top of Mount Crumpit, the Grinch discovers that he has not robbed the Whos of their Christmas spirit even though he has robbed them of virtually everything else. As he hears their singing, he becomes aware that the spirit of Christmas "doesn't come from a store" (Grinch). He realizes that while Christmas may be associated with consumerism, the meaning of Christmas comes from giving, not receiving. Readers witness the Grinch's transformation as this new understanding of things dawns on him. Beyond stating that the Grinch's "heart grew three sizes that day" (Grinch), Seuss alters the Grinch's physical appearance. His closing illustrations reveal a kinder, gentler Grinch. They contrast sharply with earlier depictions, particularly the one that illustrates the moment the Grinch conjured the idea to rob the Whos. There he has a perfectly malign smirk; the pupils of his eyes even look like devilish horns. In the final illustration, however, the Grinch's countenance is softened with a smile, and a wreath sits behind his head like a halo. His eyes are closed in satisfaction rather than glowering, and he actually looks like a Who, not a monster, a visual feature that facilitates a shift in reader identification and motivates positive empathic response.

Once again, Seuss has used varied mechanisms to arouse empathy for an unlikely target. His story has brought us around to *feeling as* and *for* a character who we don't initially like, and with whom we do not expect, or even want, to align. With his narratives Seuss shows his readers that even unsympathetic figures have their own stories; he kindles our concern for them by shifting both our emotional alignments and our cognitive ones. Using a complex combination of linguistic and pictorial cues he moves his readers not merely to feeling but to the appreciation of fairly explicit moral messages regarding the way we should (and should not) treat others and the way we should (and should not) behave ourselves.

OVERCOMING BIAS WITH EMPATHY

> We're exactly like you!
> . . . We're all just the same.
>
> *—The Sneetches*

This pattern continues in *The Sneetches* where Seuss works to disable a broader type of bias—namely, bias against social groups defined by physical type. *The Sneetches* opens by distinguishing two types of Sneetch from one another: the "Plain-Belly" and the "Star-Belly." Apart from the presence or absence of a small star on the abdomen, Sneetches look exactly the same. This is no accident. Nor is the fact that they are more birdlike than humanoid, or that there is no easy protagonist with whom to identify in the story. As Seuss's narrator states at the start, you might think that having a star on one's belly "wouldn't matter at all." However, the narrative quickly makes it clear that it does.

The narrative reveals that in Sneetch society physical appearance is a basis for social differentiation and claims of superiority. The Star-Belly

Sneetches occupy a position of privilege. They marginalize the Plain-Belly Sneetches because they don't have stars; they have "nothing to do with the Plain-Belly sort"—they do not talk to them, they do not let their children play with them, they do not permit them to participate in social gatherings. This pattern of segregation is not occasional. It is maintained "year after year." Not surprisingly, the Plain-Belly Sneetches do not like being marginalized. Unfortunately, their desire to possess the star that would grant them social access leaves them open to mistreatment of another sort. Ironically, it comes at the hands of a Fix-It-Up Chappie named Sylvester McMonkey McBean. McBean arrives on the Sneetches' beaches with a machine that will place stars on the bellies of those so unfortunate as to be born without them. He announces he will provide this service for a mere $3. The Plain-Belly Sneetches quickly seize the opportunity and brag to the Star-Bellies, "We're all just the same, now, you snooty old smarties! / And now we can go to your frankfurter parties" (Sneetches). Predictably, the Star-Bellies aren't ready to surrender their superior status, and they don't have to do so; the Fix-It-Up Chappie is there to serve them as well. McBean offers to take their stars off with the machine, but this service costs more. Tightening the frames over consecutive illustrations so readers can fully appreciate the heightening tension among the competing Sneetches, Seuss's narrator states knowingly to the reader, "Of course, from then on, as you probably guess, / Things really got into a horrible mess" (Sneetches). And a mess it is. Seuss depicts the Sneetches careening round and round in a foreshortened infinity symbol, running through the machine again and again until "neither the Plain nor the Star-Bellies knew / Whether this one was that one . . . or that one was this one / Or which one was what one . . . or what one was who" (Sneetches). When McBean drives off with all of the Sneetches' money, it seems as if he has had the last laugh. However, Seuss makes it clear that he has not. Though McBean contends that "you can't teach a Sneetch," Seuss's narrator refutes his contention. He asserts that the Sneetches "got really quite smart on that day," discovering that, regardless of appearance, "Sneetches are Sneetches" (Sneetches) and no type is better than any other.

Visual mirroring is evident in the final illustration—in this case, double mirroring. On the right side, there are two adult Sneetches, one with a star and one without; they shake hands with one another, and their bodies and expressions reflect one another almost exactly. On the left-hand side, that same parallel pattern of representation is present, save for the fact that it is instead two young Sneetches. The reader is shown the ideal state of affairs and encouraged doubly to empathy by this mirroring pattern. Seuss even adds a fish for visual emphasis. It is shown looking approvingly on the show of solidarity between the Sneetches, thus reinforcing, in a different manner, the message implicit in the figures—namely, that empathic concern and equal treatment are morally superior to indifference and injustice.

Structurally, the dynamics of empathy differ in *The Sneetches*. Though empathic response is elicited for all of the Sneetches eventually, a strong point of reader identification is not established at the start. There is no clear-cut protagonist for the reader to identify with, and the fact that the characters are birdlike and their problem seems trivial discourages close reader identification and, consequently, high levels of empathic response. One might think it unusual for Seuss to cultivate this distance when the text has such an obvious and important message. However, the distance is critical to the sort of understanding that the text seeks to develop; it is the critical distance necessary for revelation.

As Martha Nussbaum notes, literature has a unique heuristic capacity not only because we can become immersed in it but also because it affords us an opportunity to observe situations in which we have less of a personal interest, interest that might motivate unconscious bias and thereby obscure rather than reveal. As she states, literature "free[s] us from certain sources of distortion [in judgment] that can frequently impede our real life deliberations. Since the story is not ours, we do not find ourselves caught up in the 'vulgar heat' of our personal jealousies, or anger, or in the sometimes blinding violence of our loves."[13] Oddly enough, if the characters in *The Sneetches* were human and their conflict was about skin color, the text might seem too didactic and some readers might not be as ready to embrace its message. Sometimes it is easier to see a truth about ourselves if it is first presented as a truth about someone else. Seuss sets readers up to observe the Sneetches as another type of being, as much as to immediately identify with them. As quickly as readers are inclined to empathize with the alienated Plain-Bellies, Seuss shows those same Sneetches succumbing naively to the wiles of a charlatan; reader response is immediately transformed. While readers might still feel for the susceptible Sneetches, they also see their mistake clearly and know that nothing good is going to follow from their efforts to change themselves.

Seuss ingeniously interrupts audience alliance with the Sneetches again before the climactic scene by having the narrator speak directly to the reader in the second person. This maneuver fosters alignment between the reader and the literary figure of the narrator, distancing the reader enough from the Sneetches that he or she is able to view their actions critically. The fact is that readers, regardless of their age, are likely to have an unconscious bias toward their in-groups, against out-groups, and against the notion that they possess bias; realism in representation may actually make it difficult to raise these biases to awareness if it is structured in a manner that motivates unconscious defenses to be engaged. In *The Sneetches*, the degree of abstraction afforded by the cartoon illustrations and the fantastic scenario proves an effective vehicle for consciousness raising. Just as it dawns on the Grinch that he might have misunderstood the Whos, most readers of *The Sneetches* eventually see themselves in the Sneetches; however, they do so at the end of the narrative after the creatures have become smarter and nicer, a time when identification is easier. This identification compels a retroactive association that invites the reader, particularly in the course of postreading activities, to identify empathically with the Sneetches and become smarter and nicer as well. The reader is encouraged to face the fact that they, too, might have problematic biases but is moved to do so more readily because the message wasn't shoved down their throat.

EMPATHY AND CONCERN (NOT THNEEDS!): "WHAT EVERYONE, EVERYONE, EVERYONE NEEDS!" (LORAX)

Like *The Sneetches*, Seuss's *The Lorax* has a strong moral message and seeks to widen the scope of empathic response and the sphere of compassionate concern. Indeed, it goes further than *The Sneetches*, encouraging the extension of empathy and concern not only impartially to members of our own species but also to other sentient beings and the environment in general.

The Lorax opens ominously. The dark title page depicts a threatening pair of eyes peering through a boarded-up window at a vulnerable-looking character readers will later come to know as the Lorax. The colors darken as the reader turns to the first page of the story. The scene is a barren field at night. The vulnerable figure of a young boy stands alone on a foreboding-looking path. The vegetation is wilted and askew. There is little evidence of life or joy. A tilted streetlight bears a sign that reads, "The Street of the Lifted Lorax." It is a dystopian scene that primes readers to experience concern and identify with the boy as he navigates the threatening surroundings.

As the story progresses, the boy walks toward a dilapidated house. Seuss compounds the mystery established by the cryptic sign with interrogative phrasing: "What was the Lorax? / And why was it there? / And why was it lifted and taken somewhere?" (Lorax). Seuss then amplifies the suspense by introducing an enigmatic character: "the Once-ler." Like the setting that surrounds him, the Once-ler is cast in disquieting terms. He is never shown to the reader throughout the entire course of the text, a structural feature critical to the effects that Seuss achieves. Just as his figure is kept secret, he is described as being secretive and unpleasant. He "lurks" in the house as if awaiting unsuspecting victims.

The Once-ler takes over the role of the narrator after the boy pays him to tell the story of the Lorax. As the narrative transitions to the Once-ler's tale, another change occurs: the boy is removed from the illustrations, only to return in the final two. This shift decisively moves the reader to simulate the boy as the Once-ler now speaks directly to him or her. There is also a significant shift in the quality of the illustrations at this point. They introduce the reader to a completely different world. The setting is lush. Bright colors replace the somber hues present in the opening illustrations. The landscape is brimming with varied forms of life. Readers are presented with a portrait of nature unspoiled. In the first illustration of this Eden, attentive readers will notice only one artifact of human engineering: the "Once-ler wagon." However small the Once-ler's wagon first appears, it does not take long for his impact to be felt: "In no time at all, [he] had built a small shop. / Then . . . chopped down a Truffula Tree with one chop" (Lorax). The Once-ler cuts down the trees so he can make "thneeds," odd multipurpose items that he says "everyone needs."

A conscientious objector to the Once-ler's enterprise, our title character immediately reacts to the Once-ler's action. The Lorax appears spontaneously from a Truffula stump. Despite his fantastic entrance, the Once-ler's description of the Lorax is negative. Although the Once-ler offers an unflattering description of the Lorax, the Lorax doesn't actually look bad. He has a round and kind-looking face. Moreover, he says that he "speak[s] for the trees," which suggests that he (unlike the Once-ler)

acts in the interest of others, not out of self-interest. This disparity between the appearance of the Lorax and the description offered by the
Once-ler contributes to the "(controlled) cognitive dissonance"[14] that fiction can so effectively create and that strongly influences empathic reactions. It moves reader alignment to the Lorax. Thus, when the Lorax
characterizes the Once-ler's thneed as foolish and accuses the Once-ler of
being "crazy with greed," readers are more likely to believe him. Seuss's
introduction of the Lorax decisively moves positive reader engagement to
him and creates antipathy for the Once-ler.

Successive scenes reinforce this shift. Over the next thirty-two pages
readers observe the devastating impact that the Once-ler's thneed business has on the entities that populate the Lorax's domain and the environment itself. As the frames progress, the color scheme returns to the dismal
one that was present at the opening of the narrative. This color symbolism
establishes a clear visual link between the action of the Once-ler and the
depleted landscape. The Lorax appears repeatedly, petitioning the Once-
ler to stop cutting down the trees, explaining the impact that their loss has
on other members of the ecosystem. He explains that the Brown Bar-ba-
loots are starving without the Truffula fruits and that the smog from the
factory is choking the Swomee-Swans. Readers are moved to feel both
for and *as* these creatures by various aspects of Seuss's narrative. Though
the creatures are not human, they are depicted more humanistically than
the one human who now occupies the narrative. Their plights are also
described in familiar terms: They want clean water and air. They do not
want to suffer. They do not want to leave their homes. These are desires
with which most readers can identify. Indeed, they can identify with these
feelings just as, perhaps even more readily, as with the Once-ler's desire
for financial gain. As theorists note, fiction arouses empathy more readily
when it presents readers with characters who have "a name and a face."[15]
Whereas the animals are developed and made highly sympathetic, the
Once-ler is not. The animals have adorable faces. Conversely, readers
don't ever see the Once-ler's face and are never told his name. Thus,
when he rejects the Lorax's pleas and displays indifference to the affable
creatures readers now empathize with, readers are moved to feel antipathy toward the Once-ler. This feeling is amplified when he declares that
irrespective of the adverse effects of his actions, "Business is business!
And business must grow" (Lorax). Through varied means, Seuss's story
conveys the message that individual actions have an impact due to the

interconnections that exist in natural systems. He makes it clear that because of this interconnectedness businesses cannot survive if they deplete the resources upon which they depend. Seuss drives this message home with the "sickening" sound of the last Truffula tree being cut, a sound that signals the end of the Once-ler's business and sets the stage for the closing scenes of the narrative.

The text closes with the same barren setting that opened the story. The shortsighted and egotistical action of the Once-ler is established as the cause of the environmental catastrophe and concomitant loss of animal life and human flourishing. With the landscape in ruin, the Lorax lifts himself out of the scene, leaving just a small pile of rocks with one word, *Unless*. At this point, Seuss returns the boy to the narrative's illustrations. The Once-ler says to him, "Now that *you're* here, / the word of the Lorax seems perfectly clear / UNLESS someone like you / cares a whole awful lot, / nothing is going to get better. / It's not." (Lorax)

Happily, the narrative does not end with this cautionary statement. It offers hope. Just as the Once-ler's action initiated a chain of events that led to disaster, in the final scene he takes a step that could lead to renewal and that restores the reader's empathic relation to him. Here, he throws the last Truffula seed into the boy's hand. Seuss moves the figure of the boy out of the frame. In this way the reader can more readily identify himself or herself as the "you" in the Once-ler's speech. By returning and then removing the boy, Seuss assigns the message of environmental responsibility first to the future generation represented by the boy and then to the reading subject, actively integrating the reader into a narrative that both illustrates the high stakes of apathy and incites emotional engagement with the entities that need protection.

FOSTERING FEELING

Seuss's best-known stories actively command empathic response. Recent research on empathy suggests not only that there are various types of empathy[16] but also that different types of empathy are "partially dissociable"[17] and may be motivated by divergent causes. Seuss's use of multiple devices that tend to arouse empathy heightens the potential that empathy will be successfully elicited regardless of differences that obtain between individual readers. Studies also indicate that literary sources may have a special ability to elicit empathy because of the way in which they can manipulate features conducive to the response.[18] For example, research indicates that imaginatively simulating the mental state of another person increases the degree of empathic response as well as the likelihood of prosocial behavior.[19] Clearly, reading literature expands our understanding of others not only by creating opportunities for readers to access the private thoughts of other subjects[20] but also by creating opportunities for them to simulate the mental states of those others that are "not [as] readily available in life."[21]

In the four stories examined here, Seuss uses multiple mechanisms to encourage empathic response. He draws heavily upon the normal tendency for readers to identify with the main character of a story, a tendency anchored in the fact that our own lives possess a narrative structure, one in which we are the main character. Seuss reinforces this tendency to identify with the main characters sometimes in order to compel us to identify with different ones by using other means. These include the use of "grammatological"[22] structures, such as first- and second-person pronouns, which foster identification to the extent that we associate their use with ourselves; other literary devices, such as direct dialogue to the reader; and pictorial cues, such as the removal of figures from the frame so as to facilitate reader identification. Importantly, Seuss skillfully manipulates empathic response in order to motivate not merely the simulation of another's experience but also to widen the range of this sort of response, expand the scope of compassionate concern, and increase moral understanding and action.

As noted, in addition to cultivating empathy, Seuss's stories also encourage the development of concern. Like empathy, concern is receiving increased attention in empirical studies. It is defined as a feeling for others that does not entail the process of emotional or imaginative simulation of their situation. While fiction can produce "strong empathic response,"[23] it is not the only impact it can have. When it comes to the heuristic ability of fiction, particularly its ability to improve us morally, empathy is not the only factor in the equation. It is not because "increases in empathy do not necessarily make us behave more morally."[24] Though studies establish that "concern and empathy are positively related"[25] to prosocial behavior, they also identify "concern, and not empathy, [as] the primary motivator of moral thoughts and actions."[26] Thus, to genuinely be instructive, it is critical that texts inspire concern as well as empathy.

Throughout the four stories examined, Seuss encourages not only empathy but also concern for individuals and the situations they confront. While empathy can serve to enhance our appreciation of the experience of others, empathy alone is no guarantee that our understanding or responsiveness to others will genuinely be augmented. It is not because empathy is subject to bias; we are simply not as ready to empathize with some people as others.[27] Moreover, if empathy arouses too much personal distress, it can "debilitat[e]"[28] rather than enable prosocial responses. Finally, even if we experience empathy for someone, our mental simulation of the thought processes of that other person does not genuinely guarantee the transparent disclosure of those processes or their situation to us. Instead, as Thomas Nagel argues in his famous "What Is It Like to Be a Bat?" empathy may merely give us the opportunity to imagine what it is like for us to be those others.[29] If we don't recognize this fact, empathy can promote unwitting psychic colonialism due to a feeling of emotional congruence that masquerades as understanding of the other when it is in fact largely projection.[30] Concern for and appreciation of the particularity of the other's experience is a necessary complement to empathy. Characters in fiction are conceptual structures that are designed, among other things, to facilitate the appreciation of other people's perspectives through simulation. They help us develop an awareness of the stark difference of those perspectives from our own. Indeed, literature's unique ability to acquaint us with different perspectives, often by shifting the target of empathic identification and by cultivating sympathy as much as simulation, is what helps it motivate the development of concern and understanding alongside empathy.

EMPATHY AND ITS PARTNERS

From a moral standpoint, concern is a necessary partner to empathy. Though moral theorists tend to place a positive value on empathy, few (if any) make empathy a prerequisite for moral understanding or action. Rather, most assume that being moral entails the ability to be sensitive and responsive to others even in its absence. Morality does, however, presume concern and understanding, and Seuss's works develop concern for others, notably others who might lie outside our standard sphere of interest. He does so by crafting highly detailed stories that develop our sense of those individuals and portray them in sufficiently evocative terms so that we are literally drawn to feel sympathy for them.

Seuss also employs cognitive means to evoke and enlarge the sphere of feeling and to encourage moral development. As many theorists of emotion note, though not all emotions are belief dependent, some are, and certain emotions can be elicited, amplified, or eradicated on cognitive grounds. Theorists such as Martha Nussbaum, David Novitz, Jenefer Robinson, and Susan Feagin, among others, note that while literature does not instruct principally through propositional statements, it certainly can use these sorts of assertions, or other intellectual means, to facilitate the development of understanding, to convey a moral viewpoint, or to depict hypothetical situations in such a way as to influence the reader to experience belief-sensitive feelings such as empathy and sympathy.[31] Seuss not only employs mechanisms that arouse pathos with regards to characters but also invokes logos. He appeals to reason in addition to emotion, and the capacity his works have to instruct is as dependent upon the former as the latter. For example, in *The Sneetches*, Seuss purposefully crafts a situation in which individuals who are equal in everything but an incidental, indeed trivial, feature are treated inequitably in order to appeal to the reader's implicit sense of justice. Seuss frames his narrative to present the reader with a situation that appeals to reason because it defies logic: if A is equal to B, then A should not be treated in a manner contrary to that in which B is treated and A should not mistreat B. It is this recognition, as much as the appealing expressions of the Sneetches, that arouses the reader's empathic response, compassionate concern, and moral growth.

In addition, Seuss's stories would not be as instructive without their aesthetic appeal, an appeal derived from a host of factors, including their engaging illustrations, their humor, and their captivating and almost involuntarily memorable rhyme. As theorists confirm, individuals are more susceptible to empathic response and other changes in perception when they experience higher degrees of aesthetic response than when they do not.[32] Whether this is simply a function of the fact that we are more open to influence by things that we like, and more likely to retain a connection to things we enjoy, remains to be seen. It seems clear, however, that Seuss's beloved narratives are made more influential by their aesthetic appeal, appeal that extends beyond the reader's immediate experience of the text.

As recent literature suggests, "Fiction may change how, not just what, people think about others."[33] In doing so, it changes us. It might prime us for important social skills like empathy;[34] it might enhance our moral conscience.[35] While all of its effects have yet to be understood, it is clear that our "reactions to fictional characters are integrated into broader response patterns in daily life."[36]

Seuss's four stories—"What Was I Scared Of?" *The Sneetches*, *How the Grinch Stole Christmas!*, and *The Lorax*—all invite the powerful empathic response that has so recently commanded empirical interest in literature and its effects. Importantly, they also reveal that empathy is "variable, complex, and dynamic"[37] and that the beneficial effects of fiction, including the advancement of prosocial behavior and moral understanding, are likely irreducible to empathy alone, instead being a function of the careful and coordinated solicitation of feeling, the cultivation of concern, and the delivery of explicit moral messages.

10

HEARING WHOS AND MINDING OTHERS

Care Ethics in Dr. Seuss

Janelle Pötzsch

I meant what I said, And I said what I meant . . .
An elephant's faithful one hundred per cent!
—Dr. Seuss, *Horton Hatches the Egg*

Gladly I serve my friends, but alas I do it with pleasure.
Hence I am plagued with doubt that I am not a virtuous person.
—Friedrich Schiller, *Xenia*[1]

German playwright Friedrich Schiller (1759–1805) might have been one of the first but surely would not be the last to poke fun at the rigid moral philosophy of Immanuel Kant (1724–1804), which was all about what people *ought* to do. Tongue-in-cheek, Schiller raised an important point when it comes to our dealings with other people: Does all the high-minded philosophical talk about rights and duties really capture what's at the heart of our social relations? This question, so tentatively posed by Schiller, was to meet a convinced "No!" in the years (read: centuries) to come. I suppose Horton, the gullible elephant whom a lazy bird talks into hatching her egg, would give an answer along these lines as well. His first reaction to Mayzie's request is not only negative but also strictly logical: "*I* haven't feathers and *I* haven't wings. / ME on your egg? Why, that doesn't make sense" (Hatches). But, eventually, Horton succumbs to something even more compelling than logic: the persuasive power of pitiful (and idle) Mayzie.

But what exactly made her appeal so powerful that Horton gives way? Had he aligned with Kant, he would have checked whether his action (or Mayzie's demand) aligns with the categorical imperative Kant devised. This is an ethical principle that asks us to "act on no other maxim than that which can also have as object itself as a universal law."[2] And since we cannot want gullible elephants to be regularly entrapped by pleasure-seeking birds too lazy to hatch their own eggs, Horton should have turned down Mayzie's request. Yet the fact that he did not suggests that there is something more (or something different altogether) than abstract talk about claims and duties that drives our interactions—or specifically, our granting of favors.

That morality isn't something one can reason about was also the conviction of one of Kant's most ardent critics, German philosopher Arthur Schopenhauer (1788–1860). His stance was very similar to Schiller's point in the lines given above: Why talk about duties when we can witness everyday that people actually *want* to act morally, and do so quite artlessly?

Just recall how spontaneously the characters in Dr. Seuss respond to the pleas of others: Thidwick, the Big-Hearted Moose, answers the bug's request for giving him a ride on his antlers by stating, "I'm happy my antlers can be of some use. There's room there to spare, and I'm happy to share!" (Thidwick). Unsuspicious Horton is butter in Mayzie's hands (or, rather, wings), and when he encounters the Whos, his consideration is roused well before he can even be sure that there's a living thing on the small speck of dust—in a way, he acts on conjecture, but clearly not on careful deliberation.

What these examples show is that both Horton and Thidwick are able to put themselves in the shoes of others and judge a given situation from their perspective: even though Horton sees absolutely nothing on that small speck of dust he comes across at the pool, he imagines there to be "[s]ome sort of creature of very small size, [t]oo small to be seen by an elephant's eyes . . . some poor little person who's shaking with fear" (Horton). Similarly, he sees Mayzie's point that it would be nice to have a short(!) time off after having sat on an egg so long, which is why he agrees to look after it for her. And poor Thidwick identifies to such an extent with his (mostly uninvited) guests that he keeps telling himself that "a host, above all, must be nice to his guests" (Thidwick), no matter how intolerable the situation eventually becomes for him. His degree of self-sacrifice is surpassed only by honorable Horton, who ultimately cares so much about Mayzie's egg that he doesn't even flee from the hunters who come after him: "Shoot if you must / But I won't run away! / I meant what I said / And I said what I meant . . . / An elephant's faithful / One hundred per cent!" (Hatches).

The willingness of Horton and Thidwick to put themselves out for others clearly sets them apart from their less obliging environments. To add insult to injury, it's not only lazy Mayzie and the animal squatters they have to deal with but also the disapproval of their friends. However, far from making them reconsider their decisions, the rejection they meet seems only to strengthen their selfless choices.

But precisely what makes Thidwick and Horton so oblivious to their own self-interest? This question is all the more pressing given that selfishness seems to be so hardwired in all the other animals—including us humans, as Schopenhauer would be quick to point out. He was convinced that only two motivating forces propel all our actions: egoism and malice. It was mere egoism that made the other animals settle on Thidwick's antlers and that prompted Mayzie's preposterous request that an elephant should hatch her egg. And the only reason poor Horton isn't shot by the hunters is their sudden change of mind to "sell him back home to a circus, for money!" (Hatches). Malice is also on full display in Dr. Seuss, especially when Horton tries to protect the Whos. In this episode, the sneering kangaroos are surpassed only by the eagle that flies "[a]ll that late afternoon and far into the night" (Horton) only to hide the clover on which the Whos live from Horton.

Why do the bad examples of the others fail to have any impact on both Horton and Thidwick? They neither decline their help nor succumb to the social censure their commitment provokes. And, unlike their surroundings, they seem void of egoism and malice. As Schopenhauer has it, there is only one thing that makes us suspend our egoism, no matter how strong this tendency might otherwise be: our ability to feel compassion. This not only prevents us (at least from time to time) from pursuing our self-interest at the expense of others but also serves as the basis of all of morality—even of such seemingly abstract notions as justice.

According to Schopenhauer, the sympathy we feel for others operates in two ways: for one, it makes us aware of the suffering an unjust act might bring unto others, which in turn makes us refrain from carrying it out. Once we are aware of the sufferings our mischievous acts inflict on other people, our sympathy causes us to make such refraining from harmful behavior into a guiding maxim to respect people's rights. Yet much more important, as the characters of Dr. Seuss demonstrate, is the second way sympathy functions: beyond making us desist from evil-doing, it also entails bringing about actions that *benefit* others. Recall that Horton didn't confine himself to not harming the Whos; he actually wanted them to be well and therefore saved them. That's because sympathy gives rise to humanity (*Menschenliebe*, as Schopenhauer puts it), an attitude that actively seeks to improve the well-being of others. And as if working in practical philosophy isn't frustrating enough in and of itself, Schopenhauer has the nerve to claim that "ethics is actually the most simple of all sciences"[3] because everyone has the necessary (emotional) provision for deriving moral rules for all kinds of cases. And clearly neither Horton nor Thidwick bothered to go to grad school; yet their conduct is nothing short of admirable (albeit maybe just a little bit too trusting). Interestingly, although Schopenhauer claims that empathy is a basic human function, he asserts that women surpass men in this respect (tell that to Mayzie!). That's because the grounds for empathy are "mainly illustrative and hence appeal directly to pity, for which women are definitely more receptive than men."[4]

TENDING THE NEST

Ponderings about the differences between men and women not only blessed us with the assuring wisdom that "men are from Mars, women are from Venus" but also brought about some real food for thought: namely, Carol Gilligan's book *In a Different Voice* (1982),[5] which set up what's known today as care ethics, a feminist branch in moral philosophy that seeks to establish a counterweight to traditional moral theories. As the title of Gilligan's book indicates, she claims that women approach moral problems differently than men due to their different life experiences. Life experiences differ due to traditional gender expectations, which specify which kind of bearing seems appropriate for which sex. And even those unfamiliar with the range of products in an ordinary toy store recognize that society expects *very* distinct things of men and women. Specifically, women/girls are encouraged to focus on the so-called private realm of family (not to mention their looks), whereas men employ themselves in the manly world of business, the public sphere. It is because of these divergent areas of life that Gilligan thinks men take to an ethics of justice, which focuses on abstract reflections concerning people's rights and aim to set up general principles (if you will, the Kantian approach mentioned at the beginning of this chapter), whereas women, Gilligan argues, have a different approach to ethics, one grounded in their special responsibility to care for others, family members in particular. (Needless to say, such "responsibility" is socially channeled rather than biologically determined—otherwise, Mayzie couldn't enjoy herself so much in Palm Beach.) Women, therefore, tend to adopt an ethic of care.

Those who subscribe to an ethics of care highlight that it captures the actual situation of human beings more adequately than former ethical theories: "Moralities built on the image of the independent, autonomous, rational individual largely overlook the reality of human dependence and the morality it calls for."[6] Because, like it or not, all of us are at least during some times of our lives highly dependent on others, especially as infants and elders. People with disabilities might be in need of care their whole life. And given their unbelievably small size, the Whos will always depend on the good will of persons like Horton. By ignoring our vulnerability and dependency, ethical theories that celebrate autonomy and rationality are optimistic at best, and at their worst callous and insensitive to genuine, variable human needs. But what precisely does "caring" mean? First and foremost, it stands for a kind of *work*—one usually associated with women (and which Mayzie refuses to accomplish). Recall the dry remark of the authorial voice in the episode when Horton and Mayzie meet again at the circus: "The work was all done. Now she wanted [the egg] back" (Hatches). Caring for those who are dependent on you is work. It's labor intensive. Some care ethicists highlight the labor aspect of care,[7] but care also entails a special kind of motivation, or attitude (which Mayzie clearly lacks).

According to one definition, to care about others means to be emotionally sensitive to them.[8] Horton's anxious "I can't let my very small persons get drowned! I've got to protect them!" (Horton) is a very good example of a caring attitude that pays attention to people's needs. More precisely, to care means to be "concerned about the situation a given person is in, and one's focus is on the individual herself."[9] So an ethic of care discerns what should be done in a *specific* situation to meet the needs of those involved (i.e., not to rely on general principles suitable for any scenario, but rather to decide situationally)—if no one else is around, an elephant will hatch an egg, even if it doesn't make much sense.

Yet it's not just about simple "caring." Recall how Horton and Thidwick are being exploited and made fun of—in a way, they have fallen victim to their otherwise praiseworthy feelings. This is especially true of Thidwick, the too-big-hearted moose, whose extreme empathy for the other animals makes him ignore his own interests. We therefore need an *ethics* of care instead of mere "care" to ensure that otherwise laudable emotions don't backfire or become misguided. So even if proponents of an ethics of care view traditional moral theories skeptically for their focus on abstract general principles, it's not that an ethics of care implies ad hoc or relativistic decisions on moral issues. Instead, "expressions of care and caring relations need to be subjected to moral scrutiny and *evaluated*, not just observed and described."[10] Without such moral analysis, caring could bring about self-denial, as in the case of Thidwick. Not only care ethicists seem to take issue with that situation: in the books on Horton, Dr. Seuss is quite lenient with the morally lacking characters—the kangaroos repent and join Horton in caring for the Whos, and Mayzie simply has to do without her chick, which returns home with Horton. But in the case of Thidwick, the animal squatters who exploited and endangered poor Thidwick end up on the Harvard Club wall: "All stuffed, as they *should* be" (Thidwick). Such an ending is more than simply a powerful verdict on free riders; it also throws an interesting light on the social implications of an ethics of care. Recall that care ethicists reject former moral theories for drawing an incomplete picture of human life. Given our dependency on others, it's more adequate to see us as relational rather than self-sufficient and autonomous. We might think and act as if we were independent, but we rely on a wide network of social relations in doing so. Without Horton, Mayzie, as a mother-to-be, wouldn't have been able to go on holiday. The animal squatters enjoy their free living space literally on Thidwick's back and even compel him to stay on the side of the lake *they* prefer, despite the lack of moose-moss to eat for Thidwick. Their "fair" vote on whether to leave the northern shore of Lake Winna-Bango is a bad caricature of political decision making. In this regard, this episode also illustrates the shortcomings of the ideal of personhood that is at the heart of most moral theories and that may be dubbed best as "liberal individualism"—that is, the idea that we're all free and autonomous and able to choose whether to associate with each other.[11] This sounds a bit as if our social relations are as easily entered into (and as easily rejected) as eco-nomic transactions—voluntary bargains with hardly any strings at-tached.[12] Such a view, however, ignores the dependencies and duties that come with social existence.

Our relatedness to others makes it very difficult, if not impossible, to renounce the obligations our relations give rise to. Once Horton has agreed to take care of Mayzie's egg, there's no way back; he has to endure the bad weather, the mockery of his friends, and eventually even the hunters, who ship him off to America. And as Thidwick's lot illus-trates, our relations (and the responsibilities they imply) are not necessari-ly freely entered into, either. Some of them are forced upon us; some of them we acquire by mere accident, as in the case of Horton and the Whos, not because the world's unjust (well, not *always*) but simply because of "our embeddedness in familial and social and historical contexts," which "often calls on us to *take* responsibility."[13]

This embeddedness is double edged, for it both empowers and makes dependent, giving rise to cooperation as well as obligations. Since we're not all as self-directing as some moral or political theorists imagine us to be, the way our integration into society affects our lives, whether it em-powers or weakens, and to what extent, depends on social and historical contexts. Due to our highly diverse backgrounds and life experiences, some people are more autonomous than others and enjoy more, or differ-ent, privileges. Others again, like those animal squatters on Thidwick's antlers, succeed in having their wishes fulfilled by simply being pushier than others. An ethics of care takes such varying social intricacies into account when deliberating about moral guidelines, which is also why it aims for situational decisions rather than set principles.

Dr. Seuss seems to have had such an idea of the person as socially embedded in mind. After all, it's not the indulgent Thidwick who's pre-sented as a warning ("Dear children, that's what happens to you if you can't say no!") but the animal squatters who took unfair advantage of his leniency. The idea is that it's wrong to exploit another person's eagerness to be of help. But you should still help! In Thidwick's case, this eagerness is combined with a shockingly low self-esteem, which makes him neglect his own needs, and a weird understanding of what's socially appropriate. No matter what the squatters take the liberty to do, Thidwick sticks to his mantra that "a host, above all, must be nice to his guests" (Thidwick).

But are the animal squatters really the only blameworthy party? Some philosophers would warn us against viewing Thidwick as faultless, or even admirable. Recall that Gilligan devised her moral theory as a response to what she considered the male point of view in ethics, a point of view that didn't appreciate women's approach to moral issues. Critics argue that the "different voice" Gilligan claims women have simply stems from the patriarchal, unjust traditions under which women were/are forced to live and which in turn influence the kind of values they hold or view as appropriate. We should, they warn, beware of appreciating caring practices too much—after all, those who perform them do so to their own disadvantage, as both Horton and Thidwick learn the hard way. So instead of making them poster boys of moral worth, shouldn't Dr. Seuss caution us against their excessive altruism, which borders on self-sacrifice? This question is all the more pressing given that the fates of Horton and Thidwick point out the shortcomings of an ethics of care and its uncritical celebration of caring attitudes. If we declare caring the ultimate ethical ideal that we should strive for at all costs, what do we make of exploitative relationships like the ones Thidwick finds himself in? According to one author, we act under a "diminished ethical ideal" if we withdraw from a caring relation, regardless of whether this relationship is harming us.[14] Interestingly, Thidwick is spared such a decision; luck intervenes and he loses his antlers, thus getting rid of the animal squatters and escaping the hunters. Still, the fact remains that his unwillingness to dissolve this bizarre tenancy is nothing short of suicidal, and care ethics has so far failed to provide a satisfying answer to such problems. Maybe Thidwick's plight just shows that an ethics of care cannot do without considerations of justice. I think Dr. Seuss plays with such deliberations when he writes about Thidwick's old antlers in the Harvard Club that they are "[w]here *you* knew they *would* be. His guests are still on them, all stuffed, as they *should* be" (Thidwick). Without principles of justice, it's difficult to pin down what people owe to each other and what we can legitimately ask others to do for us.

MAKING YOURSELF HEARD

Another issue raised by critics of an ethics of care touches on its applicability. With its focus on caring relations, an ethics of care might be restricted to persons we know and are in close contact with. Indeed, some care ethicists hold that a "face-to-face interaction between carer and cared for is a crucial element of the overall activity [of caring]."[15] This, however, poses serious problems in our globalized and highly interdependent world, where even seemingly innocent actions like buying a T-shirt can have tremendous effects on people at the other end of the globe—people we don't know and very likely will never meet.[16] If we pursue an ethics of care, which principles should guide our relations to strangers? How difficult it is to "care" about people we've never seen is at the core of Horton's adventure with the Whos. Despite Horton's confident "I *know* there's a person down there" (Horton), the other animals give up their horrible scheme to boil the clover on which the Whos live only after they have had (acoustic) proof of their existence: *"Their voices were heard! They rang out clear and clean"* (Horton), declares the narrative voice triumphantly. The kangaroos and the other animals behaved the way they did because they didn't believe in the Whos, who are too small to be seen and *very* difficult to hear. In a way, it's the same with us. We might have heard some disturbing rumors about the effects of our consumptive behavior, like the greenhouse effect (thanks to our love for thirsty cars and juicy meat) or brutal working conditions in distant parts of the world where our fast fashion comes from. But does any of this affect our buying decisions? Of course not! Not because we're hard-hearted brutes but simply because those issues are too abstract to have any effect on us. With things like global warming, it's a bit like with the Whos: there might be some irritating guy (be it Horton or Al Gore) blabbering about the dreadful consequences our actions might have, but where is the proof to stop me right now from enjoying myself?

Whatever the reasons for our skepticism toward those who want us to change our conduct, the fact remains that some people succumb more willingly than others—and not necessarily because they're gullible simpletons. What precisely, for instance, made Horton prick up his ears? Why didn't he dismiss the noise he heard at the beginning of the story as an acoustic illusion, a figment of his imagination on a hot summer day? I'd say that this is because he not only heard the Whos but also *has* a moral voice different from those of the other animals. In this regard, Horton's adventures demonstrate how care ethics can (and should!) complement our moral reasoning. The established, traditional moral theories have been one-dimensional in one way or another, given their respective focus on justice, liberty, or duty. This, of course, doesn't make them irrelevant; on the contrary, they give a pretty adequate picture of our moral life and the things we ought to consider (just recall that even though the other animals don't bother about the Whos, they're not moral outlaws, as they seem to live in a functioning society). But as the stories of Thidwick and Horton make clear, this picture is not complete. The tiny voices Horton hears on that speck of dust reveal that morality has multiple aspects, all of them being expressed by different voices. These voices don't make traditional moral theories obsolete but draw attention to what so far have been blind spots. Like the Whos who try to make themselves heard, an ethics of care opens our ears to those voices we seldom hear and that run the risk of getting trampled ("Humpf!" says the sour kangaroo).

THINK YOU'RE A BIRD?

This also helps to answer the question you might've already considered: If care ethics has its roots in feminist thought and is meant to supplement the "male point of view" on morality, how do Horton and Thidwick fit in? After all, they're *boys*! Yet Thidwick is as selfless and accommodating as the kind of devoted mother one might come across in a nineteenth-century manual on female decorum. And Horton even surpasses the females he comes across, like Mayzie and that obnoxious kangaroo. Is Dr. Seuss trying to brainwash our children by (gasp!) "gender mainstreaming"? Not necessarily. That former moral theories (most of which were developed by men) have been dominating moral discourse doesn't mean that alternative ethical approaches can (or should) be classified as belonging to a specific group of people, be it women or elephants. Rather, care ethics is simply about pointing out that other moral voices haven't been listened to properly. In this regard, adding care ethics to our moral vocabulary is like building a good choir: you include as many and as varied voices as possible to ensure that all vocal ranges are covered. For a pretty long time—well into the nineteenth century—the choir we listened to had been rather one-dimensional, consisting only of male voices. Little by little we expanded our casting practices to include the voices of animals, people of color, and women (yep, in that order). And like Horton and the Whos, these voices had to prove that "they ARE persons, no matter how small" (Horton). Yet, despite the title, Horton not only heard but actually

listened to the Whos, and his devotion to making the other animals attentive to them as well illustrates that an ethics of care requires and *encourages* a particular point of view. And, like the insightful books by Dr.
Seuss, the care we give to others has the power to influence and change.

The way we educate our children and the kinds of values we impart to
them affects not only the private realm of our respective families but also
our whole community.[17] Care and education imply "creative nurturing"
and hence have "the potential to shape new and ever-changing *persons*"[18]—which is why an elephant-bird hatches from Mayzie's egg!
After Horton has devoted so much time and effort to it, something of his
personality passed on to the little creature growing inside that egg. Apart
from silent affection that nudges them this way or that, children learn also
by observing and copying their parents. If your only role model happens
to be a sneering kangaroo, it takes a persistent good guy like Horton to
make you rethink your principles. If we manage to make our children
(and also ourselves) sensitive to the concerns of others, we might well
chime in with the converted kangaroo: "I'm going to protect them with
you!" (Horton).

NO KIND OF SNEETCH IS BEST

Bigotry, Dehumanization, and Rehumanization
in the Stories of Dr. Seuss

Bertha Alvarez Manninen

I'm quite happy to say, that the Sneetches got really quite smart on that day. The day they decided that Sneetches are Sneetches. And no kind of Sneetch is the best on the beaches. That day, all the Sneetches forgot about stars and whether they had one, or not, upon thars.

—Dr. Seuss, *The Sneetches*

Take many sheets of paper and write something different on each one—then they do not resemble each other. But then take again every single sheet; do not let yourself be confused by the differentiating inscriptions; hold each one up to the light and you see the same water-mark on them all.

—Søren Kierkegaard, *Works of Love*[1]

In recent years, the immigration debate in the United States has become increasingly polarizing and, at times, violent. In our family, the prevalent rhetoric against persons of Hispanic origins is particularly painful given that I am Cuban and my children are half-Hispanic. When my oldest daughter was a toddler, I went shopping with her and, as is typically the case when I am alone with my children, I spoke Spanish to her. This act was met by glares from others, and as I was putting my groceries away in the trunk of my car, another car blazed by while screaming racial slurs at us. I remember thinking that I was so grateful she was little and didn't understand. But she understands now. Recently, her peers in school told her that all "Spanish people" will be going back to their country. She asked whether I would be deported to Cuba, and what would happen to her and her little sister, who are "half-Spanish." It might have been easy to appease her fears by explaining to her that her mother was born in the United States and that she and her immigrant (but permanent resident) parents were all here legally. But, for reasons that I will explore below, I did not want to introduce dehumanizing language and concepts by denoting some persons as "illegal" into her lexicon or consciousness. Instead, my husband and I used this opportunity to begin an age-appropriate discussion with her about the dangers of bigotry. In their book *Nurture Shock*, authors Po Bronson and Ashley Merryman note that nonminority parents are hesitant to talk to their kids about race or racism because they genuinely wish to raise children who are "color blind." Yet this often ends up backfiring on them—kids will naturally end up noticing that different people have different skin colors, and, without an explicit conversation about race, they will form their own conclusions based on both tacit and overt cultural stereotypes and will gravitate more toward people who look like them.[2]

Thankfully, parents and teachers are not without some age-appropriate tools to discuss these delicate issues with our children—Theodor Seuss Geisel (Dr. Seuss) provides a wealth of literary opportunities to do so in many of his children's books. It is important to note here that Dr. Seuss deliberately wrote many of his children's books to have deeper social messages, and some of them represented a shift in his own moral views. For example, *Horton Hears a Who!* (which will be discussed below) represented a departure from Seuss's view of the Japanese during World War II. During the war, he felt a deep animosity toward them, going so far as drawing and publishing several anti-German and anti-Japanese editorial cartoons.[3] Yet after his post–World War II visit to Japan, particularly to Japanese schools, "where the importance of the individual was considered an exciting new concept,"[4] he was inspired to write *Horton*, in which the importance of acknowledging the moral status of even the "smallest" person is paramount. And in fact the book was dedicated to a Kyoto University professor, Mitsugi Nakamura, whom Seuss considered a close friend. Indeed, one analysis of *Horton Hears a Who!* is that Seuss was attempting to "redress the American image of Japan."[5] *Horton*, therefore, is Seuss's redemption story, and just one of the many stories he wrote where the perils of bigotry are starkly portrayed for the reader.

"THEY HAVE KINKS IN THEIR SOUL!" (BUTTER): EXPLORING CHARACTER-CONDITIONED HATE

In *Oh, the Places You'll Go!* Dr. Seuss writes about different scary scenarios that the reader is likely to encounter on their journey through life and uncharted domains, things that will likely "scare you right out of your pants"—for example, "Hakken Kraks." In *Oh, the Thinks You Can Think!* the reader encounters a scary creature as well, called a "Jibboo." It's normal for us to be on guard when encountering something that scares us, and when something or someone threatens or hurts us or those we love. It is typical, and understandable, that we develop negative feelings about that person in return. Psychologist Erich Fromm, in his book *Man for Himself*, distinguishes between what he calls "rational hate" and "character-conditioned hate"[6] and argues that the former is the kind of hate we may feel toward someone or something that poses a real danger to our health, safety, or livelihood. But character-conditioned hate is something else altogether. Gordon Allport describes it as "a continuing readiness to hate."[7] This is the kind of hatred at the root of our most bigoted behavior, and therefore the one that concerns us for this chapter.

Bigotry typically functions by highlighting an alleged negative characteristic of a person, or groups of people, that, ultimately, proves irrelevant for their moral worth. A human being's moral status, and moral and legal rights, are ultimately rooted in the fact that she or he is a human being, a person, someone who can be harmed or benefited, and has interests that can be advanced or thwarted. Chairs and desks do not possess any intrinsic moral status because they are not the kinds of things that can be harmed or benefited—but human beings can be harmed or benefited on the basis of their sentience and their status as rational beings (and for many philosophers, the possession of sentience is sufficient for moral status, which means many nonhuman animals, though perhaps not rational beings, possess moral status as well). Traits such as skin color, religious affiliation, ethnicity, or gender (and some philosophers would even add "species membership" to this list) are simply irrelevant when it comes to determining a person's worth or moral status.

At least two of Dr. Seuss's books emphasize the absurdity of the kinds of bigotry-causing demarcating lines humans often tend to draw. In *The Sneetches*, the title characters have segregated themselves into two groups, one with stars on their bellies and one without. Such segregation, as the narrator points out, is clearly inane.

> Now, the Star-Belly Sneetches had bellies with stars. The Plain-Belly Sneetches had none upon thars. Those stars weren't so big. They were really so small. You might think such a thing wouldn't matter at all. (Sneetches)

There is nothing relevant about having stars on bellies that mitigates the Sneetches' moral status, moral rights, or their personhood. Yet, as a result of this decoration, the Star-Bellied Sneetches consider themselves superior to the ones without, and therefore they "would sniff and they'd snort, 'we'll have nothing to do with the Plain-Belly sort!' And whenever they met some, when they were out walking, they'd hike right on past them without even talking" (Sneetches). This behavior clearly adversely affects the Plain-Bellied Sneetches. Their children are not allowed to play games with the star-bellied children and are never invited to any of their parties. But worse than that, the book implies that the society's resources were spent far more on the Star-Bellied Sneetches than the plain-bellied ones, and that this disparity lasted for many years; the Plain-Belly Sneetches were "left . . . out cold, in the dark of the beaches. They kept them away, never let them come near. And that's how they treated them year after year" (Sneetches). Unsurprisingly, multiple studies have indicated that victims of bigoted treatment often suffer some degree of psychological damage, some so severe as to be on a par with post-trauma disorders.[8]

In *The Butter Battle Book* (an antiwar story in which Seuss criticizes the nuclear arms race during the Cold War era), the warring factions have demarcated themselves not due to some sort of biological difference but to what amounts to a difference in social or cultural customs.

> On the last day of summer, ten hours before Fall, my grandfather took me out to the wall. For a while he stood silent. Then finally he said, with a very sad shake of his very old head, "As you know, on this side of the Wall we are Yooks. On the far other side of this Wall live the Zooks." Then my grandfather said, "It's high time that you knew of the terribly horrible thing that Zooks do. In every Zook house and in every

Zook town every Zook eats his bread with the butter side down!"
(Butter)

Seuss never goes into the history of these prejudices—that is, he never explains to the reader why it matters to the characters on which side the bread is buttered or how belly-stars came to represent superiority. It may be, however, that the reason he omitted this is because there *is* no real reason; individuals who practice character-conditioned hatred often may not even *understand* the reasons why they feel such deep animosity for members of an "out" group. As Allport writes:

> [Character-conditioned hatred includes] a continuing readiness to hate. The sentiment has little relation to reality, although it may be the product of a long series of bitter disappointments in life. These frustrations become fused into a kind of "free-floating" hatred—the subjective counterpart of free-floating aggression. The person carries a vague, temperamental sense of wrong which he wishes to polarize. He must hate *something*. The real roots of the hatred may baffle him, but he thinks up some convenient victim and some good reasons. [9]

The Zooks and the Yooks not only despise the "other" because of how they butter their bread but also extend this hatred to the point of decrying each other's moral character or trustworthiness because of this simple, and ultimately irrelevant, difference. In doing so, they simultaneously exalt *their* way of doing things as being the *obviously* correct way. At no time does either side stop to analyze whether the other way of buttering bread may be equally legitimate—instead, the "other" is simply disregarded as being bad (this occurs with the Sneetches as well, since the ones with the stars exalt themselves at the expense of the ones without).

> "But we Yooks, as you know, when we breakfast or sup, spread our bread," Grandpa said, "with the butter side *up*. That's the right, honest way!" Grandpa gritted his teeth. "So you can't trust a Zook who spreads bread underneath! Every Zook must be watched! He has kinks in his soul!" (Butter)

Edward Wilson writes that the tendency to turn benign cultural (or biological) differences into an assessment of moral value, a kind of xenophobia, is "the dark side to the inborn propensity to moral behavior." [10] Moral sentiments, Wilson argues, are cultivated over years and years of humans learning that cooperative behavior is instrumental for their survival, and one reason we tend to "prefer" members of "our kind" is because "personal familiarity and common interest are vital in social transactions" and therefore it makes sense that our "moral sentiments evolved to be selective."[11]

In a diverse society, however, this very quickly devolves into bigotry and fear of those who are different. In another of Dr. Seuss's stories, "What Was I Scared Of?" our main character finds himself constantly encountering a pair of pale green pants that walks around even though there is no occupant in them. Confronted with something so utterly different than him and his expectations, he reacts with abject fear and does everything he can to avoid the pants. Wilson writes that this is the kind of behavior that leads to xenophobia:

> People give trust to strangers with effort, and true compassion is a commodity in chronically short supply. Tribes cooperate only through carefully defined treaties and other conventions. They are quick to imagine themselves victims of conspiracies by competing groups, and they are prone to dehumanize and murder their rivals during periods of extreme conflict. . . . The complementary instincts of morality and tribalism are easily manipulated. Civilization has made them more so.[12]

This kind of manipulation is clearly seen in both *The Butter Battle Book* and *The Sneetches*. Both the Zooks' and the Yooks' governments send others off to fight their wars with increasingly bigger, more destructive, weapons, even if it causes pain and takes lives (note that the government officials create the weapons but never themselves go off to fight the war). The hatred between the two groups grows so strong that members of their respective society cheer on their war even if it entails their own destruction ("fight, fight for the butter side up; do or die!" [Butter]).

In *The Sneetches*, a fellow by the name of Sylvester McMonkey McBean comes into the Sneetches' society with a machine designed to turn Plain-Bellied Sneetches into star-bellied ones, thereby making it impossible to tell the difference between the groups. In reaction to this change, the original Star-Bellied Sneetches use the same machine to have their stars removed in order to reclaim their superiority (which illustrates that the stars themselves, ultimately, really are irrelevant). This process continues for a lengthy amount of time, encouraged by McBean, who is profiting from the Sneetches' prejudices.

> Through the machines they raced round and about again, changing their stars every minute or two. They kept paying money. They kept running through. Until neither the Plain nor the Star-Bellies knew, whether this one was that one, or that one was this one, or which one was that one, or what one was who. (Sneetches)

In both *The Butter Battle Book* and *The Sneetches*, character-conditioned hatred is massively exploited, causing the latter society extreme financial loss and the former potential complete eradication.

"A PERSON ON THAT? . . . WHY, THERE NEVER HAS BEEN!" (HORTON): THE CONSEQUENCES OF DEHUMANIZATION

As Wilson notes above, one key aspect of what causes xenophobic violence is the human tendency to dehumanize the "other." We do this when we mentally deprive human beings of the traits that we tend to associate with personhood or moral worth. When a human being commits a heinous act, for example, we tend to say things like "he's not human; he's a monster!" Of course, we do not literally mean this—he remains a member of our species. What we mean, instead, is that he is not really a person, not someone who is worthy of any moral consideration. Dehumanization occurs quite frequently when dealing with prejudice or bigotry. One of the functions of this dehumanization, as Allport explains, is to render one's hatred toward the "other" justifiable. If one views the "other" as nonhumans, as individuals unworthy of moral consideration, then one can psychologically distance oneself from the hated persons; they no longer regard these people as fellow humans to whom they have ethical responsibilities and a duty of care or compassion.

> There is a kind of economy in adopting an exclusionist approach to human relations. By taking a negative view of great groups of mankind, we somehow make life simpler. For example, if I reject all foreigners as a category, I don't have to bother with them—except to keep them out of my country. If I can ticket, then, all Negros as

comprising an inferior and objectionable race, I conveniently dispose of a tenth of my fellow citizens. If I can put Catholics into another category and reject them, my life is still further simplified. I then pare again and slice off the Jews . . . and so it goes. The prejudiced pattern, involving degrees and kinds of hatred and aggression, takes its place in the individual's world view.[13]

One prevalent way that dehumanization occurs is via the use of racial and ethnic slurs or epithets (as is the term *illegal*, which is why I refused to introduce it into my daughter's lexicon) or by using language that refers to human beings as literal animals. While writing about how Americans and their allies dehumanized German and Japanese soldiers during World War II (something of which Seuss was also guilty, given the content of his editorial cartoons), David Livingstone Smith writes that the latter "were considered animals, and were often portrayed as monkeys, apes, or rodents, and sometimes as insects . . . the Japanese were looked upon as something subhuman and repulsive, like cockroaches or mice"[14] (indeed, in some of Seuss's cartoons, the Japanese are portrayed as literal animals—for example, as sly alley cats or monkeys doing Germany's bidding). Richard Delgado writes:

The racial insult remains one of the most pervasive channels through which discriminatory attitudes are imparted. Such language injures the dignity and self-regard of the person to whom it is addressed, communicating the message that distinctions of race are distinctions of merit, dignity, status, and personhood.[15]

Slurs effectively function to erase someone's humanity and personhood, rendering him nothing more than a figurative animal, as subhuman, and therefore a member of a group one distrusts or hates.

[S]lurs provide a simple but toxic shorthand for marking boundaries between groups. [Individuals who used racial slurs] reified demeaning stereotypes and established lines across which "others" should not cross. . . . All of this talk helped draw lines between groups, forming us/them boundaries.[16]

The consequences of dehumanizing others can be severe—primarily for the victim, but also for the perpetrator. According to one study, when persons are dehumanized they become "deindividuated, [they] lose the capacity to evoke compassion and moral emotions, and may be treated as means toward vicious ends."[17] In other words, one consequence of dehumanization is that the "other" is rendered, in a sense, invisible—they are not seen as persons of moral significance, which, in turn, renders it more likely that they will be victims of violence. Persons who engage in bigoted thoughts or behaviors may either partake in this violence or become bystanders to violence. Allport highlights this concept:

> There is a good reason why out-groups are often chosen as the object of hate and aggression rather than individuals. A human being is, after all, pretty much like another—like oneself. One can scarcely help but sympathize with the victim. To attack him would be to arouse some pain in ourselves. Our own "body image" would be involved, for his body is like our own body. But there is no body image in a group. It is more abstract, more impersonal. . . . We are less likely to consider [the subject] an individual, and more likely to think of him only as an out-group member.[18]

In his book, Smith relays many stories of atrocities done from one human being to another as a result of dehumanization. The Holocaust is "the most thoroughly documented example of the ravages of dehumanization,"[19] but there are others as well. Just as we dehumanized the Japanese, they exalted themselves as "the highest forms of human life" and committed atrocious acts against their enemies as well; for example, they "killed, mutilated, raped and tortured thousands of Chinese civilians."[20] During the Rwandan genocide in 1994, the Hutus slaughtered hundreds of thousands of Tutsies within a one-hundred-day period, referring to them as "cockroaches" that needed to be exterminated. The primary victims of dehumanization are those who are harmed, but those who engage in dehumanization are also adversely affected; Smith notes that "dehumanization isn't a way of talking. It's a way of thinking . . . it acts as a psychological lubricant, dissolving our inhibitions and inflaming our destructive passions."[21]

There are various subtle examples of dehumanization in Seuss's books. In *Horton Hears a Who!* Horton is the only one who sees the Whos as persons, and therefore he is the only one who cares about their welfare. To everyone else, especially to the "sour kangaroo" and her joey, who lead the push to discredit Horton, the Whos are invisible—they quite literally do not exist at all from their perspective. This can be interpreted as a literal exposition of the abovementioned psychological consequences of dehumanization—the "other" is erased from your moral consideration. In Ralph Ellison's *Invisible Man*, the narrator describes the experience of being a black man in 1930s America as almost a literal invisibility:

> I am an invisible man. No, I am not a spook like those who haunted Edgar Allen Poe; nor am I one of your Hollywood-movie ectoplasms. I am a man of substance, of flesh and bone, fiber and liquids—and I might even be said to possess a mind. I am invisible, understand, simply because people refuse to see me. Like the bodiless heads you see sometimes in circus sideshows, it is as though I have been surrounded by mirrors of hard, distorting glass. When they approach me they see only my surroundings, themselves, or figments of their imagination—indeed, everything and anything except me.[22]

Because the Whos are not recognized as persons by the rest of society, everyone else, except Horton, is willing to destroy Whoville. Horton repeatedly tries to get others to see what he sees, to recognize the Whos' "humanity," and to plead for their safety from what would essentially be their genocide.

> "Believe me," said Horton. "I tell you sincerely, my ears are quite keen and I heard them quite clearly. I *know* there's a person down there. And, what's more, quite likely there's two. Even three. Even four. Quite likely a family for all that we know! A family with children just starting to grow. So please," Horton said, "as a favor to me, try not to disturb them. Just please let them be." (Horton)

The others regard Horton's insistence on bringing the Whos into their society as crazy and disruptive to their "peaceable jungle," as the sour kangaroo puts it. At her command, everyone else in the jungle attempts to imprison Horton to get him to stop, all the while threatening to burn down the Whos' society (indeed, history shows us that those who fight for the rights of the oppressed are typically subjected to imprisonment and assassination attempts). *Horton Hears a Who!* can serve as a cautionary tale as to what happens when we deprive a group of individuals of their personhood and moral status. When we fail to see them as persons, if we render them invisible to our moral sensibilities and our community, we are far more likely to harm them. Yet when we recognize their humanity, as Horton does, we will fight to protect them.

In *The Butter Battle Book* the Zooks and the Yooks so vilify each other that they are willing to destroy each other in an all-out war. In *Horton Hears a Who!* the Whos' invisibility almost renders them victims of a genocide. Although bigotry can result in horribly violent acts, in our everyday lives bigotry can manifest itself in quieter and more insidious ways. This can be seen in "What Was I Scared Of?" where the narrator, clearly afraid of the unknown, starts drawing negative conclusions about the likability of the pale green pants:

> Those empty pants! They kind of started jumping. And then my heart, I must admit, it kind of started thumping. So I got out. I got out fast as fast as I could go, sir. I wasn't scared. But pants like that I did not care for. No, sir. (Scared)

Never does the pair of pants threaten or harm our narrator—his proclamation of dislike comes solely from the fact that the pants are different from him, unlike anything he has ever before encountered. The narrator takes great pains to avoid the green pants, and when he finally realizes that he cannot, he starts to cry out for help.

> Those spooky, empty pants and I were standing face to face! I yelled for help. I screamed. I shrieked. I howled. I yowled. I cried, "OH, SAVE ME FROM THESE PALE GREEN PANTS WITH NOBODY INSIDE!" (Scared)

Seuss appears to be making a commentary on how fear of the unknown quickly devolves into something more dangerous. Fear fuels dislike, and this dislike, in turn, fuels a desire for separatism. In society, this desire for separatism can translate into segregationist policies. Moreover, blindly acting, and relying, on fear has led to several human rights violations here in the United States. For example, there were the Japanese internment camps during World War II—an abhorrent practice that some individuals have proposed reviving, this time targeting individuals of Middle Eastern or Arab descent. [23]

"What Was I Scared Of?" is not only a story about the dangers of impulsively acting on fear and letting this color how one approaches the unknown. The end of the book also teaches about the first steps we have to take to combat fear and bigotry in our lives: we have to rehumanize those we have dehumanized.

"BECAUSE AFTER ALL, A PERSON'S A PERSON NO MATTER HOW SMALL" (HORTON): THE PROCESS OF REHUMANIZATION

This chapter began with a quote from Danish philosopher Søren Kierkegaard's *Works of Love*, a book devoted to the analysis of the biblical commandment to love your neighbor as yourself. Kierkegaard notes that humans, as a rule, tend to practice what he calls "preferential love"—that is, we tend to restrict our love only to people whom we prefer and are part of our chosen social circle. Yet this kind of love, Kierkegaard argues, is still selfish, for this kind of love still has the self as the center of the moral universe. The reason I love my *my* kids, *my* parents, *my* spouse, *my* country, *my* race is because of the relationships these persons have *to me.* Christian love, the kind of love that seeks to follow God's command, seeks to practice unconditional love of the neighbor, which is "love of all men, unconditionally all."[24] The way to do this, Kierkegaard argues, is to focus on our commonalities rather than our dissimilarities. This is the sentiment reflected in both of the opening quotes in this chapter. According to Kierkegaard, our differences should

> hang loosely on the individual, loosely as the cloak the king casts off in order to show who he is, loosely as the ragged costume in which a supernatural being has disguised himself. When distinctions hang loosely in this way, then there steadily shines in every individual that essential other person, that which is common to all men, the eternal likeness, the equality. . . . In being king, beggar, scholar, rich man, poor man, male, female, *etc.* we do not resemble each other—therein we are all different. But in being a neighbor we are all unconditionally like each other. Distinction is temporality's confusing element which marks every man as different, but neighbor is eternity's watermark—on every man.[25]

Because Kierkegaard is writing this from a Christian perspective, he maintains that our common similarities come from our relationship to and with God. But it is also possible to find merit in Kierkegaard's words even from a secular perspective. Shredding away the differences and focusing on our commonalities is the first step in rehumanizing those we have dehumanized.

Seuss portrays the process of rehumanization beautifully in "What Was I Scared Of?" After the narrator screams to be "saved" from the "pale green pants," he is shocked to see the pants' reaction upon confrontation:

> But then a strange thing happened. Why, those pants began to cry! Those pants began to tremble. They were just as scared as I! I never heard such whimpering, and I began to see that I was just as strange to them as they were strange to me! (Scared)

The fact that the pants reacted against the narrator in the same way as the narrator reacted against the pants illustrated their shared commonality—not just that they were afraid of each other but also that the pants expressed this fear in the same way as the narrator: with tears. In reaction to their shared "humanity," the narrator was able to overcome his fear, his barrier with the "other," and reach out to the pants in a gesture of compassion and care—one that ultimately leads to friendship.

> So . . . I put my arm around their waist and sat right down beside them. I calmed them down. Poor empty pants with nobody inside them. And now, we meet quite often, those empty pants and I, and we never shake or tremble, we both smile and we say . . . "Hi!" (Scared)

It is only when the narrator starts to see the pants as just another person, another version of himself, that he is able to see past their dissimilarities and get past the fear caused by focusing on them. Jewish philosopher Emmanuel Levinas describes being confronted with the face of the "other" as a call to moral obligation; by looking someone in the eye, by recognizing the common strain of your humanity, you are called into moral responsibility with each other: "The face is a living presence; it is expression . . . the face speaks . . . it is a source from which all meaning appears . . . it speaks to me and invites me into a relation."[26] The pale green pants crying was the "face" the narrator needed to encounter in order to call him into a relationship with the entity he feared.

In *Horton Hears a Who!* the Whos are saved from their impending genocide when they are finally heard by the others in the jungle. When their voices finally come through loud enough for all of society to acknowledge them (pivotally aided by the smallest Who, who thought he had nothing to contribute—Seuss noted that this example is meant to drive home the importance of voting: "And of course when the little boy stands up and yells 'Yopp!' and saves the whole place, that's my statement about voting—*everyone* counts"[27]), the sour kangaroo wastes no time in correcting her previous perspective:

> Finally, at last! From that speck on that clover, *their voices were heard*! They rang out clear and clean. And the elephant smiled, "Do you see what I mean . . . ? They've proved they ARE persons, no matter how small. And their whole world was saved by the Smallest of All!"
>
> "How true! Yes, how true," said the big kangaroo. "And from now on, you know what I'm planning to do? . . . From now on, I'm going to protect them with you!" (Horton)

As Kierkegaard puts it, loving the neighbor as the self involves the "duplicating of one's self."[28] And once you see the "other" as another version of yourself, you are, as Levinas writes, immediately called to action to care for them: "The face opens the primordial discourse whose first word is obligation."[29]

ENDING BIGOTRY: SELF-AWARENESS AND THE NEXT GENERATION

One important thing to note while studying Seuss's history and his work is that he was just as guilty, at times, of perpetuating the bigotry that he maligned in his stories. This, again, can be seen in his World War II editorial cartoons. Richard Minear writes:

> Perhaps it is no surprise that American cartoonists during the Pacific War painted Japan in overtly racist ways. However, it is a surprise that a person who denounces anti-black racism and anti-Semitism so eloquently can be oblivious to his own racist treatment of Japanese and Japanese Americans. And to find such cartoons—largely unreproached—in the pages of the leading left newspaper of New York City and to realize that the cartoonist is the same Dr. Seuss we celebrate today for his imagination and tolerance and breadth of vision: this is a sobering experience.[30]

One way to understand this seeming paradox when it comes to Seuss is to admit that this is likely something of which we have all been guilty at some point. Even the most tolerant of persons has likely had prejudicial or judgmental thoughts. One step toward becoming better human beings, working closer toward the love of the neighbor that Kierkegaard emphasizes, is to be honest about our shortcomings, and to remain self-aware and self-critical.

Elliot Aronson notes that the prejudiced personality is often formed during the formative childhood years when kids seek to identify with their parents; if the adults are themselves prejudiced, "a child might consciously pick up beliefs about minorities from his or her parents because the child identifies with them . . . many people may have learned a wide array of prejudice on Mommy's or Daddy's knee."[31] Smith prefaces the first chapter in his book with two quotes: one by Rabbi Ovadia Yosef, "Arabs are the same as animals. There is no animal worse than them," and a second one that states, "Palestine is our country. The Jews our dogs." The second quote is particularly heartbreaking because of its source—a Palestinian nursery rhyme.[32]

That prejudice is often learned by children from their parents and surrounding society is clearly displayed in *Horton Hears a Who!* by the baby kangaroo, who has spent the entirety of the book in his mother's pouch, listening intently to her refusal to recognize the Whos' existence and mimicking her prejudice by always saying "me too" whenever she derided them. Toward the end, however, when the mother kangaroo pledges to care about and respect the Whos, her child is as quick to mimic her care and compassion as he was to mimic her bigotry. *Horton Hears a Who!* ends with the voice of a child, who promises that "from sun in the summer. From rain when it's fallish, I'm going to protect them. No matter how smallish" (Horton). The baby kangaroo serves as a representation of how children are always listening to the adults in their world, and how they are capable of learning either virtue or vice from those adults. This forces the reader to confront how easily prejudice and hate can be passed down, but also how easy it is to pass down care and compassion. By choosing the latter at the end of the book, there is a generational shift in values—the new generation will now devote themselves to caring for the vulnerable. This is in stark contrast to how *The Butter Battle Book* ends, with both the Yooks and the Zooks dangling a bomb over each other's side of the wall, both threatening to detonate it. At the bottom of the last page we see a Yook child witnessing the confrontation with an utterly terrified look on his face, waiting to see who will drop the bomb first.

With these two books, Seuss paints a stark contrast: Either the next generation can help end bigotry or we may end up destroying ourselves, and them, instead. How our "tale" ends is entirely up to us.

12

THE *OTHER* SNEETCHES[1]

Cam Cobb

> In a sense, the power of normalization imposes homogeneity; but it individualizes by making it possible to measure gaps, to determine levels, to fix specialties and to render the differences useful by fitting them one to another. . . . It is a normalizing gaze, a surveillance that makes it possible to qualify, to classify, and to punish.
>
> —Michel Foucault[2]

> When the Star-Belly Sneetches had frankfurter roasts
> Or picnics or parties or marshmallow toasts,
> They never invited the Plain-Belly Sneetches.
> They left them out cold, in the dark of the beaches.
> They kept them away. Never let them come near.
> And that's how they treated them year after year.
>
> —Dr. Seuss, *The Sneetches*

You are standing on a wide beach. The sky is clear and a gentle breeze sweeps across the waves and over the sand. A small group of approximately twenty stands huddled together. As various individuals mingle, the group quickly divides itself into two factions. Peering closer, you realize that the two clusters are identical in every way . . . save for one visible aspect. You then wonder if it was by comparing their physical appearances and pinpointing this one characteristic that the group divided itself up.

From the body language and facial expressions you observe, it seems that one of the factions feels superior to the other. They certainly *act* superior. Those in the first group hold their heads high, noses pointed up in the air, scowling at their counterparts. They seem to see themselves as worthy; on this beach, they are empowered. Meanwhile, those in the second faction behave as though they are inferior. Their heads are drooping down with their shoulders slouching, and their eyes looking forlorn, as though they are somehow lesser than their counterparts. Unsurprisingly, the second cluster appears to be out of sorts. It is as though the folks in the second faction long to have the same status as their peers. You cannot see it, but the individuals in this second faction are even thinking about altering their bodies so they might look exactly like their peers and climb out of their unpleasant social position.

If you are familiar with the work of Dr. Seuss, this scenario likely gives you a feeling of déjà vu. And so it should. It has been adapted from one of his popular stories, *The Sneetches*.[3] In this chapter, I discuss the social phenomenon of othering and consider how Dr. Seuss portrays it, as well as its consequences, in *The Sneetches*. When the story opens, the Sneetches with stars on their bellies mistreat their peers who don't happen to have stars on their bellies. What follows is a tale of discrimination, *othering*, and shifting identity.[4] To examine othering in relation to the story, I have organized this chapter into three parts, or questions: (1) What is othering? (2) What is power? (3) What are the implications?

WHAT IS OTHERING?

Just as communities may be completely inclusive, they may also be completely exclusive. Yet inclusion and exclusion often exist on a spectrum, rather than in a state of binary opposition. Within this spectrum, there are a great many points between the two poles. *All* communities fall *somewhere* on this continuum. In a community, wherever it falls on the continuum, *some* individuals may feel like outsiders. Or, more to the point, *they may be made to feel like outsiders*.

When one experiences othering, that person, in one way or another, *feels like an outsider*. Perhaps it has something to do with their physical appearance. Perhaps it is somehow tied to their behavior. It may be related to their cultural habits and routines or to their faith customs. There are many ways in which othering may occur. It begins with a focus on what is different. As critical legal theorist Martha Minow notes, "When we respond to a person's traits rather than their conduct, we may treat a given trait as a justification for excluding someone we think is 'different.' We feel no need for further justification: we attribute the consequences to the difference we see. We neglect the other traits that may be shared. And we neglect how each of us, too, may be 'different.'"[5] As such, othering isn't purely a matter of noticing difference—rather, it is a matter of focusing on what is different rather than what is shared. Yet you may wonder to yourself: If othering is all about difference, then surely everyone is othered in one way or another. After all, isn't everyone unique?

While everyone within a community is unique, some individuals have reason to believe that their uniqueness (or an aspect of it) pushes them away from the *social norm*. A social norm is a set of expectations, or a code. Social norms are produced by habits and routines that dominate and foster a perceived sense of regularity or normalcy. They are often unwritten—what scholar Henry Giroux calls the *hidden curriculum*.[6] Drawing from the work of French sociologist Pierre Bourdieu,[7] Giroux notes that in schooling, "a child internalizes the cultural messages of the school not only via the latter's official discourse (symbolic mastery), but also through the messages embodied in the 'insignificant' practices of daily classroom life."[8] Within this framework, school rules and daily routines both regulate behavior and set benchmarks, or parameters that reflect and normalize wider social expectations and discourses.

Here, the habits and routines of a social space—namely, a school—impose a code of what is *expected* and what is *normal*. How are children expected to talk? How are they expected to behave? How are they expected to dress? What is the schedule they are expected to follow? Notions of what constitutes normal (or polite) speech, behavior, and dress may lead some children to be pushed outside the center point of a social space, depending on their own family's beliefs and customs. A Monday-through-Friday school week with an annual winter holiday (a.k.a. *Christmas break*) sets a pattern and expectation within schools. Yet what happens to students (or educators for that matter) who do their prayers during the school day (i.e., on Friday afternoons), or observe something other than Christmas? You may be reading this, and you may be thinking: yes, but, many school boards offer accommodations, so students won't be penalized if a test or exam is scheduled on Eid al-Fitr or Yom Kippur or Eid al-Adha or Rosh Hashanah, or another non-Christian holiday.

Sure, many school boards offer religious accommodations of one form (or degree) or another. Yet the notion of *accommodating difference* establishes a dynamic where there is a dominant center point, and something that exists outside that norm.[9] By creating a situation in which some need to ask for a religious accommodation to follow their faith, we create a dynamic that fuels othering. After all, within this dynamic, the identity/ habits of some exist outside the dominant center, which leads them to ask that exceptions be made. Just as a child may be *othered* within this sort of dynamic, the Star-Bellied Sneetches are othered as they are *made to feel like outsiders* when they stand on that quiet beach at the start of Seuss's story. But what does othering evoke?

Let's take one example of this social phenomenon: If I am a child in a grade 1 classroom and I peruse the picture books in my classroom library, and all the books depict families with heterosexual couples as parents, then heterosexuality becomes the *social norm*. This is called *heteronormativity*.[10] In this scenario, it is the dominant identity for families, and anything outside that dominant identity is beyond, or peripheral, to the norm. Of course, whatever falls outside the norm also falls on a continuum. Some things on the *outside* are further away from the center than others. For instance, if all (or most of) the books tell stories about families with a mom and a dad, then, if one child has a parent who has passed away, that child may feel like an *outsider*. It may be a tiny inkling of inadequacy, but an inkling nevertheless. If another child has two parents who are divorced, then that child too may feel slightly *lesser* than their peers. Possibly, because the second child's parents *chose* not to stay as a couple, that child may perceive a deeper form of othering. Yet if a child has two parents who happen to be a same-sex couple, then that child may be pushed even further outside the periphery. Consequently, that third child may experience the deepest form of othering in this scenario.

Of course, othering goes beyond heteronormativity. Let's return to the classroom library. Imagine all (or a great majority) of the stories on the bookshelf are about white families, or financially stable families, or non-immigrant families, or adventures in which the hero is a boy or a man. Imagining this, unfortunately, isn't hard to do. In such a space, numerous children would experience one form (and degree) of othering or another. It is pervasive. When normative thinking shapes a community, some of the people within that community are privileged and others are disadvantaged—depending on how their identity compares to the *dominant center*, or *center point*. Now, imagine we are back in the world of the Sneetches. What would *their* books look like? Starless Sneetches would not likely be heroes, or perhaps even represented in their stories.

At the beginning of *The Sneetches*, the community (namely, those who hold power) dictates that having a star on your belly is *normal*, and *not* having a star on your belly is *not normal*. Both are different, but only one is *not normal*. If you don't have a star on your belly, you're outside the norm—and, as such, you're seen and treated as an inferior. The social dynamic of the story is one in which one group sets the social norms, and, specifically, decides what constitutes an acceptable, or desirable, physical appearance. Those who are not included in this dominant group—the Sneetches who don't have stars on their bellies at the beginning of the story—are seen and treated as second-class citizens, something lesser than their peers. Because of their physical appearance, the starless Sneetches are always on the outside, they are always *othered*. And this isn't purely a matter of difference—*it's difference combined with normalization*. Yet there is something else going on here. Othering also fuels— and is produced by—a power system, one rooted in domination.

WHAT IS POWER?

Just as othering is a product *of difference combined with normalization*, power and domination—at least in part—are products of othering. As we delve into the idea of power, it is important to note that power may be defined in a variety of ways. Let's consider two very different views.

Some see it as something that is shared and encouraged. Brazilian advocate and philosopher Paulo Freire, for instance, encourages an approach to teaching and learning that is firmly rooted in reciprocity. While Freire recognizes that power *may* be used to dominate—in a system rooted in hierarchy, or *banking education*, for instance—educators may also foster a dynamic rooted in *dialogue* and *problem posing*.[11] When teachers and learners work together to explore problems, the learning process becomes a joint activity. From this point of view, power is communal—it is shared. In a Freirian, communal sense, teachers and learners can empower one another. Within such a dynamic, leadership, expertise, knowledge, and so on exist in the plural form, rather than being limited to the singular. Teachers and learners can ask one another for help, and they can offer help as well. They can ask advice, and they can engage in dialogue. They may switch roles in different circumstances. So, a teacher may become a learner just as a learner may become a teacher. While Freire often wrote about teaching and learning, his ideas of reciprocity and collaboration can be applied to society itself. People can support their peers and encourage them to take an active role in their lives and in their communities. From this perspective, we might see power as the ability and opportunity to express one's views, make choices, and contribute to shared decisions. Ultimately, this sort of view of power can be equated with liberty.

Yet power is also viewed as something else entirely. It is frequently seen as something quite different than liberty. Often, it is perceived as a *power over* relationship rather than *power with* relationship. From this perspective, power is a matter of domination. Domination occurs when one's freedoms, one's voice, one's actions, and one's very options are limited in one way or another. Within this dynamic, power is viewed as the ability, or opportunity, to dominate or control—to dominate others and control events. Here, rather than being shared, power is held or possessed by a select number of individuals within a community or society. Perhaps this second view of power is prevalent because power is not universally shared in so many communities and societies around the world. Domination, after all, is a global phenomenon. And it is often both a direct and an indirect result of social othering. Those who tend to dominate are not othered. They tend to have access to other powerbrokers, possess wealth, and have unequal opportunities in terms of capital, education, and employment, among other things.

If power often takes the form of *power over* (or domination)—rather than *power with* (a democratic form of collectivism)—then it is important to ask ourselves: Who tends to have (or wield) power? To approach this question, let's start by focusing on the immediate setting within which Dr. Seuss lived and wrote. Let's consider the context of early 1950s America, the place and time when Seuss wrote and first published *The Sneetches*.

At that time, those who wielded power in the United States tended to follow certain patterns. For one, they held positions of power—political power, the power to create and interpret laws and policies; the power to buy and sell the means of production; the power to buy, sell, and influence mass media; the power to join and assume leadership roles in the military, police forces, and other law enforcement agencies; the power to lead institutions of education; and so on. And if we look at the people who held these sorts of positions of power, we would see certain patterns—in terms of sex, gender, sexual orientation, race, religion, and so on. Moreover, if we were to identify these patterns, we would notice that those who held positions of power in 1950s America tended to be wealthy (or, at the very least, financially comfortable), white, Christian, heterosexual families of European descent. This group was disproportionally represented in positions of institutional authority, published literature, films, television shows, advertisements, and so on. It is important to note that although white women were better represented than nonwhite women during this era, they themselves were frequently relegated to subservient roles in the home and the workplace. So, white women were at once empowered and disempowered, privileged and dominated. [12]

When Dr. Seuss wrote *The Sneetches*, white males were more frequently put on school reading lists, they were suspended from school less frequently, and they were incarcerated less frequently. They tended to live in communities with cleaner drinking water and had better access to health care. Also, at that time, the Original People of the United States and Canada did not have the right to vote. At that time, many restaurants, washrooms, businesses, and neighborhoods were segregated. In fact, if Dr. Seuss went for a walk to take a break from writing *The Sneetches*, he might have come across buildings and businesses with signs that read "Whites Only" or "Gentiles Only." This was the world within which Seuss wrote and published *The Sneetches*. [13]

Some of you may be reading this chapter, and you may be thinking to yourselves: *Well, that was long ago. Surely that's all in the past, and we don't need to worry about those injustices anymore.* Some of you may be reading this chapter, and you may be asking: *Isn't today's society better in terms of social justice?* And I can only respond to this question by answering: *Yes, of course it is. Of course, today's society is much better in terms of social justice.* Yet that does not mean that today's society is above reproach. And it certainly does not mean that today's society is one that is just or equitable. Let's consider the matter of change. While many disturbing aspects of Seuss's social surroundings have indeed changed for the better, not everything has changed. Look around the United States and Canada today and ask yourself: Who is suspended from school more/less frequently? Who is incarcerated more/less frequently? Who tends to live in communities with cleaner drinking water? Who has better access to health care? Who holds more CEO positions? In terms of public works, who tends to hold more positions of elected office or work in the civil service? In terms of the private sector, who tends to get paid more for their work, or who tends to sit on a company's board of governors? And so on. The answers to these questions lead us to some disconcerting patterns.[14]

When creating *The Sneetches*, Dr. Seuss looked around himself, considered his surroundings, and then dramatized the phenomena of inequality and othering. On the quiet beach at the outset of the story, difference exists. It's visible—and it's a matter of variety. Yet it's more than that. On this quiet beach, difference goes far beyond variety itself. On this beach, difference is a social system where *some* members of the community are *normalized* and others are *abnormalized*, or seen and treated as the other. As such, *The Sneetches* shows us a community where there is a definite center point. In the story, that center point is determined by one's physical appearance. As the narrative unfolds, we see that othering is not just a matter of inclusion and exclusion. In the story, we have a society where there is a dominant center and those who occupy that center hold power, which they wield over those who live outside the center—those mistreated Sneetches who (at the start of the story) do not have stars on their bellies.

While Dr. Seuss was writing about conditions he observed in his own context in mid-1900s America, these observations still have relevance today. Difference still exists. Difference still leads to situations in which some are normalized and others are abnormalized. Difference still leads some to be privileged and others to be disadvantaged. And normalization and othering are still tied to a *have/have not* social system of power and domination. Because othering and inequality continue to exist, *The Sneetches* remains a tremendously relevant story.

WHAT ARE THE IMPLICATIONS?

When a society has a system of domination, one that is exclusionary, it is important to ask: *Who dominates and who gets dominated?* Posing this question, and examining its answer, can help us to identify certain patterns regarding who tends to hold power, as well as who doesn't. It can also help us to identify who tends to receive privileges as well as who tends to get disadvantaged in society. By exploring the answer to this question, we may better understand certain things about privilege and power. Ultimately, the things we learn from delving into these questions may be discomforting. Yet while these matters are certainly important, they are more of an individual matter, a matter of who is advantaged and *who holds power*. By pursuing a second question, we may delve deeper into the realm of *how*.

It is just as important, perhaps more important, that we ask ourselves: *What is the system that allows for (or fuels/maintains) this system of power?* As this second question illustrates, rather than focusing on specific individuals, or families, or groups who hold power within a society, it is necessary to consider the system itself. After all, as French thinker Michel Foucault has noted, while individual powerbrokers themselves may come and go, the system itself endures. When exploring larger questions about the social system itself, we may ask: *What is the system? How does it foster equality and/or disparity? If it fosters disparity, how does it do this?* Finally, we might ask: *Why does society support a system that fosters (or promotes) disparity? Who benefits from this? What does it mean for the community itself?* As we further consider the implications of othering while we think about *The Sneetches*, we can see the phenomenon from a variety of perspectives.

In terms of justice, othering is unjust. It unfairly leads some to receive privileges and others to be disadvantaged. It isn't fair that Sneetches with stars on their bellies are born with power and authority. What did they do to deserve that power? For that matter, why should power be something that can be lorded over others? And on the flipside, what did the starless Sneetches do to deserve their social position, their lot in life? Moreover, why should society foster such a system of domination? The power system we see at the outset of *The Sneetches* is highly divisive. It highlights division, encourages division, and maintains division. While the system is unfair for individuals, it is socially unhealthy. It creates a community that is fractured, unhappy, and unstable. If democracy is an empowering social system, then the social system within the world of *The Sneetches* isn't just unfair—it's also undemocratic.

In terms of psychology and mental wellness, othering can lead to an unhealthy state of mind among different members of a community. There are many ways that othering fosters negative or unhealthy states of mind or being. Again, let's consider the landscape of *The Sneetches*. At the outset of the story, certain Sneetches see themselves as superior. After all, they live in a world where they are empowered. In a clear system of privilege, where one's physical appearance is equated with inclusion and domination, the star-bellied Sneetches are determined to look down upon their peers. And so they do. Moreover, because they recognize their position of power and they are not worried about the inequities at play, they strive to maintain their privileges and clutch the power that they hold. As such, the empowered Sneetches strive to maintain the social system that gives them various advantages or privileges. Rather than acknowledging the inequities that are inherent in their social system, the star-bellied Sneetches strive to maintain the system. They are overcome with feelings of superiority, or supremacy, and they are dogged by feelings of worry as they fear losing their position of privilege.

Within the social system that we see at the beginning of *The Sneetches*, those who are disempowered—*the Sneetches without stars on their bellies*—may be prompted to experience feelings of frustration or even inadequacy. It wouldn't be surprising if some of them had feelings of low self-esteem. Within the Sneetches' world, *the othered Sneetches* are made to feel jealous, or envious, or regretful, or lesser. If someone is put outside the center point simply because of who he/she is, then what does that mean for that individual's sense of self-identity, self-worth, and self-esteem? Having feelings of inadequacy or low self-esteem does not make the starless Sneetches any lesser than their peers. It doesn't make them any lesser as individuals, but it *does* mean that they face a variety of unpleasant psychological and emotional challenges. In Seuss's story, this unhealthy dynamic leads the starless Sneetches to change their very identity by altering their physical appearance. In other words, in a system of othering, those who are othered may not only lose their *sense of identity* but also alter the thing that is perhaps most precious to them—*their very identity*.

YOU CAN TEACH A SNEETCH

In *The Sneetches*, Dr. Seuss exposes the ridiculousness of lookism, racism, and all sorts of discrimination—and othering. Seuss's story shows us how unfair it is to use difference to foster a social dynamic where people get othered simply because of who they are. It is so stubbornly arbitrary. As the story unfolds, we see how othering is a phenomenon that not only doesn't make sense but also is ultimately toxic—and we clearly see that it just shouldn't happen. As we see in the story, othering is unhealthy on a psychological and emotional level. Of course, some readers may be thinking: *That's just a part of learning to survive in society. People should just tough it out.* For those who are swayed more by financial- rather than humanist-oriented arguments, othering, to put it in terms of dollars and cents, is costly. On a social level, fostering a have/have-not dynamic, fueling relations that are rooted in discrimination, and creating a system of privilege and disadvantage leads to such things as social unrest, poverty, and conflict.

As a narrative, *The Sneetches* shows us how othering leads to a social system rooted in unshared power and domination. Seuss initially wrote *The Sneetches* as a satire to show how anti-Semitism and discrimination are not simply unjust but also toxic—and socially unhealthy and inhumane. We may read the story as a warning against any sort of othering that persists in society—anti-Semitism, Islamophobia, racism, homophobia, sexism, and so on. In a simple story, Seuss shows us the who, what, why, and how of social othering—all the while exposing the wider social implications. Although social othering may not be the same as it was in Seuss's day, the phenomenon and issue still lingers, pestering communities all around the world.

Part IV

Us!

Living with others is often a pain,
Everyone looking for only their gain.
So we need to decide how to set up a stable
State where each member is sat at the table,
Where each gets a chance to realize her dreams,
Ensuring we don't go to any extremes.

We need to consider rights, power, and law,
We need to ensure a fair order for all.
Our rights from the state we must surely protect,
A just legal system we'll need to erect.
No force or undue use of state power,
We must have protections for when things turn sour.
And noting that none of us are quite the same,
We'll do so while speaking diversity's name.

But sometimes the state will need to chime in,
To save us from trouble without and within.
Decisions are needed about matters most grave,
War, death, and destruction, and who will be saved.

So as we continue, remember this fact,
Living with people's a balancing act,
My rights against yours, my welfare, your care,
Let's all do our best to ensure a fair share.

13

OH, THE MISTAKES YOU'LL MAKE WHEN YOU'RE FREE

Coercion, Power, and Liberty in Dr. Seuss

Kevin Guilfoy

"Put me down," said the fish. "This is no fun at all."
"Put me down," said the fish. "I do not wish to fall."
"Have no fear," said the Cat. "I will not let you fall. I will hold you up
high as I stand on a ball."

—Dr. Seuss, *The Cat in the Hat*

Humiliating to human pride as it may be, we must recognize that the
advance and even the preservation of human civilization are dependent
upon a maximum of opportunity for accidents to happen.

—F. A. Hayek[1]

It struck me as odd when I was first asked to write a chapter on coercion
for this book about Dr. Seuss. But with just a little thought I realized how
fitting this subject is. Children are rigorously and systematically coerced
in every aspect of their lives. Who feels more viscerally the anguish of
having their desires thwarted? Who suffers more acutely when their will
is bent to that of another? When you are three years old and your life plan
is to wear the cat *as* a hat, you have a sharp lesson to learn. Dr. Seuss
feels your pain. When your deepest and most meaningful personal goal is
to eat ice cream for dinner and Dad gives you broccoli, you are powerless. As a parent, I have goals and values and hopes for the lives of my
children. Part of me wants them to do everything I say. The rest of me

knows that children need the liberty to make mistakes, and suffer consequences, if they are to become autonomous and happy adults. It is a
constant struggle to acknowledge that I may not know what is best, that
even when I do know better, controlling people is bad for them and for
me. Humility is a virtue that runs deep in Dr. Seuss. Coercion is a lack of
humility.

It may also seem odd that I have chosen to use the ideas of F. A.
Hayek (1899–1992) to bring out the depth of Seuss's thought. Hayek, the
libertarian philosopher and Nobel Prize–winning economist, is most famous for *The Road to Serfdom*, an occasionally paranoid diagnosis of
Hitler's rise to power. But few remember that Dr. Seuss was a biting
editorial cartoonist in the 1940s; like Hayek, he aimed his most critical
barbs at those who did not see the existential threat posed by Hitler.
Hayek and Seuss both understand the risks posed by men with grand
plans for a new world. If they are different, it is because Hayek lurches to
extremes in finding subterranean threats to liberty, while Seuss imagines
extremes of whimsy, silliness, and even catastrophe in the exercise of
liberty. Hayek works at a societal level, advocating that the individual
live free from state coercion. Seuss brings this message of liberty and
experimentation to children. In all types of coercion, the coercer believes
that he knows what is right or best; the coerced has different plans.
Parents assume the child is less intellectually able to make the right
choice. Hayek cautions us against a state that makes the same assumption
of adults.

The two also share a worldview. Hayek describes a social world created by the spontaneous choices of millions of individuals. The result is a
spontaneous order, wondrously efficient but totally bizarre. For Hayek,
"every change creates a 'problem' for society" that is "gradually solved"
by those who "have little idea why they are doing what they do and no
way of predicting . . . an appropriate move . . . or suitable answer."[2]
Civilization is the evolving result of choices made by people who do not
know what they are doing. That is why it works. I suspect Seuss would
agree. The real world, like the world of Dr. Seuss, is beautiful and complex, but not the product of rational design. This is why Hayek opposed
coercion and promoted liberty. The best world is created through the trial
and error of people who do not know everything.

YERTLE HATCHES A PLAN

Yertle the Turtle, Seuss's metaphorical Hitler, has a plan. He wants to build a huge stack of turtles so that, from the top, he can be king of all that he sees. It is his vision, and he forces Mack and the others to pile themselves up. Assuming that Yertle threatens punishment for noncompliance, his actions illustrate the basic elements of Hayek's theory of coercion and coercive state power: "Coercion is when one man's actions are meant to serve the other man's will, not for his own, but for the other's purpose."[3] Mack's actions serve Yertle's purpose, and he gets nothing from the deal. Coercion does not require force or restraint. Nor does coercion imply a lack of choice or free will. Coercion occurs when one person arranges the consequences of alternative choices to make them less preferable to another.[4] Yertle coerces Mack by making other alternatives unacceptable. Mack may have free will in the metaphysical sense, but he is not choosing to go along with Yertle because it is part of his own rationally chosen plan. Yertle's manipulation means that Mack cannot "use his own knowledge in authentic circumstances" to pursue the goals he desires for himself.[5] This is bad for Mack, of course, but it is also bad for Yertle. "Power does not corrupt when it is the power to achieve our own aims. The power that corrupts is the power to bend the will of others to our own."[6]

This clear case of coercion can be contrasted with three others. When King Louis Katz employs a subordinate to hold his tail, the subordinate is not coerced. The tail holder in fact employs his own tail holder, who then employs his own tail holder, and so on, as each subsequent subordinate selects a supported tail. The first tail holder chooses to assist the king in his goal because he gets something that allows him to further his own goal: money. The scheme collapses when the ultimate tail holder can find no one to hold his tail. Tail holders must perform a service for another before they can follow their own plans. They may get nothing of personal value out of the job. Unlike Yertle, the king is not manipulating the circumstances to make a particular choice preferable. Nor is the worker who decides he does not want to hold tails. A worker who demands a higher wage than an employer will pay does not coerce the employer.[7] Hayek sees greater risk of workers coercing employers, but the converse holds. An employer who offers less than an employee would like does not coerce the worker. This is just negotiation.

But the market can, without manipulation, create an opportunity for coercion. If it is "crucial to my existence or the preservation of what I most value" that I remain employed or purchase a service, I can easily be coerced.[8] The coercer exploits the fact that under authentic circumstances I will suffer horribly without the job or the service. Hayek seems to acknowledge that threatening to kill and threatening to let die are morally equivalent when the threat is part of gaining cooperation in a voluntary transaction. Such organic conditions are "not impossible" but would be rare "in a prosperous competitive society."[9]

How about the North- and South-Going Zax? Each has a rational life plan: to walk in one direction without swerving. Their paths collide. They stand their ground, refusing to swerve one inch, while the world goes on around them. Hayek explicitly addresses this case: "A person who blocks my path on the street does not coerce me."[10] He does not cite Seuss, but he condones Seuss's resolution. Although each Zax is an insuperable obstacle to the other, neither is coerced. The choice each makes to stand, waiting for the other to die, is simply commitment to their goals. The desires and goals of other people, and the actions they undertake in pursuit of these goals, are part of the authentic circumstances that we each must work in. We may be limited, or even constrained, by the actions of others, but this is not coercion.

My daughter thinks the Zax are stubborn fools who would be happier if they just moved around each other. She is full of the hubris that inspires coercion. She cannot know what will make the Zax happy. Yet she would force each to take one step to the right. This seems fair to her, but it coerces both Zax. They may proceed unabated, but neither would have achieved their goal. They would have been forced to do what she thinks is best. For a third party, the state, to step in and move one or both of them infringes on their liberty.

Controversially, under this definition of coercion, the animals forced to flee the Lorax's forest are not coerced. The suffering of the Humming-Fish, Swomee-Swans, and the Brown Bar-ba-loots is a failure of institutions. They have no property rights that protect them against the incursions of the Once-ler. The Humming-Fish's desire to swim conflicts with the Once-ler's desire to manufacture thneeds. The pond is a resource that both want, only one can use, and neither owns. The Once-ler's actions drive the fish away, but they are not coerced. The fish are not forced to work toward the Once-ler's goal. Sure, his plan involves poisoning the water, but the Once-ler has no desires whatsoever concerning the activities of the Humming-Fish. His actions have made their home inhospitable, but this was incidental. This is obviously not a good result. But Hayek would oppose the bald assertion of state power to correct it. He is not insensible to the immediate suffering of the animals. Yet, having survived the rise and fall of National Socialism, he is genuinely more terrified of the consequences that follow from the exercise of state power in order to guide people's actions or to protect the interests of a particular group.[11]

Property rights are not absolute or natural, according to Hayek.[12] He would not recognize a right of ownership just because the Humming-Fish were in the water first. Under an established system of property rights the Humming-Fish could have owned the pond. This recognition of property rights is the first step in the delimitation of a private sphere that protects us against coercion.[13] Under the rule of law, the liberties protected in this private sphere allow a property owner to pursue their own chosen goals. So, had the fish owned the pond, they would have been at liberty to use and enjoy the pond as it fit their life plan. In this scenario, the Once-ler could offer to buy the pond. His plans will be thwarted, but he will not be coerced, if the fish refuse to sell. The institution of property rights under the rule of law is part of the authentic circumstances that shape everyone's options.

Ideally, we would all be at liberty to pursue our own rationally chosen plans within the authentic circumstances we find ourselves in. Coercion is the manipulation of those circumstances to force a particular choice. A coercer may have their own plans, and no regard for the desires of others, or they may genuinely think they know what is best. Either way, they bend your will to their own by making you an offer you can't refuse. The loss of liberty is bad enough for an individual. A society where people are routinely coerced into making particular choices loses the experimentation, vitality, and creativity that spawn all great human achievement.

WHERE IS A LORAX TO SPEAK FOR THE POOR?

But, you object, the powerless Humming-Fish are doomed from the outset. Hayek assumes equal power and bargaining positions. Seuss is not the only one describing a fantasy world. There are so many other examples. What about poor Gertrude McFuzz, hopelessly deficient in the natural endowment of feathers? Bartholomew Cubbins is not able to negotiate as an equal for his increasingly fabulous hats. Hayek is not totally unmoved by inequality. But inequality is quite low on his list of problems. Equality is correspondingly low on his list of values. Hayek plays the Once-ler to this Lorax for the poor. When inequality is the result of the legal structure, or when inequality can be addressed without infringing on liberty or coercing others, then it should be.[14] But inequality is a necessary, and in many ways a good, feature of a free society. Hayek's dismissive approach to inequality assumes we are talking about an affluent society where the depravations are relative, not absolute. But he is fully aware of the seriousness of relative inequality.[15]

The Once-ler is rich. He has a world of opportunities the Humming-Fish do not. Their lower quantity of eligible life options is not the result of coercion by the Once-ler or anyone else. Liberty is not increased or decreased by the quantity of options one can choose from.[16] If the Humming-Fish cannot afford the pond when it is put up for sale, they will have to leave. The fish are in an unenviable position relative to the Once-ler but are at liberty to use what resources they have to pursue whatever goals seem reasonable to them under the circumstances. "Though the alternatives before me may be distressingly few, and my new plans of a makeshift character, yet it is not someone else's will that guides my actions."[17]

Gertrude McFuzz and Bartholomew Cubbins may be more favorable illustrations of Hayek's view. Gertrude laments that she has only one tail feather. When she learns that eating a magic pill-berry will grow new feathers, she eats them all. This ends badly, but Seuss has little sympathy for Gertrude. The moral of her short tail[18] is self-acceptance. We don't have equal talents and abilities. Hayek would draw two lessons: First, efforts to address this kind of inequality are a slippery slope. When we have equality of tail feathers, we will still be unequal in something else. Once we are committed to equality as a goal, we can never stop.[19] The more controversial lesson Hayek draws is that society is better off if the more talented are at liberty to pursue their wider range of options.[20] The only equality we can hope to achieve is equality under the rule of law. We can establish general rules protecting each person's liberty to pursue any of the options open to them by the circumstances the actual world presents. If we falsely equate equality before the law with the spurious notion of metaphysical equality, we run the risk of making "equality" meaningless, and of losing all the innovations that arise from the greater abilities possessed by the few.[21]

Physically and intellectually, Bartholomew Cubbins may be superior to his king. He has an amazing talent, but he is economically disadvantaged. He can produce impressive hats; yet he seems to have no choice but to accept the king's offer of five hundred gold pieces. This is pocket change for the king. Yet Bartholomew could live his greatest dreams for half that. The relative marginal value of money may make it seem that the much poorer Bartholomew is compelled to accept the king's offer. This initial problem is easily handled. Bartholomew could charge more. Under the rule of law, he could refuse to sell altogether. Even the king could not compel him. And if the king did not manipulate those circumstances to make Bartholomew sell the hat, he would not be coerced. (We know very little about the political economy of Didd. Hayek warns us not to make a "fetish of democracy." It is possible to have a monarchy that operates under the rule of law.[22]) Hayek is fully aware that the poor have fewer eligible opportunities than the rich. But, as with the Humming-Fish, he does not think this is a limitation on their liberty, nor does he see this as an abuse of power by those with more resources and opportunity.

While we may feel for Bartholomew, Hayek sees a social advantage to the king and his class. From collecting hats, to walking on stilts, to having their tails held, the kings in Seuss's worlds employ their resources on silly pursuits and decadent luxuries. They form an intellectual and cultural elite.[23] For everything from ice cream to indoor plumbing, the luxuries of the rich quickly disseminate to the rest of society.[24] Their ability to pursue decadent and absurd frivolities helps society advance. The misers and the greedy, the Once-lers, do not. "It is doubtful whether a wealthy class whose ethos requires that at least every male member prove his usefulness by making more money can adequately justify its existence."[25] Hayek notes that America "has produced a propertied class that lacks intellectual leadership and a coherent defensible philosophy of life."[26] America produces Once-lers. The problem is quite serious. The Once-ler's shallow pursuit of profit does not make the world better. Nonetheless, rather than limit the liberty of the next Once-ler, Hayek would use him as a cautionary example. As individuals, we can learn a lesson from the Once-ler's self-destruction and apply it to our own circumstances. But the lesson is only valuable if we are at liberty to learn from it on our own.

The best we can hope for is a system of strong institutions that allow the Once-ler to hurt himself without damaging others too much.

Our natural talents and economic status are part of the authentic circumstances that can limit our options. We mostly have to work within those limitations. Yet even with fewer options available, we are not coerced into any one of these options. Sometimes our options are limited by the desires and actions of other people. This is a more difficult issue.

HORTON: COERCED INTO CONFORMITY

All his troubles start when Horton hears a Who. No one else hears anything. Horton listens and devotes himself to the protection of the dust ball that serves as Who-ville's planet. Horton believes in a "reality" that others cannot perceive. This is weird, but in Thomas Jefferson's (1743–1826) often-quoted formulation about religion, Horton's devotion to Whos "neither picks my pocket nor breaks my leg."[27] Nonetheless, he suffers social and state coercion for his devotion.

In a world without social coercion Horton would only suffer the opportunity costs of his devotion to the Whos: he would be unable to do other things with his time. Instead, he is ridiculed by judgmental kangaroos. The kangaroos' behavior manipulates the circumstances to increase the penalty Horton suffers for his beliefs. John Stuart Mill (1806–1873) is deeply concerned by this form of moral coercion. He saw great problems with people punitively expressing their negative judgments of the harmless choices made by others. Hayek thinks Mill "overstated the case for liberty." He balks at calling "the pressures that public approval or disapproval exerts to secure obedience to moral rules" coercion. The "milder forms of pressure society applies to non-conformists" play an "indispensable role" in establishing a "flexible background of more or less unconscious habits that serve as a guide to most people's actions." On balance, there is some small element of coercion in the kangaroos' actions, but moderate enforcement of a clear social framework helps more people than it hinders in pursuing their goals.[28]

Like all social systems, the norms and customs in the Jungle of Nool are the product of generations of people using the knowledge of their own desires and circumstances to negotiate the best outcomes for themselves. "Rules have grown from trial and error in which the experience of each successive generation has helped make them what they are."[29] When we follow these norms, we benefit from the cumulative application of knowledge that we could never possess. These traditional norms are not good in themselves. Hayek is a skeptic, not a conservative. Their continued general acceptance shows merely that they have met people's needs in the past. We can never know enough to understand how and why. Norms need to continue evolving, but violating them should not be without consequences. Because social rules are voluntary—there is no state sanction for violating them—nonconformists like Horton are at liberty to decide whether breaking them is worth the social cost.[30] Hayek tolerates judgmental kangaroos. They signal a presumption in favor of conformity. When the monkeys steal Horton's dust ball, they have gone too far. The social coercion that Hayek chooses to ignore quickly metastasizes into state coercion.

Under the rule of law, Horton's private sphere includes his dusty sphere. He may be laughed at, but he should be at liberty to continue listening to it unimpeded by angry monkeys. Horton's actions are weird, but well within what ought to be the protected sphere of privacy. Unfortunately, the Jungle of Nool is not under the rule of law. Although he is the victim of theft, Horton is tried and imprisoned. The kangaroo, as judge, decrees that there is a proper use of dust balls and all other uses will be punished. Horton is not at liberty to pursue his own rational life plan with his dust ball. This is state coercion.

In Mill's spirit, Hayek notes, "Religious beliefs seem to be almost the only ground on which general rules seriously restrictive of individual liberty have ever been universally enforced."[31] Religious groups more often find themselves in a majority, able to wield the coercive power of the state. But one lesson of *The Road to Serfdom* is that any ethnic, cultural, or political group may unite to use the coercive power of the state to implement its own values. Without checks on governmental power, any group might use the power of the state to coerce others into living out their preferred conception of the good. Such majorities have a tool for imposing their will on nonconformists: democracy.

THIDWICK: BIG-HEARTED BUT OUTVOTED

There is a common misconception that if power is held by the people, liberty will be protected. There are many good reasons for power to be in the hands of the people. This is not one of them. "We can no longer be sure . . . that democracy is an important safeguard of individual liberty."[32] It is simply too easy for majorities to vote themselves privileges at the expense of minorities. Democracy is a good answer to the question: Who should wield state power? But this is the second question we should ask. The first question is: What is the scope of state power?[33] Getting this answer right will protect liberty regardless of the form the government takes. As Thidwick discovers, it is dangerous to answer these questions in the wrong order.

Thidwick the moose invites a Bingle-Bug to ride on his antlers as he walks through the forest. This bug invites a friend, who invites a friend, who brings his family. Birds pluck hair from Thidwick's head to build nests. Woodpeckers drill holes in his antlers. Squirrels hide nuts in the holes. Thidwick's friends abandon him because he won't evict his guests. When the food runs out and the other moose cross lake Winna-Bango for the winter, Thidwick's guests do not want to go. The Bingle-Bug puts the question to a vote. Thidwick loses. The majority has decreed that Thidwick must starve.

Thidwick and his guests assume that a vote justifies any result. They have mistaken the means—democracy—with the end—legitimate state action. Thidwick has been coerced by a democratic majority because they forgot to answer Hayek's first question. They have not established the scope of state power before attempting to govern. Hayek would suggest that the government respect individual liberty and the rule of law. In the first place there ought to be rights of the individual that are above state interference.[34] Specifically, "the private citizen and his property should not be at the disposal of the government."[35] The guests should not be able to outvote Thidwick on the use of his body to promote their goals.

Thidwick has the right to vote. He has the right to speak. He has the full slate of political liberties. His guests have not tried to take these away. But Hayek notes, rightly, that inner freedom and the right to vote "will not make the slave free."[36] Thidwick needs more mundane economic freedoms: the liberty to use his property as he wants provided he follows the same general rules applicable to everyone else. "Freedom of action even in humble things is as important as freedom of thought."[37] The liberty to pursue our mundane day-to-day activities is how we pursue our goals and build meaningful lives. So how are we supposed to do this when everyone else is pursuing their own goals and building their own lives?

WHO SPEAKS FOR THE FISH?

The Cat in the Hat is a dark cautionary tale for our neoliberal age. Most readers miss this point. Sally and her brother share their moribund and stagnant home with a contented fish. Mother is a good libertarian governor operating under the rule of law: she is mostly absent. In sweeps the Cat in the Hat. Let the creative destruction begin!

The Cat is the unbridled force of liberty and creativity. His games are not much fun. This chapter opens with a quote from a game the Cat calls "Up, Up, Up, Up." Brother finishes this sad tale: "That is what the Cat said. . . . Then he fell on his head. He came down with a bump from up there on the ball, and Sally and I, *we saw all the things fall*" (Cat). A more activist mother would have been there at the beginning to stop the Cat as soon as he thought of hoisting the fish on a rake. She would have kept Thing One and Thing Two in their box. So much senseless damage could have been avoided. At least it is flattering to human pride to think so.

As Hayek would have it, the advance of human civilization depends on the Cat's liberty to stand on a ball with a book on his head. In the real world, Dr. Seuss is the Cat. After the relative lack of success of *And to Think That I Saw it on Mulberry Street*, and Seuss's other early books, a wise person might have told him to stick to editorial cartoons. But he was at liberty to try and fail. My copy of *The Cat in the Hat* has a blurb from a 1966 *Detroit Free Press* review praising the book as a "karate chop to the weary little world of Dick, Jane, and Spot." This book was an assault on the simplistic and moralistic world of children's literature. No one could have known beforehand that it would touch something so vital in our culture. Our world is a better place because Seuss was at liberty to pursue his questionable dreams.

Seuss's behatted Cat is less successful, but still a good ambassador for neoliberal change. Unlike the Once-ler, the Cat cleaned up his own mess. This is how it should be, although it rarely happens with kids, cats, or failed capitalist ventures. Sure, Mother could have barred the Cat from the house and coerced the children into doing what she believed was best. But a lesson learned is more valuable than an order followed. And, as Hayek might say, mothers cannot have all the relevant knowledge necessary to enact a proactive plan that will distribute resources and make children happy.

Still, where is the Lorax to speak for the fish? The fish is content. His world is exactly as he would choose it to be. Yet as long as the Cat is at liberty, the fish cannot enjoy his world. The Cat's first venture fails, but he comes back. Again, and again, and again. He has vision and ideas. As we have seen, Hayek is a supporter of tradition, but only insofar as tradition is the embodiment of practices that allow people to satisfy their desires, use resources adequately, and be happy. The Cat's liberty to fly kites in the hall upsets everything the fish values. The children, however, are intrigued. Change is unavoidable. They will all approach the problem of redistributing resources and organizing their lives in a halting and haphazard way. They do not know what they are doing, but if they are to be happy on their own terms, they need the liberty to try.

The fish is suffering the dynamic upheavals of neoliberal social change. He illustrates perhaps the hardest problem for an individualist to face: no fish is an island. So why does Hayek side with the Cat? If the children choose to build a rational life plan around what the Cat offers, the fish is unable to live his preferred life plan but remains free to find a second-best option of his own choosing. However, for the fish to live his rational life plan, the children must be coerced into specific life choices they would not otherwise make. For the fish to prevent the children from playing with the Cat simply to protect his own way of life would be coercive. And according to Hayek, the children need not be bothered by the fact that their choices disrupt the life of the fish. They are under no obligation to advance the fish's goals.[38]

The simple fact is that most people desire comity as part of whatever else we desire. When change occurs, this comity will be realized through trial and error and complex social negotiations. These complex social negotiations cannot be rationally planned. Only the individuals involved can know their desires at any moment. Only they can decide on a compromise that is acceptable. One lesson from the Once-ler is to listen to the complaints of others if you hope to live well yourself.

ON ZOOS AND CIRCUSES

With Mack and Horton, and most alarmingly Thidwick, Dr. Seuss has shown the dangers of state coercion. With this background in mind, Seuss offers us two competing visions for the design of the state. *If I Ran the Zoo* is a dark tale of the dangers of coercive social planning. *If I Ran the Circus* is an optimistic story of voluntary collaboration.

The zoo is popular. The zookeeper too. But Gerald McGrew has a plan for the zoo: "I'd open each cage. I'd unlock every pen, let the animals go and start over again" (Zoo). His lion will have ten feet, not four. An elephant-cat will stand watch at the door. He will gather and hunt every new, bigger, better, and more gawkworthy creature to be found. The people will love it. The people will love him. He has a good plan. The impulse to organize the social world for the common good is a noble one. Gerald is not Yertle. Gerald wants what is good for everyone. But he is doing the same thing Yertle does, and his plans are doomed to failure.

The zoo, as an institution, like society, evolved. It was not rationally designed. The zoo is the result of generations of zookeepers trying things, compromising, and learning from their mistakes. Gerald has the benefit of all that accumulated knowledge. The knowledge is embedded in the cultural tools and institutions that we habitually follow without knowing why.[39] We cannot improve on these cultural structures by imposing new and trendy ideas.[40] "It is only our profound and comprehensive ignorance of the nature of culture that makes it possible for us to believe that we direct and control it."[41] Hayek is not building an argument for stultifying traditionalism. Imposing trendy ideas is very different from offering trendy ideas the way the Cat does. Gerald should organize an expedition to Hippo-no-Hungus and bring back a Bibbo-no-Bungus if he thinks people will prefer that to the bonobo exhibit.

But Gerald is foolishly confident that he knows what future zoo patrons will like. He sets all the animals free and starts over. It is too simplistic to point out that even a boring old four-footed lion might suddenly become much more exciting when set loose into the neighborhood. Hayek's objection is much deeper than pointing out the potential for unintended consequences when you "improve" a system you don't understand. Gerald claims to have knowledge of what people want. He claims to know what they will like, and what will make them happy. Such knowledge is impossible. The knowledge of each person's marginal desire—how much they would prefer a ten-footed to a four-footed lion—is uniquely particular. Only the individual knows their own preference at a particular time. No social planner can know with any certainty beforehand exactly what another person will desire.[42] Gerald is trying to improve a system that he does not understand in order to satisfy people's future desires, which he cannot know. The situation calls for humility instead.

Gerald makes the same error as every legislator with a social vision. In addition to being incorrect, the imposition of a social vision by law is coercive. Gerald assumes a "common good." In his case, he assumes it is simply a fact that ten-footed lions are better. Like all social planners, he assumes that his judgment of what is good is correct. When a social planner implements their vision for the distribution of goods or roles in a society, they assume there is a single scale of values that everyone will agree to and that can guide state action. In a diverse society, this is simply not the case. There is no agreed-on value system that a policymaker can appeal to when making the needed policy tradeoffs. There is no single scale ranking values and goods that everyone would agree to and that could guide state action. Quite simply, in a diverse society there is no "common good."[43]

The lesson Hayek draws from this skepticism about common values is that we must be at liberty to pursue our own values.

> This is the fundamental fact on which the whole philosophy of individualism is based. It does not assume, as is often asserted, that man is egoistic or selfish or ought to be. It merely starts from the indisputable fact that the limits of our powers of imagination make it impossible to include in our scale of values more than a sector of the needs of the whole society, and that, since, strictly speaking, scales of value can exist only in individual minds, nothing but partial scales of value exist—scales which are inevitably different and often inconsistent with each other.[44]

We cannot know how and why social structures and norms evolved. We cannot know the marginal desires of other people. There is no universal scale of values to guide our decision making. The case for individual liberty, warts and all, rests firmly on this recognition of our human ignorance.[45]

What is Gerald McGrew with his vision to do? He should be more like Morris McGurk. McGurk sees a derelict lot behind Sneelock's store. He envisions cleaning up the property and opening what he thinks would be an amazing circus. Gerald McGrew roamed the world himself collecting animals because he knows what people like. Gerald is a bit of a control freak. Morris McGurk considers employing others to utilize their own talents. In the beginning, McGurk hopes Sneelock "might like to help." Sneelock jumps in with both feet. Billed as the Brave Colonel Sneelock, he wrestles the Spotted Atrocious and dives thousands of feet into a fish bowl. How does he manage this feat? "Don't ask me how he'll manage." McGurk asserts, "That's his job. Not mine" (Circus). When McGurk raises the circus tent, he has created a framework where Sneelock can pursue his own dreams. Far from having a grand plan, McGurk has no idea how Sneelock does it.

McGurk even shares Hayek's overly optimistic view of the other circus workers: "My workers love work. They say 'work us please work us!'" (Circus). Such is the delusion of Morris McGurk. The workers bring back the issue of inequality. They do not run the circus, and they are not the star. They are Bartholomew, Gertrude, and Mack. They follow McGurk's direction, not their own plans. My daughter, a very skeptical reader of Seuss, doubts the authenticity of the workers' enthusiasm. It is likely that the workers are inflating their eagerness so as to win the boss's favor. This reflects their lower status in the social order. Lacking the resources of McGurk and the talent of Sneelock, they have to sell their labor to McGurk. Their situation is unenviable, but they are not coerced. It is worth noting that they have the opportunity to work at the circus because of McGurk and Sneelock.

The poor have fewer social and economic options. Do you have a plan for fixing this? Are you sure your plan will give people what they want? People need help. Other chapters in this book describe Seuss's message of compassion or care. This discussion of Hayek may seem pinched, even mean, as he warns us to temper even our kindest ambitions. But humility is a virtue that should temper our ambitions.

The virtue of humility promoted in Seuss is the honest humility that comes from knowing our own ignorance. Yertle lacks humility. Other turtles are merely tools used to advance his own interests. But so does Gerald McGrew. Without consultation, Gerald does what he thinks is best for other people. Thidwick's guests, the monkeys of Nool, and even the fish are all willing to force others into choices that will make themselves happy with little regard for Thidwick, or Horton, or Sally and her brother. They all overestimate their own knowledge and abilities and show little regard for the desires and plans of others.

Coercion grows out of the feeling that we know what other people want, need, and value, and we know how to give it to them. This is knowledge we could never have. Coercion assumes that our individual scale of values is universal. This is hubris. People at liberty will do dumb things. There will be conflict as they negotiate their various paths. The solutions they come up with may appear irrational to everyone else. Forcing people to choose what we think is best may prevent some spectacular accidents, but it precludes even more wondrous possibilities. Seuss wrote a book called *Oh, the Places You'll Go!*, not *Oh, the Places I'll Take You!*

14

STATE POWER AND INDIVIDUAL RIGHTS IN DR. SEUSS

Aeon J. Skoble

He who attempts to get another man into his absolute power, does thereby *put himself into a state of war* with him.

—John Locke[1]

And the turtles, of course . . . all the turtles are free, as turtles and, maybe, all creatures should be.

—Dr. Seuss, *Yertle the Turtle*

King Yertle of Sala-ma-Sond and King Derwin of Didd are quite different in many respects, but despite one being a turtle and the other a human, they are more alike than different: they are kings—and they are kings who think that the power of their office is absolute and unlimited and that their subjects have no rights.

The nature of political authority, and the relationship between the state and the individual, are perennial questions for political philosophy. Unsurprisingly, we can look to the works of Dr. Seuss for scenarios that, underneath their children's-story appearance, illuminate some key aspects of these problems. As we shall see, some of the same issues that arise for monarchies also present problems for democratic institutions.

YERTLE THE TURTLE TYRANT

King Yertle is a straightforward case, so we begin there. Yertle's reign is initially benevolent—the turtles of Sala-ma-Sond are all happy and have everything they might need. Given this utopian arrangement, it's not clear just what Yertle's reign consists of, but in any case the other turtles accept his authority as monarch. When he commands them, they obey. The troubles begin when Yertle starts to crave greater majesty. Being the ruler of all that he sees is great, but it occurs to him that he doesn't see very far. He orders nine turtles to form a stack, and when he sits on top of them, he can see much farther and is delighted that his kingdom now extends not just over the pond but approximately for a mile in circumference.

The nature of Yertle's authority is at this point even less clear. As monarch of the turtles in the pond, he has authority largely because the other turtles accept this authority—he really is their ruler, inasmuch as he issues commands that are in fact obeyed. So when he says, "I am the ruler of all that I see" (Yertle), that's correct. But it is a descriptive claim, which he erroneously takes as normative. He is in fact the ruler of the pond, and that's all he can see, but it doesn't follow that if he could see more, he'd be the ruler of more. When he gets on the nine-turtle stack, he can see a cow, a mule, and a cat, but there's no evidence that he now commands them. He still *claims* to be the ruler of all that he sees, but it's an empty claim. He can declare himself to be ruler of the cow, mule, and cat but does not in fact command them. However, since none of them challenge his "authority," he thinks he has expanded his kingdom and calls for a two-hundred-turtle stack so that he can expand his realm yet again.

On the two-hundred-turtle stack, he can see over a forty-mile circumference, and he concludes he is also king over birds and bees. Again, though, there's no reason to think he actually commands them. He is persisting in his mistaken inference that since all he could see in the pond was the pond, which was his realm, seeing more would expand the realm. Craving even more "power," he commands a turtle stack of 5,607. He thinks this would give him control of the moon, which is obviously false.

Of course, Yertle's plan doesn't come to fruition anyway. Even if his fallacious theory of authority based on range of vision were correct, sitting higher requires that his subjects suffer the weight of the stack. (His rule is literally built on the backs of his subjects!) When Mack, the turtle on the bottom, protests, he is told that he has no right to complain. Indeed, his interests are assumed to be subordinate to the king's. Yertle thinks that he has the right to command them to form a stack just to satisfy his desire for greater height and thus power. Mack's insistence that all the turtles have rights doesn't dissuade Yertle, but a simple act of rebelling— burping—will disrupt the stack and force Yertle back into the pond.

The relatively simple parable of Yertle contains several key points for political philosophy. The turtles acquiesce when the monarch's reign is benevolent but may rebel when it becomes abusive. Monarchical power must be based on something other than empty claims. People (here represented by turtles) should have equal rights and be free. All of these principles play out in the works of influential philosophers. For example, the seventeenth-century philosopher John Locke (1632–1704) argued that, by nature, there is a fundamental moral equality of persons that entails that the only legitimate basis for authority is consent, and that one can only rationally consent to regimes that respect and preserve that natural equality in the form of rights.[2] Locke's argument was explicitly appealed to in the writing of the American colonists' Declaration of Independence. As Jefferson put it, "Governments . . . [derive] their just Powers from the Consent of the Governed, [and] that whenever any Form of Government becomes destructive of these Ends, it is the Right of the People to alter or to abolish it."[3] Sala-ma-Sond is a microcosm of the revolution, and just as the tea being dumped into the harbor was symbolically dumping the king's authority, so, too, was Yertle dumped back into the pond.

KING DERWIN THE DESPOT

The kingdom of Didd is a more advanced society than Yertle's pond (and is actually populated by humans), though, like Yertle's, it is a monarchy. The behavior of its King Derwin, about whom we have two stories, is also illustrative. In both stories, King Derwin is contrasted with the commoner Bartholomew Cubbins. Like Sala-ma-Sond, Didd seems to be a well-functioning society, although with greater class stratification. In Sala-ma-Sond, there was general equality between turtles other than the king, and Yertle's "throne" was a rock in the pond. King Derwin of Didd lives in a mountaintop palace, from which he has a view of the full range of classes: "From his balcony, he looked down over the houses of all his subjects—first, over the spires of the noblemen's castles, across the broad roofs of the rich men's mansions, then over the little houses of the townsfolk, to the huts of the farmers far off in the fields" (Hats). Despite the wealth inequality, the people of Didd seem to acquiesce to monarchical authority much as the turtles of Sala-ma-Sond do. Derwin feels important, and the people of Didd all exhibit proper courtesy and respect.

Derwin first meets Bartholomew on a day when Bartholomew has come to town to sell his cranberries. He happens to get to town just as King Derwin is riding by. In Didd, the custom is to take off one's hat before the king, and what catches Derwin's attention about Bartholomew is that he has a hat on his head. When scolded for the breach in etiquette, Bartholomew notes that he *has* removed his hat. Mysteriously, though, whenever he removes his hat, a new one pops into place. Oblivious to the fact the Bartholomew keeps taking his hat off, King Derwin finds it infuriating that the boy persists in having a hat on his head, and he orders Bartholomew arrested.

While perhaps less megalomaniacal than Yertle, Derwin's rage about what is at most a minor faux pas is indicative of a ruler who feels naturally entitled not only to power but to all the trappings of power. The breach in etiquette is seen as a threat to Derwin's ability to rule. Yertle's authority over the turtles was manifest in their obeying his commands and disintegrated when they refused. If Derwin cannot get the hat removed, perhaps this would be seen as a similar weakening of his authority. But every time Bartholomew removes his hat, another one pops into existence.

When they are back at the palace, King Derwin enlists everyone he can think of: the royal hatmaker, the wise man Nadd, Nadd's father and grandfather, the Grand Duke Wilfred, the Yeoman of the Bowman—and none of them succeeds in getting the hats to stay off Bartholomew's head. Recognizing that the hat's continued reappearance must be magic, he summons his staff of magicians and orders them to cast a spell to remove the hat. We actually never learn whether this would've worked, for they tell Derwin that the spell will take ten years to work and Derwin is impatient to get the hat removed. Ultimately, King Derwin orders the palace executioner to remove Bartholomew's head.

The scene with the executioner illustrates another principle political philosophers have found fascinating—the function of laws. It turns out that there is a rule in Didd that says that the executioner "can't execute anyone with his hat on." But of course, every time the executioner removes the hat, another one appears. So the executioner says, "I can't execute you at all" (Hats), shakes Bartholomew's hand, and sends him back to the king. When Bartholomew explains why he hasn't been executed, the king *doesn't protest*—he is exasperated with the situation but doesn't order the executioner to proceed in contravention of the rule. Derwin acquiesces to the rule of law despite his status as monarch. The idea that even a king may be constrained by the laws goes back at least to Plato, who argued that this was one of the distinctions between a king and a tyrant.[4] Interestingly, Derwin may have the authority to execute Bartholomew for the refusal to remove his hat, but he lacks the authority to command the executioner to violate the rules concerning the manner of executions.

Although the executioner cannot decapitate Bartholomew, Grand Duke Wilfred offers to push him off the high tower, which Derwin finds satisfactory. Fortunately for Bartholomew, as they scale the stairs to the tower, the hats begin changing each time they come off, getting fancier and more elaborate. By the time they reach the tower, the hat on Bartholomew's head, the five hundredth hat, is "the most beautiful hat that had ever been seen in the Kingdom of Didd. It had a ruby larger than any the King himself had ever owned. It had ostrich plumes, and cockatoo plumes, and mockingbird plumes, and paradise plumes. Beside *such* a hat even the King's Crown seemed like nothing" (Hats). Derwin is so taken with the hat that he stops the Grand Duke from killing Bartholomew and offers to buy the hat. Again, one is perhaps surprised that while the king has the authority to order the death of the boy for the breach of etiquette, he lacks the authority to take the hat. (Perhaps the kingdom of Didd, despite its social stratification, has stable property rights, as Locke suggested.) In fact, he offers five hundred pieces of gold for it, which Bartholomew agrees to. As it happens, this time the hat does not replace itself, and so the story resolves: Bartholomew has removed his hat before the king, the king has acquired a majestic new hat, and Bartholomew returns home with a lot more money than he would have received for the cranberries he had originally gone to town to sell. It is as if the magic of the hat was sensitive to the mutually beneficial effects of trade.[5]

KINGS DON'T APOLOGIZE

But King Derwin is not immune to the madness of power that we observed in King Yertle. Getting angry about a breach in etiquette is one thing, but the next time we meet King Derwin, he is upset about something more ridiculous: the sky. He decides that it's boring to only receive snow, fog, sunshine, and rain, and he wants something new. "Every year the *same* four things! I'm mighty tired of those old things! I want something NEW to come down!" he complains to Bartholomew Cubbins, whom he has now apparently hired as a page. Bartholomew sensibly replies, "That's impossible, Your Majesty. You just can't have it." Derwin finds this unacceptable—since he's the king, he feels entitled to get what he wants. Bartholomew points out, "You rule all the land. And you rule all the people. But even kings can't rule the *sky*" (Oobleck). Derwin swears to be the first king to make something new come down.

Several days later, King Derwin realizes he could order his magicians to make the sky do something new. Bartholomew counsels that Derwin may regret this, but the king summons the magicians nevertheless. The magicians tell Derwin that they can make oobleck. They don't actually know what it will look like because they've never made it before. Bartholomew points out that this is not likely to end well and he implores the king not to do it, but Derwin orders it anyway. Sure enough, the oobleck starts falling the next day, and it's a disaster: oobleck sticks like glue to everything and threatens to destroy the kingdom.

No one can stop the oobleck, and Bartholomew eventually loses his temper and tells the king, "This is all *your* fault! Now the least you can do is say the simple words, 'I'm sorry.'" Derwin had previously been ready to execute Bartholomew for not removing his hat, and he takes this scolding the same way: "ME . . . *ME* say I'm sorry! Kings *never* say 'I'm sorry!' And I am the mightiest king in all the world!" Bartholomew replies, "You may be a mighty king, but you're sitting in oobleck up to your chin. And so is everyone else in your land. And if you won't even say you're sorry, *you're no sort of king at all!*" (Oobleck). Bartholomew here is representing the idea that the justification for the monarch's authority is benevolence: the king's "job" is to take care of his realm. The monarch exists to serve the realm. In the view of Thomas Hobbes (1588–1679), the monarch fulfills this duty by maintaining social order, a guarantor of security.[6] This is a much more minimalist standard of justification for authority than, say, that of Locke, but Derwin is failing to meet even this minimal standard. His stubbornness and vanity are about to destroy the kingdom.

Fortunately, Derwin realizes that Bartholomew was right, and he starts to cry and says that he is indeed sorry—"awfully, *awfully* sorry!" (Oobleck). And sure enough, the oobleck stops falling and melts away. Like the magic of the hats, the magic of the oobleck seems to have as its object the betterment of the monarchy. King Derwin has learned to be content with the sky being the way it is and also to accept responsibility for his actions, possibly realizing something about what it means to be a good king. One suspects he will be less stubborn and vain and listen to Bartholomew more. This is a different sort of problem with monarchy: Mack the turtle's objection was that tyrannical rulers like Yertle ignore the rights of the individual. Derwin is an illustration of a different problem: even if you're not trying to be a tyrant, being king doesn't mean you have the wisdom to rule justly. If you have a wise and just monarch, the realm may be ruled wisely and justly, but if you have a stubborn, vain, and impetuous monarch, you get oobleck.

AT THE BOTTOM WE, TOO, SHOULD HAVE RIGHTS

Monarchies, then, might be a less desirable form of government. In both Athens and Rome, monarchies were replaced with democratic institutions, and in the seventeenth and eighteenth centuries, democratic reforms took hold in both Europe and North America. The Lockean narrative of the equality of persons, and its instantiation in America, seems to imply that everyone should have an equal say. No one person should have that kind of power over others. Power, again, requires the consent of the governed.

Unfortunately though, it turns out that democratic institutions are not effective guarantees against the problems of monarchy. Just as the monarch may act wrongly or stupidly, as in Derwin's case, a democratic majority can act wrongly or stupidly as well. And just as a king can be a tyrant who ignores the rights of the individual, as in Yertle's case, so, too, can a democratic majority ignore the rights of the individual. We see both outcomes in the case of Thidwick the moose. Thidwick allows several smaller creatures to sit on his antlers, who in turn bring in more creatures, and eventually they claim the right to tell Thidwick what to do since there are more of them and they have outvoted him.[7] This arrangement manages to ignore Thidwick's rights as an individual, as it will lead to him starving to death, *and* is stupid, as it leads to hunters getting all of the other creatures.

The trick, it seems, is to come up with institutions that facilitate social living, safeguard individual liberty, and promote peace and prosperity. Kings cannot be trusted, but democratic majorities can't, either. A robust conception of rights might work better. When a society has a political/legal order that recognizes and protects individuals' rights, then state power is checked, whether democratic or monarchical. A familiar example would be the Bill of Rights added on to the US Constitution, which specifies spheres of individual autonomy, such as freedom of speech or religion, which the government—even by majority rule—cannot override. Morally speaking, we can understand rights as rationally justifiable claims. If these are written into the political/legal order, then they serve as protections against unjustifiable power. A king commanding everyone to have the same religion is no different from a majority vote that everyone have the same religion, an infringement on personal autonomy. But the fact that one could make a moral argument against such a command doesn't actually protect us. It has to be embedded in the social order somehow, typically by being codified into the structure of the legal system such that they block other commands. In Didd, there are rules built in that apparently even the king cannot override (for example, no chopping off heads unless the hat is removed). Even though King Derwin has ordered Bartholomew's execution, the executioner says he cannot comply—and Derwin accepts this. In the United States, a ban on newspapers would be met with a legal (not just moral) challenge to the authority of the legislature. In principle, rights serve as protections of individuals against unjustified uses of state power and limitations on the state. This presupposes that the rights aren't contingent on state power in the first place, of course. The Lockean approach is to suggest that our basic moral equality as persons is conceptually prior to any institutions of government, so governments (either democratic or monarchical) cannot legitimately violate that equality.

While the problems of state power, authority, and rights have vexed philosophers for generations, some of Dr. Seuss's examples point in a helpful direction. As Mack the turtle noted, all turtles are morally equal, so the ones at the bottom have rights too. If we understand rights as rationally justifiable claims, then surely King Yertle has no legitimate claim to demand that Mack and the others suffer the weight of the turtle stack just because he says so. The inhabitants of Didd may have laws requiring hats off before the king, but they also have certain procedural safeguards and stable property rights. It would probably be even better if their king didn't have unilateral power to declare executions or use sorcery to change the weather—the former to protect individual rights and the latter to limit the danger to the public of poor decision making. So steps in the right direction seem to include limits on state power (whether monarchical or democratic) and protections of individual rights predicated on the moral equality of persons. It's true that a king who won't say he's sorry is no king at all, but it is even better to limit the range of things they might be sorry about.

15

THE FAILURES OF KINGS DERWIN AND YERTLE

Authority, Law, and Civil Disobedience
from Didd to Sala-ma-Sond

Jacob M. Held

Boy, don't you dare tell me what I can or cannot have! Remember . . .
I am King!

—King Derwin of Didd

True law is right reason in agreement with nature.

—Marcus Tullius Cicero

Throughout his career, Dr. Seuss dealt with tyrants. Most famous is Yertle the turtle king. But before Yertle, there was King Derwin of the kingdom of Didd. King Derwin isn't as memorable as Yertle. Perhaps because he is human, perhaps because the stories about him don't rhyme, or perhaps stacking turtles is just more entertaining and memorable than oobleck or threatening to behead a young boy for refusing to remove his hat. Regardless, Seuss often dealt with failed kings—that is, tyrants. And considering tyrants, like Derwin and Yertle, can shed light on issues such as the nature and role of law, power and authority, and civil disobedience.

Whenever Seuss deals with kings, whether they be human or chelonian, he inevitably deals with abuses of power, with tyrannical kings imposing their wills, cruelly or thoughtlessly, on their citizens. For example, King Derwin in *The 500 Hats of Bartholomew Cubbins* goes so far as to condone Bartholomew's beheading merely for his failure, through extraordinary circumstances, to remove his hat. Clearly, pursuing the death of one's subject for a simple breach of etiquette is harsh. We see King Derwin again, as well as Bartholomew, in *Bartholomew and the Oobleck*. In this tale, King Derwin, bored with the weather, charges his magicians with making something "new" fall from the sky. They create oobleck. King Derwin's shortsightedness and his stubborn, self-interest almost leads to the devastation of his entire kingdom. King Derwin wields great amounts of power, perhaps too much, and he too often, from what we're told, wields his power thoughtlessly or even cruelly. And then there is Yertle the turtle king. Yertle causes great suffering among his subjects, demanding that they stack themselves merely so he can satisfy his desire for conquest. It's only through a simple act of civil disobedience that Mack spares his comrades and puts Yertle in his proper place.

What these instances of kingly excess demonstrate is that great power lies in the hands of those who administer our governments, but also that there are and must be limits to that power. There are limits to what ought to be decreed, limits to authority, and there are limits to what can be expected of the citizenry. These kings thus serve as helpful guides in understanding some fundamental issues surrounding the idea of the law and the rule of law.

MAYBE I'M ONE KING WHO CAN! (AUTHORITY)

Let's begin by talking about authority. Now obviously King Derwin is the authority in the kingdom of Didd; he's the king. When Derwin gives an order it is law, it is to be followed, and if it is not, there are consequences. So if the king says to remove your hat, you had better remove your hat, and the next one, and the next one, and so forth: "Hats off to the king!" (Hats). And if you don't or can't, then it's off to the executioner with you. But is this all we mean when we say somebody has authority—that they can behead you if you fail to obey? Is authority simply a threat backed by force? No. That's not what we mean by authority. When we speak of authority, more often than not what we mean is *legitimate* authority; that is, it is a person or institution in charge that *ought* to be in charge. So a decree from this authority is reason enough to do whatsoever is decreed merely because it was so decreed by the authority. Legitimate authority is different from simple power. "To have power is to have influence, to be able to influence people's actions and their fortunes. A person has effective authority if he is powerful, if he can influence people. . . . Legitimate authority can be defined as justified effective authority."[1]

Consider King Derwin and Bartholomew. King Derwin is powerful; he can affect Bartholomew's future, his fortune. When Bartholomew is unable to remove his hat—or rather, whenever his removed hat is immediately replaced by another—the "impudent trickster" is put entirely under the king's power. He is brought to the throne room. He subsequently has arrows shot at him, is nearly beheaded, and is almost pushed off the castle tower by the Grand Duke Wilfred. King Derwin exercises power over Bartholomew. He has effective authority. But is he justified? That is, should we do as he says merely because he says so? Do we have a *good reason* to obey King Derwin? Given his record, his propensity to rage, his short-sighted and ill-fated plans motivated by pure self-interest or even boredom, probably not. The people of Didd would do well to have some checks and balances in place. They can't always rely on luck or a particularly vocal pageboy. And this is how we ought to think of authority.

To paraphrase Joseph Raz, quoted above, one has justified authority if his decreeing that one ought to perform some action has normative force; that is, it is a reason for us to do that very thing.[2] This appeal to reason indicates something important about how we, as humans (or rational chelonians in the case of Sala-ma-Sond), view authority and practical activity generally. We are motivated by reasons. As rational creatures we want an explanation for why we do what we do, or why you want us to do what you decree we ought to do. Force alone may compel, but it is far from compelling in a normative sense. Sure King Derwin can behead Bartholomew, but that fails to address him as a rational being, so it fails to convince Bartholomew to do as he is told. And Bartholomew knows he's done nothing wrong; that's why he's so calm as Derwin rages. "Still . . . the King can do nothing dreadful to punish me, because I really haven't done anything wrong" (Hats). Bartholomew is right in a sense. The king can't *justly* punish him, but he can still have his head removed from his body, justified or not. Derwin is powerful, but he is not authoritative, or at least he is not a justified effective authority. Insofar as we are guided by reason and motivated by reasons, authority must rest to some extent on its ability to appeal to our reason, to be a reason for us to do what it demands we ought to do. What is needful is a legitimate authority, one that is in charge and so effective, but also justified such that its command for us to do something is a reason for us to do that thing.

MAGIC IN THOSE SIMPLE WORDS (THE ROLE OF LAW)

An important point to note, however, is that authority is necessary. We may disagree with or dislike King Derwin, and Yertle is downright despicable; yet somebody has to be in charge, has to be the authoritative voice when it comes to law. Law is a fundamental social institution necessary for regulating social life.[3] The law, or the king's decree, instills order. "A legal system is a coercive order of public rules addressed to rational persons for the purpose of regulating their conduct and providing the framework for social cooperation."[4] The law provides the necessary, basic structure of our social life, but not everybody will always conform to the law, and the stability of the system needs to be maintained in the face of occasional breaches. "For this reason alone, a coercive sovereign is presumably always necessary, even though in a well-ordered society sanctions are not severe and may never need to be imposed."[5] Some authoritative figure or body is necessary in order to administer the legal system.

Now we don't know how King Derwin ascended to the throne, how he became the one in charge of running Didd. Was he elected? Did the religious authorities or his magicians proclaim him king as God's representative on earth? Did he slaughter his rivals and lay waste to their lands? Did he club King Bertram of Binn to death with his own stilts in trial by combat? It really doesn't matter too much. As John Finnis notes, "The tendency of political thinkers to utter legalistic fictions about the original location of authority has its . . . occasion. . . . It remains true that the sheer fact that virtually everyone *will* acquiesce in somebody's say-so is the presumptively necessary and defeasibly sufficient condition for the normative judgment that that person has . . . authority in that community."[6] Political philosophers may speak of social contracts, original positions, ratifications, or any other genesis event whereby an authority is first acknowledged. But such stories or histories are ultimately irrelevant. What is relevant is that at some point the authority has been and still currently is accepted as the authority, and tradition and time has solidified this practice.

Consider a constitution. It can't give itself legitimacy. A constitution can't prove itself constitutional. Yet all our legal systems in constitutional forms of government rely on the constitution's legitimacy, its authority. What grants a constitution its privileged place, its authority, is that a bunch of people, the "right" people, said it would be authoritative in some symbolic act, and we still accept that and act accordingly, as if it has authority, and so it in fact has it. Well, what gave those people the right to make such a declaration; when did they become authoritative? Why should we care? We can digress infinitely. But the fact is that the constitution is accepted as the authority, and so it is. Thus, the people of Didd have King Derwin. He is king. The fiction surrounding his kingly status notwithstanding, he is authoritative for the kingdom of Didd. But with this status comes responsibility. After all, people will only accept your authority for so long if you fail to do what, as an authority, you're supposed to do.

We noted above that authority is necessary to coordinate social activities and order social life. Without a stopping point, without a place where the buck stops, there would be no decisive action, clear and intentional policies, or the ability to coordinate the complex operations that constitute a community. So there needs to be an authority. But as an authority, whose purpose is coordination, there are certain criteria that need to be met if one is to be legitimately authoritative—that is, justified in adopting the position of head coordinator, head honcho, or king. Finnis continues, "The authority of rulers derives from their opportunity to foster the common good."[7] We seek authority to assist in coordinating our social endeavors, but our social endeavors are oriented toward a singular goal: the good of the community of which we are a part. We seek authority, we justify it, as necessary to organize our collective projects toward the good of all. King Derwin seems to be a decent king in this regard. His people seem to be doing just fine—that is, until a young boy wearing a hat at an inopportune time upsets his little ego, or his boredom leads him to put his own entertainment ahead of the welfare of his subjects. In such cases, even though he wields power and may be the "mightiest man that ever lived!" Bartholomew is right when he says King Derwin is in fact "*no sort of a king at all!*" (Oobleck). Legitimate authority must be oriented toward the common good if it is to remain legitimate. With the common good as the goal, and social coordination as the means to achieve that end, authority must be exercised in a particular way. There must be a rule of law.

ANYTHING YOU SAY, SIRE (THE RULE OF LAW)

People often speak about the "rule of law," or the notion that we, as Americans, are a nation of laws, not of men. But very few actually contemplate what the rule of law is, what it means, and why it's valuable— that is, until your leader calls down oobleck, tries to behead a young boy for a minor breach in etiquette, or insists on stacking you and your fellow citizens 5,607 high in order to be higher than the moon. When these things happen we say, "There ought to be a law." Or "He can't do this!" Or "I have rights!" All such declarations are implicit references to the rule of law. We've seen above that kings, and law, need to be justified, and part of law being justified is that law must take the right form. Laws need to tell us the right way to do the proper thing. "The great aim of the movement against arbitrary power was, from the beginning, the establishment of the rule of law."[8]

The point of law is to guide behavior. "Therefore, if the law is to be obeyed *it must be capable of guiding the behavior of its subjects*. It must be such that they can find out what it is and act on it."[9] And when it comes to acting on it, our actions should promote our good and the common good. We don't simply want rules to follow, but rules that make sense in terms of coordinating our social lives both to our benefit and the benefit of the community. Thus, the point of a rule of law is also "to secure to the subjects of authority the dignity of self-direction and freedom from certain forms of manipulation. The Rule of Law is thus among the requirements of justice."[10] The rule of law thus binds governmental administration, even kings, in a way that allows those under the authority of the law to predict the uses of coercive power, plan their lives accordingly, and thus direct the courses of their lives as they see fit. "The rule of law entails, in other words, an unequal struggle between officialdom and the rest of us. It places burdens on the law and on its officials that it does not place on ordinary folk."[11] The rule of law binds kings (officials) so that we may live as dignified, autonomous adults. King Derwin is simply mistaken when he scolds Bartholomew, saying, "Boy, don't you dare tell me what I can or cannot have! Remember, Bartholomew, I am King!"

(Oobleck). He is king. He has great effective authority. But, as we'll see, the very nature of law sets limits to what he can legitimately have. The rule of law is thus a necessary feature of any legal system if we desire to respect people as self-directing, mature beings worthy of leading their own lives: "Legality 'maximizes individual freedom within the coercive framework of law.'"[12]

If the goal of the rule of law is to maximize self-direction (or liberty, for lack of a better term), then we should spend some time considering the structure of law. How does law need to be formulated in order to maintain order while respecting those subject to it as self-directed beings? John Finnis states:

> A legal system exemplifies the Rule of Law to the extent . . . that (i) its rules are prospective, not retroactive, and (ii) are not in any other way impossible to comply with; that (iii) its rules are promulgated, (iv) clear, and (v) coherent one with another; that (vi) its rules are sufficiently stable to allow people to be guided by their knowledge of the content of the rules; that (vii) the making of decrees and orders . . . is guided by rules that are promulgated, clear, stable, and relatively general; and that (viii) those who have authority to make, administer and apply the rules . . . are accountable . . . and . . . do actually administer the law consistently.[13]

His definition is consistent with most articulations of the rule of law. And we can see why these requirements would apply to the necessary structure of any legal system if a legal system is about guiding the behavior of rational human beings. The law, as rules for guiding behavior, needs to be able to be followed by those to whom it applies; thus laws can't be secret or convoluted. Laws must be public and easily understandable by the people to whom they apply. And they have to be stable, in place, and constant so as rational beings we can plan our lives according to them, expecting them to remain the same so as to provide a modicum of guidance and predictability.

Lon Fuller offers an allegory to demonstrate the problem with failures in the law; he offers the allegory of Rex, a king who believes he can do better than the current legal system under which he operates. Rex is King Derwin, with even worse judgment. Believing he can do better and fix the problems within the legal system, Rex dismantles it and tries to rebuild it from scratch.[14] Fuller thus describes the ways in which a legal system can fail insofar as it fails to align with the rule of law. He outlines his "eight routes to disaster."

> The first and most obvious lies in the failure to achieve rules at all, so that every issue is dealt with on an ad hoc basis. The other routes are: (2) a failure to publicize . . . (3) the abuse of retroactive legislation . . . (4) a failure to make rules understandable; (5) the enactment of contradictory rules or (6) rules that require conduct beyond the powers of the affected power; (7) introducing such frequent changes in the rules that the subject cannot orient his action to them . . . (8) a failure of congruence between the rules as announced and their actual administration. [15]

When law fails in these ways, the individual is unable to guide his behavior according to the law. As a consequence, the subject, the person, is open to arbitrary or excessive coercive activities of the state, his liberty is significantly impacted or curtailed, and thus the good of the populace as rational agents fails to be promoted. The law thus fails in its purpose. In many ways Dr. Seuss's kings emulate these failures.

Consider, again, King Derwin in *The 500 Hats of Bartholomew Cubbins*. The rule that one remove one's hat when the king passes by is not in any way problematic in itself. It seems perfectly reasonable. A simple show of respect for the office of the crown, and easy enough, under normal circumstances, to obey. Clearly, it is also a well-known rule. Everybody knows the expectation, and everybody obeys. But then there's Bartholomew. He tries to remove his hat. He knows the rule. But he can't. He tries and tries, and he fails (or succeeds each time depending on your perspective). Yet Derwin, still seeing a hat on Bartholomew's head, sees this as a failure to abide by the rule and is incensed. Cubbins will remove his hat! But in this case, given the unique circumstances, Derwin is requiring the impossible. Bartholomew can't remove his hat; yet he is ordered to under threat of beheading. Here we have a problem. A rule is imposed that cannot be followed. How can it guide Bartholomew's behavior? He *can't* obey it. Given the circumstances, the rule must cease to bind poor Bartholomew; it must be altered to accommodate the new circumstances, for to hold young Cubbins to the order is to demand of him the impossible and thus to force upon him obedience to an ill-formed law. Yet Derwin persists.

In dealing with Bartholomew's "disobedience" to the law, King Derwin has become the worst kind of tyrant—a capricious, brutal bully. In the end, Bartholomew is saved only by luck. After removing 499 hats under duress, the five hundredth hat comes off, and he sells it to the king for a pretty profit. So no harm, no foul. Right? Well, we did see something about King Derwin—he is a petty dictator, a small man wielding great power. The only constraint on his power would be the rule of law. And in fact we see a bit of this in Bartholomew's interactions with the executioner. When he is sent down to be beheaded, the executioner informs him, "First you've got to take off your hat . . . it's one of the rules." When he realizes that Bartholomew is always wearing a hat even if his current one is removed, he declares, "Fiddlesticks! . . . I can't execute you at all." Bartholomew informs the king that "my head can't come off with my hat on. . . . It's against the rules." To which the king responds, "So it can't" (Hats). Oddly enough, King Derwin does seem to recognize that the rule of law is necessary and that even he can't go against extant laws or rules. His power does have some limits. And this highlights an important point: "*If* one is going to have a legal system, it had better be a rule-of-law legal system."[16] Yet, additionally, "The rule of law . . . requires that all laws conform to certain principles."[17] We don't just need rules; we need rules that conform to certain principles. So what might those principles be?

KINGS CAN'T RULE THE SKY (NATURAL LAW)

Before we begin, it's necessary to discuss legal positivism. Some legal scholars, positivists, maintain that the law is merely a social technique; it's about ordered living, and so it is neutral in terms of content. What makes a law a valid law, or a law in a legal system, is simply whether it was generated in the proper way—its source, not its moral content or merit.[18] In evaluating a law to determine whether it is valid, positivists merely ask about how a law was written, instantiated, and enforced, not its content. And to their credit, a law formed in the proper way will be a law in the sense of a command or an order backed by sanctions. But that's kind of an uninteresting point to make. When we ask about valid law, we are asking about meritorious law, laws that ought to be laws, laws that are justified in being laws as holding authority over us and guiding our conduct. As Cicero notes, "The most stupid thing of all, moreover, is to consider all things just which have been ratified by a people's institutions of laws. What about the laws of tyrants?" He continues, "If justice were determined by popular vote or by the decrees of princes or the decisions of judges, then it would be just to commit highway robbery . . . if such things were approved by popular vote." His conclusion: "We can divide good laws from bad by no other standard than nature."[19] We ask about law because we want to evaluate it. Thus, positivists don't ask questions pertinent to our topic. So, we'll consider the natural law tradition.[20]

We can begin simply enough: law is a rule or measure that guides our action, necessary for coordinated social activity. And the first principle of our action is to promote our good and avoid that which is harmful. As Saint Thomas Aquinas (1225–1274) put it, "The first principle in practical matters . . . is the last end, and the last end of human life is bliss or happiness. . . . Consequently, the law must needs regard principally the relationship to happiness."[21] Happiness here indicates our greatest good, not simple joy or contentment. Rather, it is about what is good for us, as the kind of thing that we are. In addition, given that we are one among many, this good is defined in terms of our social nature, with reference to community and respecting the same good for all. So if we want to know what the law ought to say, we need to consider what is good for human beings as human beings, and then how to best realize this in community.

Finnis opens his discussion of natural law by considering basic values, basic goods common to all humans and universal in application. He takes these values to be self-evident, objective, and foundational. They are self-evident insofar as they do not need demonstration but are obviously valid; ideas such as "knowledge is a good." In addition, they are objective insofar as the denial of them is straightforwardly unreasonable, and they are foundational in that any discussion presupposes them. As he notes, "In every field there is and must be, at some point or points, an end of derivation and inference."[22] One cannot question *ad infinitum*. At some point one must stop at foundational truths, as Aristotle noted with logic and the principle of noncontradiction. Some things need to be accepted before further discussion is possible. Finnis continues, "I am contending only (i) that if one attends carefully and honestly to the relevant human possibilities one can understand, without reasoning from any other judgment, that the realization of those possibilities is, as such, good and desirable for the human person; and (ii) that one's understanding needs no further justification."[23]

Perhaps this is a leap of faith necessary for law to function as law. We need to believe in the law for the law to be authoritative and effective, but this leap of faith only makes sense if the law is worth having faith in. A law that appeals to us as humans, that speaks to our good, is a law worth believing in. When the law speaks to us, when the law appeals to the best in us, then it is worth supporting, even if the support we give the law is the only thing supporting the law itself. The law will only exist as an effective authority so long as we act as though it is a justified legitimate authority, and to do so it needs to be worthy of our support.[24] Faith in the law puts it in a position to be the rule, to be law, but its content determines whether it is worthy of such belief and support. If King Derwin routinely acted as we see him in his dealings with Bartholomew or the oobleck, at some point support for him would erode among the people of Didd. If that lack of support reached a critical mass and turned into outright resistance, he'd cease to be king from the point of view of legitimacy. He'd be left only with force to maintain his rule, and, historically, that leads to tenuous rule at best. So what are these goods, these possibilities that are self-evident, or foundational, or undeniably good? What are these basic values that should orient and define the law?

First, there is a common good for humanity, an objective "better than," self-evident through human experience. There is a common good "inasmuch as life, knowledge, play, aesthetic experience, friendship, religion [or metaphysical orientation/meaning], and freedom in practical reasonableness are good for any and every person." In addition, "There is a common good of the political community, and it is definite enough to exclude a considerable number of types of political arrangements, laws, etc."[25] Once we know what is good for humans, while recognizing that humans are necessarily social creatures—having to achieve their ends within community whether in collaboration with or in spite of other humans—certain laws and political systems will be ruled out of hand. This is the basis of natural law. "The principle concern of a theory of natural law is to explore the requirements of practical reasonableness in relation to the good of human beings who, because they live in community with one another, are confronted by problems of justice and rights, of authority, law, and obligation."[26] What specific principles a society should adopt and how it will pursue the common good in a way consistent with each person's human good is variable. It will depend on resources, traditions, and myriad other contingent stipulations, but the overriding guiding criterion is the objective human good for each and all within a community.

King Derwin's major failing in *Bartholomew and the Oobleck* is his failure to respect nature. He is tired of the four things that fall from the sky and wants something new. He goes against the natural order, the nature of things, to impose his will via his magicians and call down oobleck. But Bartholomew is right: "Kings can't rule the sky" (Oobleck). And when he tries, when he goes against the natural order, he disrupts it and causes great pain and suffering. The only way to stop the oobleck is through words, not magic words, but "plain, *simple* words." As Bartholomew tells the king, "This is all *your* fault! Now, the least you can do is say the simple words, 'I'm sorry.'" And he closes, "And if you won't even say you're sorry, *you're no sort of a king at all!*" (Oobleck). King Derwin relents and says "sorry." The oobleck subsides, and we are told that King Derwin created a holiday in honor of the "four perfect things that come down from the sky" (Oobleck). King Derwin tried to make law by ignoring the nature of the world around him. He thus went against the grain and caused great suffering. The only solution was for him to say the right words, to undo his foolish decree, to realign himself with nature, with the four perfect things that fall from the sky, and thus bring his decrees in line with the nature of the world around him. He learned that true law, proper law, is reasonable and in accord with nature, as noted by Cicero in one of the quotes that opens this chapter.

Fuller notes, "These natural laws have nothing to do with any 'brooding omnipresence in the skies' . . . They remain entirely terrestrial in origin . . . like the natural laws of carpentry."[27] Natural law isn't about God's law. It's about the structure of reality. What is good for people is good for people because of the kind of thing people are. "To embark on the enterprise of subjecting human conduct to the governance of rules involves of necessity commitment to the view that man is, or can become, a responsible agent, capable of understanding and following rules, and answerable for his defaults."[28] Human beings are amenable to, and in fact guided by, practical reasonableness, seeking their good. We commit to values, to an ideal of humankind. We aspire to greatness, or at least to betterment, and this ideal gives us purpose, a reason to act. But "to live the good life requires something more than good intentions, even if they are generally shared; it requires the support of a firm base line for human interaction, something that—in modern society at least—only a sound legal system can supply."[29] Thus, a few simple demands are clear—for example, the demands of duty (that we give one what they are owed[30]) and equality (that all be treated with equal concern). We commit to these values as necessary and foundational; we use them as the first check against the content of laws to evaluate them as fitting or flawed. Thus, we ask whether law is befitting our shared humanity. In assessing political arrangements and rulers, "the ultimate basis of rulers' authority is the fact that they have the opportunity, and thus the responsibility, of furthering the common good by stipulating solutions to a community's coordination problems."[31] In so doing, often we find the law or our leaders lacking, as we saw with Bartholomew's assessment of Derwin as being *"no sort of a king at all!"* But what if Bartholomew isn't there to save us or to speak truth to power? What if those in positions of authority are deaf to our cries?

PLAIN LITTLE LADS GET A LITTLE BIT MAD (CIVIL DISOBEDIENCE)

If the goal of law is to promote the common good, what happens when law goes amiss? Natural law theory is known for the misattributed quote, "An unjust law is no law." This claim seems to indicate that an unjust, or otherwise deficient, law is not proper law. And this claim is misleading, for if it means that an unjust law is not law insofar as it is not enforceable, then it is clearly wrong.[32] History bears witness to the use and abuse of unjust laws. What is truly meant by the natural law tradition's denial of status to an unjust law is that an unjust law is seriously defective. Finnis notes how Aquinas, quoting Augustine, states, "Unjust laws . . . are 'more outrages than laws,' 'not law but a corruption of law' . . . More precisely, he says that such a law is 'not a law simpliciter [i.e., straightforwardly or, in the focal sense], but rather a sort of perversion of law.'"[33] And insofar as law gains its legitimate authority from promoting the common good, such defective laws lose their authority, and in this sense, although they may be enforceable, they fail to be laudable or to compel or deserve a subject's loyalty or obedience.

If a law truly is unjust, then it is immoral; that is, it affronts the objective morality underlying the very intention of law—to promote the common good through the promotion of the individual's good. And it is this good that directs all human action insofar as we are practically minded creatures. Thus, an unjust law may be a decree from an effective authority, but insofar as it contradicts the good, it is an affront to our human nature and the functioning of our community. Hence, it is immoral and not a demand of practical reasonableness. In fact, one could go so far as to say it is irrational. To obey it would be to actively harm oneself in direct contradiction to the purpose of our practical reason, which is to guide us toward the good. Such laws are unworthy of us as human beings; they are perversions of law. Such laws ought not to be followed and cannot rationally or coherently be obeyed or respected.

So what might such an unjust law look like? There are some basic guidelines given the purpose of law, the role of the lawgiver or executive, and the constraints of human nature. Laws may be unjust if they use the full authority of the king or sovereign without aiming at the common good or, in fact, are detrimental to it. Consider Yertle the turtle king.

Yertle is king of all the turtles of Sala-ma-Sond. And his authority seems to be clearly recognized and respected. After all, when he calls, the turtles come. They stack themselves at his behest and remain as his throne. In fact, it takes quite a bit before anyone (in this case Mack) questions that authority. So Yertle has great effective authority. He calls nine turtles, stacks them and sits. They remain. It's not until noon that Mack sighs and wonders, "How long must we stand here, Your Majesty, please?" (Yertle). Mack is rebuffed, and he remains. Then Yertle stacks more: "'bout two hundred!" Again Mack utters his discontent, a bit more forcefully this time: "We turtles can't stand it. Our shells will all crack!" (Yertle). But he stays when he is again scolded for his impudence. As the stack grows toward the moon, it's too much, and Mack resists. He burps. "And his burp shook the throne of the king!" And Yertle "fell off his high Throne and fell *Plunk!* In the pond!" (Yertle). Left to be merely king of the mud.

Yertle's rule is marked by injustice. His laws, his rule, is not aimed at the common good of the turtles. He is not stacking them for their benefit. He is not considering their good at all. In fact, he ignores their plight. Every time Mack raises a legitimate grievance about cracked shells or starving, his claim is rejected out of hand. Yertle cares nothing for his subjects.

In addition, laws may be unjust if they fail to meet the minimum criteria of the rule of law, as outlined above. Here, as noted above, we see

King Derwin as he enforces his rule about doffing one's hat in the presence of the king. That law, in the case of Bartholomew, fails to meet the minimal criteria of the rule of law insofar as it is unfollowable. To punish him for failing to do what it is not in his power to do is to unjustly punish him, to abuse one's position of authority.

Finally, laws may be unjust if they place undue burdens on the citizens or subjects of the law. If the role of law is to promote the common good, then imposing undue burdens, burdens out of proportion in terms of the cost they require to the benefit they bestow, are poorly formed laws.[34] Here we see Yertle again. His command that the turtles stack themselves at the expense of great pain and potentially cracked shells places a ridiculous burden on his subjects, and for no reasonable benefit other than to placate his gigantic ego. Yet kings are to promote the common good. "His power . . . is limited, in that in relation to the free men subject to him . . . he can do only such things as promote the common utility . . . the emperor possesses no power that is perilous to the common good."[35] Or, to bring it back to Yertle, "And the turtles, of course . . . all the turtles are free. As turtles and, maybe, all creatures should be" (Yertle). Yertle forgets (or, rather, never acknowledges) this fact. Although he does have power in the sense that he can resort to force, he lacks power if by power we mean legitimate, or moral, authority.

If an unjust law is a perversion of law, if it fails in a significant and specific way, then it follows that it would also fail to compel us to obey it.

> Rulers have, very strictly speaking, no right to be obeyed . . . but they have the authority to give directions and make laws that are morally obligatory and that they have the responsibility of enforcing. They have this authority for the sake of the common good. . . . Therefore, if they use their authority to make stipulations against the common good, or against any of the basic principles of practical reasonableness [i.e., Equality], any such stipulation . . . lacks the authority it would otherwise have *by virtue of being theirs*.[36]

Hence we get back to the misattributed "an unjust law is no law" claim. Or, as Bartholomew might say, a ruler that can't look out for the common good, or a foolish king, is "no sort of a king at all!" In such instances it might be incumbent on the subjects of these unjust laws to resist them, to refuse to obey. Thus, subjects may find it necessary to engage in acts of civil disobedience.

John Rawls (1921–2002), offering a standard account of civil disobedience, notes that such acts are probably morally justified if certain conditions are met. If one is in the presence of injustice, one may rebel, or
civilly disobey, if (1) all other appeals have been made in a good-faith
effort to otherwise reform the unjust practice. Disobedience should be a
last resort. (2) These actions should be limited to clear and substantial
violations of justice. You don't systematically disobey the law and thus
contest its authority merely because you don't like the speed limit or
because a singular instance of an injustice has occurred. It must be significant and pervasive, a real civil rights issue, like systematic chelonian
abuse. (3) You have to be willing to affirm others' rights to do likewise
when they see grave injustice. And, finally, (4) you need to consider
tactics and the pragmatic possibility that your actions will be effective.[37]
Law breaking with no chance of success is mere anarchy, and that does
not promote justice.

Mack from *Yertle the Turtle* is a perfect illustration of this idea. Mack
believes a grave injustice is being done to him and his fellow denizens of
Sala-ma-Sond. In the face of grave pain and maltreatment he appeals to
the king, Yertle. He asks for consideration and presents the case of the
turtles in the stack, but he is rebuffed. There is severe and pervasive
injustice being done, and it is being ignored. Yertle is in clear violation of
basic principles of justice, and gravely so. His unjust reign affects all
turtles in drastically harmful ways. There's no bias here: Mack is concerned with the general welfare of his fellow citizens, and he would offer
all of them the same right to resist if they were in his place on the bottom.
In fact, he's protesting for their own good. And his tactic, a well-placed
burp, will surely shake the throne, which can't be that stable. Turtles
aren't built for stacking. An effective act of civil disobedience, such as a
well-placed burp, strong and sure enough to shake the throne of the king
and expel him, is justified, and needful. Such an act would promote and
restore the common good and is thus morally justified. In such cases one
is right to get a little bit mad, and one must do what morality demands.

Law is necessary. It provides order and security for our collective
social life. It is also necessary that somebody have authority to interpret
and implement the law as a guide for our individual and collective endeavors. But when the law is flawed, when rulers act unjustly, then it is
up to all of us to be a check on power. We need to be diligent and make

sure that our laws speak to the best of us, all of us, or else we might find ourselves in oobleck up to our ears.

16

THE SNEETCHES, THE ZAX, AND TOO MANY DAVES

Seuss's Inclusive Answer to Diversity and Difference

Timothy M. Dale and Joseph J. Foy

> In complex, highly differentiated societies like our own, all persons have multiple group identifications.
>
> —Iris Marion Young

> And no kind of Sneetch is the best on the beaches.
>
> —Dr. Seuss, *The Sneetches*

Dr. Seuss is clearly concerned about the problem of diversity. Saying that diversity is a problem is not to say that diversity is bad, or that diversity is something that we should not want. But it is a problem. Diversity is a problem in a practical sense because differences between people sometimes make it difficult for them to relate to each other. Diversity is a problem in a philosophical sense because the essence of community is that which is in *common*, and the reality of differences challenges the idea that we belong to the same group of people. Diversity presents questions, then, for both politics and political philosophy: whether it is possible to live in a society with differences, and whether these differences are good things. In his stories, Dr. Seuss suggests that the answer is "yes" to both of these questions.

In the short Dr. Seuss story *The Sneetches*, the Sneetches have a diversity problem. Some Sneetches have a star, and others do not. The fact of this difference causes problems, particularly for those without the stars. But then their apparent savior arrives. Sylvester McMonkey McBean has heard that they are unhappy and promises that he can be the Fix-It-Up Chappie. What he promises, however, is to cure the town of diversity. In this story, diversity is the source of conflict, and the reason that some are left out of the privileges of society. To the dismay of Sylvester McMonkey McBean, we learn that the apparent solution of eliminating diversity is not a viable one for the Sneetches. As in many of Seuss's stories, *The Sneetches* demonstrates why diversity can be a challenge, but also why it produces a good society.

In several of his works, Seuss takes a position on diversity and difference that is close to the position taken by political philosopher Iris Marion Young in her writings on diversity in a democratic society. Diversity is not only possible within a community, Young argues, but also necessary for it to be successful. Young is critical of the viewpoint that a democracy requires us to ignore our differences; instead, she argues that our unique identities are central to our understanding of ourselves and our relationships with others.[1] Young's arguments about diversity and difference read alongside Seuss's writings help us understand why it is that diversity is not simply a problem to overcome but also an essential feature of life in a democratic society.

THE SNEETCHES AND THE PROBLEM OF DIFFERENCE

> But McBean was quite wrong. I'm quite happy to say
> That the Sneetches got really quite smart on that day,
> The day they decided that Sneetches are Sneetches
> And no kind of Sneetch is the best on the beaches.
>
> —*The Sneetches*

One of the problems with diversity is that it tends to create a society in which people believe that they might be better than others. As the story of *The Sneetches* begins, we learn that the Sneetches with stars on their bellies would brag that they are the best kind of Sneetches. Not only would the Star-Belly Sneetches brag and talk themselves up as special and superior, but they also tied their differences to discriminatory practices. Star-Belly children would play among themselves, not allowing Plain-Belly children to join their games. The adult Star-Bellies would hold parties and gatherings and lock out Plain-Bellies, and they were especially exclusive when it came to sitting on beaches. The physical difference of the star thus became a salient difference on which to form an in-group/out-group relationship.

Though the Sneetches' star is a seemingly absurd basis for exclusion, we are all too familiar with the type of discrimination that occurs among the Sneetches. Even further, the attempts of the Plain-Belly Sneetches to buy alternatives to change their appearance evokes the image of real-life examples of those who might attempt to appear different to fit in with a dominant group. It is common for members of an oppressed group to internalize oppression by lightening their skin, changing their hair, using lenses to alter their eye color, and engaging in other practices of masking identity. The beauty standards of dominant groups are often the easiest norms of a society to reinforce.

Just as Seuss reminds us that we should not get caught assuming differences are what essentially characterize us, Young argues that no one difference or set of differences *essentially* characterize the self. She further recommends that group differences not be taken for granted or assumed to be indispensable. Because differences are constantly undergoing changes and challenges for the individual and within the group, like we see in Seuss, no assumptions should be made about these differences prior to any interactions. Young writes that "in complex, highly differentiated societies like our own, all persons have multiple group identifications . . . thus individual persons, as constituted partly by their group affinities and relations, cannot be unified, themselves are heterogeneous and not necessarily coherent."[2] There is a wide range of differences among people and between groups, and individuals should not be understood as representing a single characteristic or association. Even further, differences should not be the basis for excluding others because they are unstable and based on other social factors.

In the society of *The Sneetches*, differences among identities are not as complex as those we find in our society, but we see that these differences are just as unstable. Because the belly stars can be removed and put back on, they do not represent a meaningful way to make judgments about who should be included or excluded from the benefits of society. Seuss's analogy shows the absurdity of creating classes of people based on superficial or incoherent differences.

DENYING DIVERSITY WITH "TOO MANY DAVES"

> Did I ever tell you that Mrs. McCave
> Had twenty-three sons and she named them all Dave?
> Well, she did. And that wasn't a smart thing to do.
> You see, when she wants one and calls out, "Yoo-Hoo!
> Come into the house, Dave!" she doesn't get one.
> All twenty-three Daves of hers come on the run!
> This makes things quite difficult at the McCaves'
> As you can imagine, with so many Daves.
>
> —"Too Many Daves"

In his short poem, "Too Many Daves," Dr. Seuss provides an indication of the problem of denying difference among individuals. Poor Mrs. McCave created all sorts of problems for herself and her entire family by eliminating the recognition of difference through naming all twenty-three of her sons "Dave." The simple call of "Yoo-Hoo! Come into the house, Dave!" led to all twenty-three rushing the house at once, and an inability to correct for the problem later in life. The lesson of "Too Many Daves" is the importance of recognizing and appreciating difference as a critical element of individuality and uniqueness. Distinctiveness is as important for Sir Michael Carmichael Zutt as it is for the one named Oliver Boliver Butt.

As Seuss demonstrates in this story, dealing with difference means recognizing that diversity is not merely inconvenient or dispensable, but it is valuable for both individuals and society. Diversity sometimes requires that we treat people differently. Therefore, practices that deny or repress difference must be reconsidered. Mrs. McCave's problems occur due to her misguided attempt at a universal standard for her children. In the pursuit of equality and universal treatment she sacrifices an appreciation of the basic characteristic that distinguishes one person from another, that of a name.

The power and oppression of universalizing standards linked to naming, although humorous in Seuss's example, is one that is often seen among immigrant communities. In attempting to fit into the dominant culture, many immigrants will either alter their names to make them more easily pronounceable or take on nicknames that are assigned to them by dominant groups for their own convenience. In extreme cases, individuals who refuse to adopt or adapt their culturally rooted name find themselves discriminated against in job, loan, or housing applications. Similar to the aforementioned examples of cosmetic efforts to fit into the dominant standards of physical beauty, the denial of heritage that comes from eliminating differences in something as basic as one's own name is symptomatic of buying into, or internalizing, oppressive standards. Internalized oppression takes on many forms, distorting one's perception of oneself and leading to psychological distress ranging from withdrawal and self-loathing to harmful and even deadly behavior such as suicide. Having simplistic notions of equality as being captured in a "melting pot" standard where difference is denied can often lead to a standard of out groups needing to conform to dominant culture, thereby leading to the problems of difference taking on a negative connotation.

Like Seuss, Iris Marion Young argues against seeking a universal or simplistic notion of equality. Rather than seeking a simple universal standpoint, Young instead suggests that equality be "an achievement of democratic communication" that can only come about as difference is allowed to flourish. Not only does a lack of diversity make it difficult to distinguish one from another (not to mention that doing so makes life less interesting), but it also makes it difficult to make judgments about social and political life. Young argues that "objectivity in political judgment [occurs through] accounts and judgments people construct for themselves from a critical, reflective, and persuasive interaction among their diverse experiences and opinions."[3] We need diversity because it is only in conversation with those different from us that we come to make decisions about the kind of world in which we want to live. Seeking a better society means making it possible to interact with others different from ourselves. This does not mean, of course, that treating people differently is always acceptable. As Seuss taught us with the Sneetches, it is possible for differences in society to produce relationships of privilege. How can we avoid some people getting to go to the beach while others do not?

Young's solution is similar to Seuss's: impartiality is about finding an alternative moral standpoint to egoism. The problem is that sometimes the establishment of an impartial ideal produces a misguided attempt at superficial equality. Young explains that "the theory of impartial reason wrongly identifies partiality with selfishness, and constructs its counterfactual universalist abstraction in order to move the subject beyond egoism." Of course, in order to have a moral approach to any situation we must move beyond egoism, but impartiality is not the only way that this can occur. The alternative, as Young describes it, is "another way the subject moves beyond egoism: the encounter with other people. A 'moral point of view' arises not from a lonely self-legislating reason, but from the concrete encounter with others, who demand that their needs, desires, and perspectives be recognized."[4] Sensitivity to others only comes about when we interact with them, even more when we interact with those different from ourselves. For Young, as for Seuss, judgment cannot be concentrated with certainty in any one body or group of people. It also recommends that when made, judgments not become so self-assured that they are beyond reproach.

AVOIDING THE ZAX PROBLEM: AN ALTERNATIVE APPROACH TO POLITICAL COMMUNICATION

> Never budge! That's my rule. Never budge in the least!
> Not an inch to the west! Not an inch to the east!
> I'll stay here, not budging! I can and I will
> If it makes you and me and the whole world stand still!
>
> —"The Zax"

As we have seen, appreciating diversity means a willingness to interact with others who have different opinions, but this is not enough. We could interact with others with whom we disagree, but if we refuse to listen, compromise, or move, we might be in a worse position than when we started. Like the unnamed character in *Green Eggs and Ham* who refused to even hear Sam-I-Am's numerous and varied offers for considering the viridescent dish, when we refuse to engage the perspective or position of others, we may be denying ourselves growth, opportunity, and even a qualitatively better life.

The Seuss short poem "The Zax" presents just such a problem. A North-Going Zax encounters a South-Going Zax, and each refuses to move. Stuck as they are, "foot to foot, face to face," neither is willing to compromise. They argue because neither is willing to move or allow the other to pass. The Zax not only disagree about their directional impasse but also fight over which is more stubborn than the other. The South-Going Zax proclaims:

For I live by a rule
That I learned as a boy back in South-Going School.
Never budge! That's my rule. Never budge in the least!
Not an inch to the west! Not an inch to the east!
I'll stay here, not budging! I can and I will
If it makes you and me and the whole world stand still! (Zax)

The result, of course, is that neither one moves, and a highway is built around the Zax. In this poem, Seuss depicts both the absurdity of a failure to compromise and the degree to which accommodating others is a key element to accomplishing our own goals. We must be willing to talk to others, and we need to be open to learning from them.

The Zax are certainly willing to talk to each other, but only to proclaim how and why they are not willing to budge. The problem here, as both Dr. Seuss and Iris Marion Young would see it, is that being open to discussion with others is not enough if we refuse to be changed by the interaction. The Zax present well-reasoned arguments, but in these arguments we see a fundamental failure in understanding what the purpose of the discussion should be. In most theories of democracy, participation is predicated upon one's ability to communicate through well-constructed arguments and reasons. These arguments must accompany other commitments, however, if we are going to get the most out of our discussions with others. We should move beyond the expectation that we are simply responsible for expressing ourselves, Young argues, so that we are also "acknowledging social differentiations and divisions and encouraging differently situated groups to give voice to their needs, interests, and perspectives on the society in ways that meet conditions of reasonableness and publicity." Young goes on to say that moving past the argument stage of public discussion also "highlights the importance of valuing diverse models of communication in democratic discussion."[5]

Young recommends expanding our view of meaningful communication to include things like greetings, rhetoric, and stories as politically useful forms of communication. Each in its own way can "aid in the making of arguments" and "enable understanding and interaction in ways that argument alone cannot."[6] Accepting these forms of communication as politically legitimate would not only open political discussion to more people but also recognize different kinds of contributions as useful for a deeper understanding of issues. Perhaps the Zax would have fared better had they greeted each other more politely or been willing to share and listen to stories of their Zax pasts.

The simple act of greeting, for example, may not appear on the surface to be a significant act in the scheme of political deliberation. As Young points out, however, there are many who engage in political interaction who feel ignored or unrecognized in the process of deliberation. As a public action to prevent this, in the act of greeting participants explicitly acknowledge each other and therefore increase the likelihood that they will treat each other with respect. This public act of recognition, even if it is only obligatory or symbolic, sets the stage for an ensuing discourse that will most likely foster improved interaction between those who have already been recognized. The way Young describes it, "Recognition is best thought of as a condition rather than a goal of political communication that aims to solve problems justly."[7]

The Zax might also have learned that a more open rhetorical mode would have led to a more productive discussion. Young includes "rhetoric" as a mode of political communication in order to move away from the presupposition that dispassionate linear argumentation is the only way to effectively communicate meaning in political discourse. In her definition, the term *rhetoric* identifies not so much what is said but how it is said. It includes the moral tone of the discourse, the use of figures of speech, and different attitudes through which speech can be communicated. The Zax, for example, begin their interaction with the North-Going Zax saying, "Look here, now! I say! You are blocking my path. You are right in my way" (Zax). The moral tone of this discourse and greeting already sets the stage for the nature of the interaction.

Rhetoric is important because it can bring a tone and terms to political communication that in some cases cannot be brought by mere reasoning. Young also points out that rhetoric can serve an important function in deliberation by motivating the move from reason to judgment. She suggests that "to make judgments with pragmatic consequences, political publics must not only believe and accept claims and arguments, but also care about and commit their will to the outcomes."[8] This commitment of the will often comes about because someone uses the right language and moral tone to cultivate and motivate it. Would the Zax have made different judgments if their rhetoric had been different?

Another important mode of speech, according to Young, is that of storytelling. The method of communication through storytelling is not usually considered to be on the same level as reasoned justification, but it is often the best way to communicate ideas. Narrative, for example, may in some cases be the only response that an excluded group has when no other communicative resources are available. Narrative is also the way that many groups express their collective affinities and desires. In addition, the recollection of a narrative might offer the only way to fully understand the experiences of others. Young states that narrative "not only exhibits experience and values from the point of view of the subjects that have and hold them. It also reveals a total social knowledge from particular points of view."[9] This "total social knowledge" offers precisely the information that can lead to more just outcomes from political deliberations.

Here, Seuss's own work proves the point that Young makes. It is through storytelling that he illustrates moral dilemmas and arguments. It is through the experience of the Zax that we learn that compromise is the best way to deal with disagreement. We also learn that uncompromising attitudes will lead to no one accomplishing their goals. The Zax should have followed Seuss's lead and offered stories of their own. Seuss and Young propose that communication can become truly inclusive only by considering other forms of communication to be acceptable political discourse. Perhaps the Zax would have moved if they had been taught to follow Young's advice.

WHY WE NEED DIVERSITY: WHAT WE LEARN FROM SNEETCHES, ZAX, AND DAVES

> Today you are you!
> That is truer than true
> There is no one alive
> Who is youer than you!
>
> *—Happy Birthday to You!*

Both Dr. Seuss and Iris Marion Young maintain that only through coming to terms with difference, as an unalterable condition of human relationships, will politics be able to more completely pursue social justice. Young argues:

> Aiming to promote social justice through public action requires more than framing the debate in terms that appeal to justice. It requires an objective understanding of the society, a comprehensive account of its relations and structured processes, its material locations and environmental conditions, a detailed knowledge of events and conditions in different places and positions, and the ability to predict the likely consequences of actions and policies. Only a pooling of the situated knowledge of all social positions can produce such social knowledge.[10]

The more diverse the community, the more important it is to be inclusive to get a fuller picture of the social landscape. We recognize with the Sneetches that differences should not mean exclusion. We discover with Mrs. McCave that too many Daves can be a bad thing. We learn from the Zax that we need to expand our idea of proper communication. Combined, in these stories Seuss is telling us that diversity can strengthen our relationships with others if we approach it with the right strategies and mindsets.

The rules of Seuss's and Young's approaches to diversity are quite similar:

1. Social morality can only understand itself in relationship with others.
2. Political judgment must not be self-assured, or concentrated in the hands of a few.
3. Respect for differences must be an ongoing product of social relations.
4. Individual identity is constantly being challenged both from within and from without.

Politically speaking, these rules mean that the boundaries of political discussion themselves must be democratized. We cannot achieve a just society without having interactions with others to negotiate this society. Finally, the transformative nature of political interaction itself needs to be appreciated. If we are situated, constituted, and different from each other, then what can be *learned* from others is just as important as the decisions that are made as a result of our discussions with them.

The consequence of Seuss's and Young's justice framework is that everyone must be able to determine their life for themselves, and to develop the capacity to realize their goals and communicate them with others. Also, just as important is the application of considerations of equality in the *processes* of social decision making as much as in their outcomes. That is, according to the principle of justice, as opposed to domination, inclusion in decision-making processes becomes as important as the equitable outcome of these processes. In stories like *The Lorax* and *Horton Hears a Who!* we find characters who recognize that as people who hold positions of power they have an obligation to advocate for, and empower when possible, those who may find themselves locked out of social discourse or are otherwise marginalized. While the ultimate goal is not to continue to entrench the power dynamic of one person or group offering a voice for others, but rather to empower all to have a legitimized spot at the table, the importance of seeing obligations based on power dynamics is critical for changing democratic processes and structures to move society toward inclusion.

According to this ideal, inclusion becomes a necessary proposition of justice. Conceived this way, democratic institutions should be more concerned with inclusion than with the parameters for predictable or determined outcomes. Just as important, inclusion should not be understood as simple acceptance through ignoring—or worse whitewashing—difference. Unlike the Sneetches, who just saw themselves as all the same in the end, the cultural particularities that are tied to racial, ethnic, gender, sexual, religious, class, and other differences should be recognized and substantively included within the broader social discourse. Likewise, if identities themselves rely on politics for both articulation and formation, our communication practices and judgments are as vital in the process of democracy as they are in evaluating the outcomes of our interactions with others. Seuss teaches us we can achieve this vibrant diversity within our society. We just have to be more like the Sneetches and less like the Zax, proving Fix-It-Up Chappies wrong by learning through our interactions with others.

17

YOOKS AND ZOOKS

The Bread and Butter of War

Jacob M. Held

The right to make war is detrimental to others, and the punishment inflicted through war is of the severest kind; therefore, that punishment ought to be inflicted with the utmost restraint.

—Francisco Suárez[1]

Here's the end of that terrible town full of Zooks who eat bread with the butter side down!

—Dr. Seuss, *The Butter Battle Book*

Let's begin with the obvious: *The Butter Battle Book* is an allegory about the Cold War. The whole premise, Zooks versus Yooks and an arms race leading to the brink of nuclear (or, in this case, Boomeroo) annihilation, is a not-so-subtle condemnation of the United States' and former Soviet Union's global struggle and nuclear arms race. A chapter on *The Butter Battle Book* could tread that ground. We could look at nuclear proliferation and the policy of MAD, or mutually assured destruction. And that's an interesting topic insofar as it relies on game theoretical approaches to warfare and concludes that rational agents wouldn't engage in actions to defeat their enemies if it also assured their own destruction. We tend to love ourselves just a little bit more than we hate even our worst enemies. This is an interesting idea, but I'm not interested in it for this chapter. I don't wish to revisit theories of nuclear deterrence. Instead, I want to look at *The Butter Battle Book* and think more broadly about war, about the use of mass violence by nations to promote national interests, from human rights and self-defense to proper butter application.

Underneath the conflict between the Yooks and Zooks as presented in *The Butter Battle Book* is the presumption that preparing for war, and planning to use force against another nation, is, under some circumstances, justified. That's wherein my interest lies. When is it permissible to unleash the dogs of war, to obliterate towns and lay waste to the Zook countryside, and what (if any) rules govern our conduct in war?

IT'S HIGH TIME THAT YOU KNOW

The Butter Battle Book has a simple story line. Two peoples, the Yooks and the Zooks, are separated by a wall and an irresolvable disagreement: how ought one to butter and subsequently eat one's bread. The Yooks see the Zooks as profligate, flawed and with "kinks" in their souls, for they eat their bread with the butter side down. The Zooks seem perfectly content with the practice, but the Yooks see it as worrisome. So anxious does the practice make them that they erect a wall and patrol it, keeping a watchful eye on the Zooks. And as the story unfolds it is the Yooks who are more often than not the aggressors, instigating conflict with the Zooks in an attempt to eradicate them and their wicked way of life. So we have an irresolvable conflict between two nations, each maintaining steadfastly that their way is best. It's the global, political equivalent of the Zax. Only in the case of the North-Going Zax and South-Going Zax, they simply refused to budge and so merely stood still. They didn't murder each other, or even threaten to. But the Yooks and Zooks allow their petty disagreement to escalate. Their concern over the other's buttering practices has led to each adopting a war footing—in the case of the Yooks, leading to them preparing to invade Zook territory with the intention of committing genocide. As for the Zooks, they simply prepare for retaliation should the Yooks invade. But this is only butter! Who cares how you eat your bread! Do they really need to resort to force? Could the Yooks or Zooks make a case for war, for mass murder and destruction, all in the name of their proclivities for buttering bread?

BLOW *ALL* THE ZOOKS CLEAR
TO SALA-MA-GOO: REALISM

Let's begin with a simple fact: war is an undeniable evil. War kills and maims thousands and even millions of people, combatants and noncombatants, soldiers and citizens, warriors and children, and inflicts injuries both physical and mental, short and long term. The human toll of war is profound and profoundly disconcerting. If the Yooks and Zooks ever use their Big Boy Boomeroos, there will be many killed, wounded, and forever damaged. The numbers of killed and injured will include children, mothers, and all others caught in the wake of war. There is also the economic impact of war, resources that might have otherwise been spent on education, public works, or other social services go to building bombs, tanks, and guns. As the Yooks and Zooks spend resources and time creating newer and bigger slingshots, triple-sling jiggers, and all their other contraptions, they are not building schools, hospitals, roads, infrastructure, and so on. In addition, war destroys infrastructure such as buildings and roads. Refugees in war-torn lands are driven from their homes. When the fighting begins, where will the Zooks go as the Yooks rain Blue-goo down upon them? So how does one begin to justify the enormity of war?

At its most basic war is mass killing, and it seems to be a result of morality breaking down. So it might seem odd to apply moral thinking to war. Obviously, we don't fight because reason and diplomacy worked, because we've found shared values and are working constructively toward resolving our conflicts. War happens because someone thought force was the only or the most justifiable or the easiest way to resolve the conflict at hand. In the case of *The Butter Battle Book*, it is the Yooks who are the consistent aggressors. After the Zook VanItch uses a slingshot to break Grandpa's poor Snick-Berry Switch, it's the Yooks who continuously invent and deploy greater and greater weapons of war. But at no point is an emissary or ambassador sent to talk peace. Violence is the first and only response considered. With such a breakdown of reason, it's hard to see how moral thinking might apply to war.

Morality and law apply to civilization, and war is a breakdown of this order. One might recollect General William Tecumseh Sherman's (1820–1891) famous dictum, "War is Hell." Or his statement in a letter to the mayor and council of Atlanta: "War is cruelty, and you cannot refine it." One interpretation of these claims is that "war is hell, because as in hell, the horrors know no bounds."[2] And the Chief Yookeroo seems to agree. He declares, "In their new great machine you'll fly over the Wall and clobber those Butter-Down Zooks one and all" (Butter). Grandpa's job is to destroy all the Zooks, every one of them. If the idea that "war is hell" is taken to mean that war is beyond moral assessment, or that moral concepts don't apply to the conditions of war due to its extreme nature, then it is traditionally tagged *Realism*. Realists hold that war isn't nor can it be governed by morality or law, and so at root war merely is about promoting one's interests and however one must do so is justified. Yooks are clearly Realists. Yooks eat bread butter side up, and they want to promote this convention at all costs. If Zooks wish to flout the proper moral order of buttering bread, if they do so publicly while decrying the Yook method, then the only way to shut them up is to blow them to smithereens. The Yooks will promote their superior way of life through the annihilation of the Zooks, *one and all*. Or so the Yook Realists would have it.

Here we find the mass killing of war justified not with reference to some overarching good or moral value such as human rights or protection of the innocent, but an expedient way to promote some other interest, an arbitrary, questionable, egotistical good, like eating bread butter side up. Such a dismissal of morality as quaint or irrelevant is troubling. One can't avoid moral reasoning, especially when dealing with a moral tragedy such as war. "[T]he truth is that one of the things most of us want, even in war, is to act or to seem to act morally. And we want that, most simply, because we know what morality means."[3] War is a human activity. Like any human endeavor, it too is amenable to reason and moral assessment. "If morality applies at all, it applies to all of our actions."[4] So if we must apply moral reasoning to war, how ought we to do it?

A VERY RUDE ZOOK: *JUS AD BELLUM*

Justifying war is a two-part process: one must justify the right to go to war, and then one must justify how to fight. One must provide "an account of just cause and an account of just means."[5] The common nomenclature used to indicate the just cause part of the account is *jus ad bellum*, Latin for the "right to go to war." *Jus in bello* is used to indicate the just means part of the account and means "rights in war."

Jus ad bellum is about a nation's right to go to war. It's the justification for using lethal force on a massive scale. The standard account goes something like this: war is a necessary evil, so the presumption is always against it. You have to have a really, really, really good reason to overcome this presumption and justify the mass killing and serious evil you are about to inflict on the world. There are many formulations of the criteria one must meet in order to successfully plead for the use of military force, but most boil down to the following: there must be a just cause for the use of force such as self-defense or the defense of others, protection of rights, or maintenance of order. Resorting to force must be a last resort after all reasonable, nonbelligerent means of resolution have been exhausted. And, finally, the means you intend to use must be proportionate to the evil being staved off through your war action. That is, war has to be worth it.[6]

The special pleadings used to justify war are fairly straightforward and follow traditional rationales for the use of violence. For example, with just cause, self-defense is an obvious legitimate reason for using violence. After all, if you have a right to life, then you should have the right to protect that right. Likewise, if nations have a right to exist, then they should be allowed to protect that right as well as the well-being of the citizens entrusted to their care. Perhaps this is what frightened the Yooks so much after VanItch sling-shotted Grandpa's switch. It was an act of aggression that could've been seen as a first strike against the Yooks. The Yooks have the right to defend themselves. But there are limits to self-defense. The threat must be immediate, and your response should be proportionate.[7] If the threat isn't lethal, lethal force is an exaggerated response, and if nonlethal or diplomatic means would resolve the matter just as well as war, then they should be used. The Yooks probably overreacted. We only get a small snapshot of the international relations between the Yooks and the Zooks, but from where we stand, it doesn't appear that the Zooks are threatening the very existence of the Yooks. Instead, the Yooks take it upon themselves to initiate hostilities, going so far as to stage incursions into Zook territory, threatening to goo all the Zooks, men, women, and children. In this case, following the idea of self-defense, the Zooks might have a case for war. Yet even if one can find a just cause for war, one also needs to consider proportion and last resort.

In terms of proportion, a nation must undergo a bona fide cost-benefit analysis to see whether war is worth it. Would a war with the Zooks bring total annihilation? If so, it is probably best to avoid war. Would it be fairly cheap and quick? Would it cost a relatively small portion of your gross domestic product, and a minimal loss of life, both Yook and Zook? If so, then it might be justified if you otherwise had a just cause. But this type of assessment needs to be done in good faith, truthfully calculating the costs and weighing the benefits. It might seem cold to calculate in this way, but we're talking about death and destruction. We need to keep track, take notice, and make a wise decision. Finally, we need to make sure that war is only used as a last resort. Given its severity, war should only be used if all other reasonable means have been tried and exhausted. If all of this has been done in good faith, and war is the answer, then so be it. But please, tread lightly.

THE CHIEF YOOKEROO'S GRIM COMMANDS: *JUS IN BELLO*

The usual nomenclature for the moral principles guiding behavior during war is *jus in bello*, or one's rights in war. Even war initiated for a just cause does not allow for the use of any means to wage it. After all, part of *jus ad bellum* is making sure the destruction required to wage the war is proportionate; once in war, this requirement still holds. War is a balancing act of weighing evils against each other. And the principles traditionally held to restrict our actions in war are the principles of proportion and discrimination. With respect to proportion, we assess our proposed actions and ask whether they are necessary, and only what is necessary, to achieve a legitimate military objective. Anything more is overkill, superfluous or unnecessary suffering, and so unjustified. In addition, the principle of discrimination secures protection for noncombatants by declaring them off limits. You can't intentionally attack noncombatants for the simple reason that they are noncombatants; they are not a threat, and, unlike soldiers, they have not entered into an arrangement where they willfully put themselves at risk of being killed.

With respect to the principle of discrimination, its moral foundation is fairly clear. One scholar notes that historically this idea stems from the idea that war is a response to a wrong done, and noncombatants have done no wrong.[8] This is the idea of noncombatant immunity.[9] Noncombatants must be shown due care and their interests acknowledged and respected, although their foreseeable deaths are excusable if they are the unintended result of necessary and proportionate military actions. You can't wage modern war without using a lot of things that make really big explosions in areas often populated by noncombatants, and since you can't evacuate everybody from all potential war zones, you'll have to either find a way to morally justify their deaths or not fight. And since fighting seems necessary at times, one must find a moral justification for the regrettable loss of innocent life.[10]

But the prohibition against intentionally targeting noncombatants is crucial. We are not barbarians. We are not bullies. One does not seek to harm or maim the innocent, even if doing so may be an undesirable and unfortunate result of otherwise justified fighting. So should you ever find yourself in the position of having to drop a massive incendiary device on a heavily populated Zook town, you have to ask yourself whether the military advantage of doing so is significant. Are your intentions pure and the innocent deaths merely an unfortunate, even if foreseeable, consequence of waging a just war? "The deaths [need to] be . . . foreseen but not intended—wanted neither as a means nor as an end to the result aimed at."[11] The Yooks are clearly at fault here. First, they have no just cause, since another person eating buttered bread offensively at you isn't a reason for war. But on top of having no just cause, their goal is genocide: they seek to wipe out all of the Zooks. Thus, the Yooks are beginning from a rejection of the principle of discrimination. They are intentionally aiming at the death of all Zooks. The Zooks, however, probably have cause to prepare for war against the Yooks. After all, the Yooks are a genocidal rogue state set on total annihilation of the Zooks.

The principle of proportion, by contrast, doesn't ask about who you're killing or what you're destroying, but whether you are doing so excessively. The principle of proportion speaks about minimal force, only using what is necessary to disable the enemy. The goal is cessation of hostilities, of a resolution as quickly and painlessly as possible. If war is evil, at least we can minimize the amount of it inflicted on the world. The Yooks and Zooks continually increase their capacity for destruction, perhaps as a deterrent to the other, hoping that the other won't strike first if they see that they'll be eradicated in retaliation. But each weapon, as it increases its capacity for death and destruction, increases the number of Yooks or Zooks it will kill or maim, combatant and noncombatant alike. Weapons of mass destruction don't discriminate. The Big Boy Boomeroo, just like any chemical, nuclear, or biological weapon, is especially problematic. Even if the Zooks had cause to use it in self-defense, "the collateral damage caused even by a 'legitimate' use of nuclear weapons is so great that it would violate . . . the proportionality limits fixed by the theory of war."[12] Similar arguments have been made to decry the Allied fire bombings of Germany and Japan during World War II, as well as the use of atomic weapons at Hiroshima and Nagasaki. As one scholar notes, "The legitimate concerns about killing the innocent in war cannot be taken lightly, and proportionality forces us to take those innocent lives quite seriously indeed."[13] Nuking the Zooks or the Yooks will kill indiscriminately so many thousands and hundreds of thousands of the other that one would need a significantly serious reason to justify it. Such destruction is almost unconscionable. The orientation at which one eats their buttered bread, top-side or bottom-side butter, is surely no justification for this amount of carnage. Beyond nuclear warfare, modern warfare, conducted using high explosives from great distances in densely populated areas—such as drone strikes, missile attacks, and so forth—doesn't fare much better under careful consideration. How many innocents have been killed unintentionally, yet foreseeably, by drone strikes? If these principles are to pose moral limits to warfare, then we need to give them the weight they are owed and seriously reevaluate the way in which we kill in wartime.

So the principles of proportion and discrimination are, theoretically, if not in actuality, moral checks on how we wage war. One scholar notes that if a war can't be fought justly (that is, while respecting the principles of proportion and discrimination), then it can't be justified in the first place, implying just cause is bound by just conduct. He asks, "Why should we think that a war that cannot, or is unlikely to, be waged with just tactics should ever be considered a just war from the outset?"[14] Here, we find the Yooks and Zooks, unable to wage war without indiscriminately killing many, and to what end? The fundamental problem with the Yooks is that their goal is annihilation of the Zooks—that is, genocide. This goal can't be a just cause, and so all of their actions in pursuit of it will be unnecessary and so disproportionate. In addition, since all their actions are aimed at all Zooks, they fail to adequately discriminate between combatants and noncombatants. Since a great deal of killing in war is indiscriminate in this way, some go so far as to maintain that no wars can be justified since the way in which war is waged is necessarily disproportionate to any potential threat and always disrespectful of the principle of discrimination. These critics are pacifists.

NO BLOOD FOR BUTTER: PACIFISM

The general sentiment of the pacifist is that the cost of war is unjustifiable. No good seemingly can justify the loss of life and resources necessary to wage war. And we see this with *The Butter Battle Book.* After all, it's an allegory for the Cold War, for the threat of global nuclear war. And what could possibly justify the annihilation of the planet and the extinction of humanity? Surely not what side we butter bread on. At least the United States and Soviet Union had good reasons, such as disagreements about who owns the means of production, how social resources are distributed, and which superpower gets to control what third-world nation for its own benefit. [15] But wars on the scale in which they historically have been fought result in hundreds of thousands and even millions of deaths, mass exoduses, refugee crises, billions and billions of dollars of damage, and long-term social and economic problems. It is easy to see how one could find the enormity of war unjustifiable.

If one begins from a simple proportionality calculation where we assess the benefits war may produce against the evil it causes, pacifism may seem obvious. Rarely has war led to fewer deaths than surrender arguably would have. One scholar illustrates this through the example of World War II. Estimating that the Allied share of deaths, both combatant and noncombatant, was around 6.5 million, he states, "No one denies that a Nazi victory in World War II would have had morally frightful results. But, according to anti-war pacifism, killing six and one-half million people is also morally frightful, and preventing one moral wrong does not obviously outweigh committing another."[16] If we take proportionality to simply be about total number of deaths or amount of destruction, Douglas Lackey seems to indicate that war is incredibly difficult to justify. Surrender would probably lead to less pain and suffering than fighting. But is war and the value of a nation's sovereignty quantifiable in terms of loss of property and life, or is there a further value being fought for when one thinks about justifying war? Isn't sovereignty or self-determination valuable? Wouldn't rule by a Nazi regime be undesirable?

Both the Yooks and the Zooks seem to think their ways of life are worth protecting. The Yooks want to promote theirs over and against the Zooks' way of life, which to them indicates "kinks" in one's soul. And who knows what elements of Zook culture and identity hinge on eating bread butter side down, but surely those values matter to them, just as anybody's identity is tied to their foundational values. But Lackey doesn't think these types of values merit the cost of war. In fact, he notes that citizens of Russia and China didn't live in bastions of freedom before or after World War II, so who ruled them was kind of irrelevant. In fact, he equates the desire to not be ruled against one's own will by Germans to be nothing more than xenophobia, a fear of or dislike for foreigners.[17] Ideas of sovereignty, for him, are simply masks for unattractive attitudes about foreigners. He concludes that our prejudices against rule from the outside can't justify the millions of deaths war results in. Note that the Yooks and Zooks prepare for war and are ready to destroy each other merely so they don't have to butter bread the way their adversaries do, or even tolerate their existence. This is a clear case of prejudice, of irrational tribalism at its worst. What side you butter bread on doesn't matter, especially since you can flip it over with minimal effort. It doesn't affect the taste. At the most eating it butter-side down is probably a bit messier than eating it butter-side up, but that's the Zooks' problem. The simple reason the Yooks hate the Zooks is because they are different; they are Zooks. And "you can't trust a Zook who spreads bread underneath!" (Butter). But buttering bread underneath is merely a convenient excuse. The Yooks are motivated by xenophobia, plain and simple. They hate Zooks because they are not Yooks, and whatever reason they give for why Yooks are better is going to be arbitrary, an after-the-fact rationalization of an irrational hatred, that when left to fester leads to what we have in the story—perpetual war and attempted genocide. So maybe pacifism makes sense, once we weigh all the pros and cons.

In addition, Lackey claims self-defense is no justification for war, since the people of the invaded country would survive conquest, even if the old form of government did not. If the Zooks surrendered, if they acquiesced to the Yooks' demands, they'd survive, and all they'd have to give up is eating bread buttered underneath. They'd live for top-side butter, but they'd live. For Lackey, what's most important when trying to justify war is minimizing pain and suffering, and war can't stand up to scrutiny. It always fails the proportionality test.

This type of pacifism makes many assumptions about the value of sovereignty, justified killing, and so forth. A full account and appropriate response is beyond this short chapter, but we can ponder a few ideas. Perhaps self-defense isn't a justification for war in some cases. Perhaps losing a small, inconsequential island is not worth millions of lives. Maybe sometimes it is more cost effective, more humane, to accept defeat rather than fight.[18] But even acknowledging this doesn't deny that there might be some cases that pass a threshold of intolerable evil. Nazis probably pass this threshold. If they don't, who could? Consider the insidious Yooks. They are hellbent on genocide! Why would the Zooks ever consider surrendering to them? They'd be annihilated, or their way of life so transformed that they wouldn't even recognize themselves afterward. Self-determination and rights may hold no value for Lackey, but some see them as constitutive of the value of human life.[19] How you live is as important as the fact that you live, so to dismiss sovereignty as a value is to dismiss something considerable to many reasonable and thoughtful people. Beyond this one could rightfully claim that the threat Nazis posed was significant and uniquely grave. As Thomas Hurka notes, "Proportionality and necessity are not always impossible to judge; sometimes there are clear cases. For example, most believe that, despite the massive destruction that resulted, the Allies were right to fight World War II."[20] One might justify this claim with reference to what's called a "supreme emergency"—that sometimes something so uniquely horrible arises that it momentarily justifies what had been previously unjustifiable. But such a threat has to be beyond any doubt. Sometimes you wager the wickedness of war against an immeasurable evil, like Nazi rule. In such a case, you go with the more palatable devil you know as opposed to the looming, terrifying devil you don't; war is better than Nazi rule. And so the Zooks must consider all relevant factors, and if top-side butter is as unpalatable as National Socialism, and if the Yooks seem poised systemically to murder them after conquest, then they're right to prepare for war. But appealing to a supreme emergency must be a last resort and only referenced in the direst circumstances. We should be wary of those who see all threats as apocalyptic and so all scenarios as supreme emergencies. Those like the Chief Yookeroo are simply too enthusiastic about war.

But we shouldn't be dismissive of the pacifist's position. After all, what some might term war crimes and what are surely horrendous acts of brutality, such as the terror bombings of Germany in World War II and the atomic attacks on Hiroshima and Nagasaki, have been justified within a traditional just war framework. We should be wary of those who see nuclear war as a viable option. Pacifism does serve as an important moral check on our rationales for war.

WE WILL SEE . . .

Clearly, the Yooks and Zooks can't justify their actions according to any reasonable interpretation of just war theory. Their disagreements are insignificant. If the Yooks and Zooks would simply return to their respective sides of the wall and continue going about their own business, ignoring the other, neither would ever have to concern itself with what was happening, or how bread was being eaten, on the other side. There'd be no threats to each other's existence. And since neither the Yooks nor the Zooks are engaged in any sort of human rights violations, there'd be no justification for humanitarian intervention. So there is simply no reason for them to be where they are in terms of hostilities, nor is there any foreseeable reason why they'd ever have to be.

But this is the problem with war thinking. If the old truism that to the man with a hammer everything looks like a nail holds true, then perhaps to the nation prepared for war everything looks like a threat. If war is an option, and the most expedient or preferable one to those who make such decisions, then diplomacy will not be tried. Why waste time with a bunch of words and compromises, or strive to live in peace (even if fragile), with those with whom we disagree when we can just bomb them to smithereens? Perhaps this is why pacifism plays an important role in war theory, and ought to play a role in our thinking. Pacifism is a check on just war theory. If we take morality's demands to heart, then we should stop and think, and think seriously, about war before we start dropping bombs. Do we have a really, really, really good reason for considering war as an option? Is it necessary, and in response to an unacceptable and grave evil? Can it be done justly, and with minimal harm? If not, perhaps we go back to the drawing board, or just stop worrying about on what side someone else butters his bread.

EPILOGUE

A Simple Answer

Jacob M. Held

... and finally now, you've come to the end,
So I'll answer the questions with which we beganned.
Do you remember what we first asked?
The questions, the queries, with which we were tasked?[1]

We mentioned the good life and suffering, pain.
We pondered o'er Marx and consumerist gain.
There was mention of knowledge and truth and diversity,
And just to confuddle us all, postmodernity.
Ethics, respect, and our old German friend.
That book was a monster! Would it ever end?
No.
Not 'til we covered yet even more ground.
Political questions often confound.
So we asked about justice and business and property,
Mentioning Rawls and thus doing so properly.
Not lastly or leastly, we talked about trees,
The Lorax and nature and our role in these.
Finally, it ended with talk of aesthetics
(that's jargon for "art," but we *are* academics).

That was a great start, as we noted back then
But more could be said, so we picked up our pens.
We penned you this book that you currently hold,
More of the same, with new truths to behold.
Yet, through every bit, as we puzzled and pondered,
we failed to address what is so often wondered;
through all of our writing and quoting and rhymes
we never once asked about God, the divine!

Since Seuss never dealt with a god or religion,
We can't use his stories to think or envision
How he would've dealt with a topic like that,
A topic that everyone needs to have at.
To end, then, it's God to which we will turn;
Theological questions, we're seeking to learn.

What is a god, and why do we care?
What do we get from a being up there?
Is he up there, or down underneath?
Is he a he, or a she, or a sneetch?
Regardless, it's God, or some divine being,
That gives many people their purpose, their meaning.
It's God and our many religious traditions
that give our lives focus, that define our missions.
That's why it matters, and why we should care
About whether there are any gods anywhere.
We *should* want to know, we should wonder out loud
And hope that just maybe some answers are found.

When thinkers or doubters or others inquire
Into the nature of God and aspire
To answer the mysteries of here and beyond,
There are certain questions that always abound.
Of course there's the question "Does God exist?"
If there isn't a God, we could stop or desist.
But assuming there is, or at least the potential,
Then other, more weighty conundrums unravel.
The problem of evil, now that's a brain twister!

Ask Job, who lost everything (all but the blisters).
Some wrongs people do and so earn their penance,
But other bad happens, a natural occurrence:
Like earthquakes and fires, and cancers and floods.
If God is the best that ever there was,
Wouldn't God stop this so we didn't suffer?
Wouldn't God care for us like our mother?
But nobody yet has found a solution
No answers to wash away doubts, no ablution.
Perhaps it's a mystery, or all for the best,
Perhaps we're too stupid, or bad things are tests.

And the deeper we dig, the more questions we find;
If God has a plan, is my life really mine?
Is all of this set, can I choose, am I free?
When God planned the world, did that include me?
If I am not free but must do what I must,
Then how can He judge me as good, bad, or bust?
And should I decide to live life as I'm told,
What book should I read? There's too many to hold!
Should I read the Qur'an, the Bible, the Vedas,
The Torah, the I Ching, the Bhagavad Gita?
Whose God is the right God? (So many to choose from.)
So many options; yet no answers come.
Or, rather, they come but are run through with doubt;
God is one thing we know nothing about.
How can we know about gods far and distant,
About gods ever absent with proof nonexistent?
The revealed word of God, revelation and faith,
Words that when spoken in mouths leave bad tastes.
We seek the truth, but we want it with proof,
and God isn't like that, He's kind of aloof.

Faith does heavy lifting in this situation,
Belief leads to knowledge some saint had once mentioned. [2]
That's all well and good when it helps you live well,
But some gods call for war, inquisitions, and still
We go on believing and fighting and kill

In the name of our god or our church or our creed.
Such gods preach division and avarice and greed.
Skeptics will focus on flaws and the bad;
They'll claim we've been duped, screaming, "You've all been had!"
By priests or authorities seeking control,
That we need to shun faith for what we can "know."
Yet the problem we're in is one of design;
We can't know a god; we can't see the divine.
But we still seek our place in the cosmos above,
We still seek security, meaning, and love.
God gave us purpose; God gave us a place,
Religion a home, church our safe space.
Where does that leave us when all's said and done?
No answers, more "whys," which is where we'd begun!

Some questions loom large and are almost unmindable,
And answers seem distant and almost unfindable.
What kind of a god could answer our questions?
What possible answer could solve our perplexions?

Questions are many, and answers are rare;
Oh, people will talk, but so much is hot air.
We bumble and mumble and blunder about,
In many ways vapid, each full of doubt.
Yet an answer's quite clear, we know what *to do*:
Treat others as equals, as you'd want to treat you.
There's no trick to this life, no secret to find;
The answer's quite simple—to all quandaries: *Be Kind!*

Too often in asking a difficult question
We're caught up in details, seeking perfection.
We might ask for science, some numbers to square,
The questions before us and up in the air.
But science can't save us; it talks about stuff,
Not about values, and goodness, and love.
We squibble and squabble, use jargon galore,
Losing sight of the reason the argument's for.
Sure, we want answers, solutions are grand,

But life's about people, and so we demand
An answer that even the "smartest" can find.
The answer is simple, it's simply: *Be Kind!*

We're wrapping up now; we've been talking of deities,
How a god or a goddess gives life its security,
A goal and a purpose, a structure for being,
A reason to live for, a life full of meaning.
Why are we here, what ought I to do?
For what can I hope, and how about you?[3]
From Socrates onward, there's many suggestions,
You've read them all, or at least skimmed the best ones,
And still here we sit, asking big questions,
As if these curt answers could give resolutions.
But the world's too big and fantastically wide;
Our brains are too small, so it can't fit inside.
We're bound to forever be stuck in a muddle:
we'll ask, they'll respond, we'll get further rebuttals.
You see . . .
regardless of answers, regardless of whys
what we have is each other, forever, our lives
together, community, life among others,
sisters and brothers, friends, fathers and mothers.
It just doesn't matter who's smarter or "right"
Who won what argument, who won what fight.
The simplest answer for all humankind
Regardless of question is simply: *Be Kind!*

So read Seuss or Seneca, Plato or Kant,
Nietzsche or Hegel, or maybe not.
Study philosophy, politics, law;
Learn science and history, knowledge galore.
Never stop learning, don't shut off your mind,
But always remember, the point is:
Be Kind![4]

NOTES

PREFACE

1. Thanks, by the way.

2. Check out the Great Authors and Philosophy series, or *Roald Dahl and Philosophy: A Little Nonsense Now and Then*.

1. ON BEYOND REASON

1. Samuel Taylor Coleridge, *Anima Poetae: from the Unpublished Notebooks of Samuel Taylor Coleridge*, ed. Ernest Hartley Coleridge (London: Heinemann, 1895), 282.

2. Yuval Noah Harari, *Sapiens: A Brief History of Humankind* (New York: Harper, 2015), 7.

3. Immanuel Kant, *Critique of Pure Reason* (New York: Random House, 1958), Axii.

4. Kant, *Critique of Pure Reason*, B29.

5. Kant, *Critique of Pure Reason*, B103, A78.

6. Milos Rastovic, "Kant's Understanding of the Imagination in *Critique of Pure Reason*," in *E-Logos* (November 2013): 6.

7. William Wordsworth, *Lyrical Ballads with Pastoral and Other Poems* (London: T. N. Longman, 1802), 2.

8. Wordsworth, *Lyrical Ballads with Pastoral and Other Poems*, 6.

9. Wordsworth, *Lyrical Ballads with Pastoral and Other Poems*, 6.

10. Samuel Taylor Coleridge, *Biographia Literaria*, ed. James Engell and W. Jackson Bate (Princeton, NJ: Princeton University Press, 1985), 304.

11. Coleridge, *Biographia Literaria*, 308.

12. Percy Bysshe Shelley, *A Defence of Poetry* (Indianapolis: Bobbs-Merrill, 1904), 12.

13. Shelley, *A Defence of Poetry*, 12–13.

14. Shelley, *A Defence of Poetry*, 90.

15. Shelley, *A Defence of Poetry*, 90.

2. ARISTOTLE AND THE CAT ON
FUN THAT IS FUNNY

1. Aristotle, *Nicomachean Ethics*, translated, with introduction, notes, and glossary, by Terence Irwin (Indianapolis/Cambridge: Hackett, 1999), 1128a, 65.

2. In Geisel's own words, "It's the book I'm proudest of . . . because it had something to do with the death of the *Dick and Jane* primers. In 1954 John Hersey wrote an article in *Life* that suggested something to the effect that we should get rid of the boredom of Dick and Jane and Spot and hand the education-al system over to Dr. Seuss! William Spaulding, who was then the textbook chief at Houghton Mifflin, read the article and asked me if I'd like to try to do a primer, and he sent me a list of about three hundred words and told me to make a book out of them. At first I thought it was impossible and ridiculous, and I was about to get out of the whole thing; then decided to look at the list one more time and to use the first two words that rhymed as the title of the book—*cat* and *hat* were the ones my eyes lighted on. I worked on the book for nine months— throwing it across the room and letting it hang for a while—but I finally got it done. Houghton Mifflin, however, had trouble selling it to the schools; there were a lot of Dick and Jane devotees, and my book was considered too fresh and irreverent. But Bennett Cerf at Random House had asked for trade rights, and it just took off in the bookstores." Originally published by Jonathan Cott in *Pipers at the Gates of Dawn: The Wisdom of Children's Literature* (New York: McGraw-Hill, 1983). Republished as chapter 12, "The Good Dr. Seuss," in *Of Sneetches and Whos and the Good Dr. Seuss: Essays on the Writings and Life of Theodor Geisel*, ed. Thomas Fensch (Jefferson, NC: McFarland, 1997), 115.

3. Aristotle, *Nicomachean Ethics*, 1106b21, 24.

4. Aristotle, *Nicomachean Ethics*, 1128a5, 65.

5. Fensch, *Of Sneetches and Whos and the Good Dr. Seuss*, 116.

6. Aristotle, *Nicomachean Ethics*, 1128a8, 65.

7. Aristotle, *Nicomachean Ethics*, 1128b2, 66.

8. Aristotle, *Nicomachean Ethics*, 115a5, 119.

9. Al Gini, *The Importance of Being Funny: Why We Need More Jokes in Our Lives* (Lanham, MD: Rowman & Littlefield, 2017), 42.

10. Fensch, *Of Sneetches and Whos and the Good Dr. Seuss*, 112.

11. Aristotle, *Nicomachean Ethics*, 1128a30, 66.

12. Fensch, *Of Sneetches and Whos and the Good Dr. Seuss*, 117.

13. Gini, *The Importance of Being Funny*, 51.

14. Aristotle, *Nicomachean Ethics*, 1106b21, 24.

3. ARISTOTLE AND EUDAIMONIA

1. All references to Aristotle will be to the *Nicomachean Ethics*, trans. W. D. Ross, http://classics.mit.edu/Aristotle/nicomachaen.1.i.html, a translation now in the public domain and available online. The citation will indicate the book and the chapter within which the quote is taken; for example, *"Nico* II.ix" refers to the ninth chapter of the second book of the *Nicomachean Ethics*.

2. Martha Nussbaum understands *eudaimonia* as "human good living" or "flourishing" in *The Fragility of Goodness* (Cambridge: Cambridge University Press, 2001), xii–xiv. *The Online Liddell-Scott-Jones Greek-English Lexicon* translates it as "prosperity" (http://stephanus.tlg.uci.edu/lsj/).

3. Rudyard Kipling, "If—," in *Rewards and Fairies* (New York: Macmillan Children's Books, 2016).

4. For a good examination of Aristotle's commitment to universal and precise answers in ethics, consult Carlo Davia, "Universality in Aristotle's Ethics," *Journal of the History of Philosophy* 54, no. 2 (2016): 181–201.

5. Aristotle tells us that we have a "nutritive" or "vegetative" function. Although biology has advanced significantly since his time and rejects Aristotle's simplistic divisions between plants, animals, and humans, this terminology has persisted in common speech: when a person is in a coma we commonly refer to this as being in a vegetative state—that is, one in which only those basic bodily functions are operating.

6. For a nice treatment of how *eudaimonic* ethics can provide a more inclusive framework of well-being than the utilitarian perspective of neoclassic economics offers, see Donald G. Richards, "Eudaimonia, Economics and the Environment: What Do the Hellenistic Thinkers Have to Teach Economists about 'The Good Life'?" *Ethics & the Environment* 18, no. 2 (2013): 33–53.

7. Aristotle uses the word *arete* in Greek to discuss "virtue," and this word roughly means an "excellence" or a good characteristic of a thing or person. Everything has some characteristic or more that can be said to make that thing good and allow it to do its work well. Those characteristics are the "virtues" of the thing. Note that there is nothing inherently "moral" about virtues in general. The virtue of a knife is that it is sharp (so it can cut well).

8. Bernard Williams disparages this element in Aristotle's ethical theory, in *Ethics and the Limits of Philosophy* (Cambridge, MA: Harvard University Press, 1985), 36: "Aristotle's . . . views on [virtue] are bound up with one of the most celebrated and least useful parts of his system, the doctrine of the Mean. . . . The theory oscillates between an unhelpful analytical model (which Aristotle himself does not consistently follow) and a substantively depressing doctrine in favor of moderation." Peter Losin (in "Aristotle's Doctrine of the Mean," *History of Philosophy Quarterly* 4, no. 3 [1987]: 329–42) defends the doctrine well against Williams, showing that reducing the doctrine of the mean to the mere idea that moderation of all things is best is crude and overly simplistic.

9. For an example of a recent but overly simplistic understanding of the doctrine of the mean, see Melina Hughes and Virginia Fitzsimons, "Lessons from Aristotle: All Things in Moderation," *Nursing* 46, no. 4 (2016): 50–53.

10. Two great essays examining the issues of character development in Aristotle are in *Aristotle's Ethics*, ed. Nancy Sherman (New York: Rowman & Littlefield, 1999): M. F. Burnyeat's "Aristotle on Learning to Be Good" and N. Sherman's "The Fabric of Character."

4. DID I EVER TELL YOU HOW
STOIC YOU ARE?

1. The full text of Epictetus's *Discourses* can be accessed at http://classics.mit.edu/Epictetus/discourses.html.

2. Zeno of Citium is not the same as Zeno of Elea, who devised the famous paradoxes of motion about 150 years before the founding of Stoicism. Ancient Greek names can be confusing!

3. For the sake of this chapter, I will focus mostly on Epictetus's presentation of Stoic philosophy, though similar themes appear in other Stoic writers.

4. Diogenes Laertius, *Lives of Eminent Philosophers* 7.86–9, from *Hellenistic Philosophy: Introductory Readings*, second ed., trans. Brad Inwood and Lloyd Gerson (Indianapolis: Hackett, 1997).

5. Seneca, *On the Happy Life* III–IV, trans. Marcus Wilson, from *The Practice of Virtue*, ed. Jennifer Welchman (Indianapolis: Hackett, 2006).

6. I borrow this way of breaking down Stoic philosophical practice from Massimo Pigliucci (in *How to Be a Stoic* [New York: Basic Books, 2017]), who adapts it from Epictetus and uses it to structure his book. I've changed Pigliucci's order slightly.

7. *Enchiridion*, chapter 8. The full text of Epictetus's *Enchiridion* (or *Handbook*) can be accessed at http://classics.mit.edu/Epictetus/epicench.html.

8. The clearest surviving explorations of these topics are in Cicero, *On Ends* 3.16–22 (in *Hellenistic Philosophy*), and Seneca, *Letter* 121 (found in Seneca, *Selected Letters*, trans. Elaine Fantham [Oxford: Oxford World Classics, 2010]).

9. *Enchiridion*, chapter 14.

10. *Enchiridion*, chapter 1.

11. *Enchiridion*, chapter 14.

12. *Discourses* II.5, translated by Robert Dobbin, in Epictetus, *Discourses and Selected Writings* (London: Penguin Classics, 2008).

13. Marcus Aurelius has several great passages that develop this idea. In one famous passage, he writes, "The mind adapts and converts everything that impedes its activities into something that advances its purpose, and a hindrance to its actions becomes an aid, and an obstacle on its path helps it on its way" (V.20, in Marcus Aurelius, *Meditations: with Selected Correspondence*, trans. Robin Hard [Oxford: Oxford World Classics, 2011]). A similar sentiment appears in IV.1: "When the ruling power within us is in harmony with nature, it confronts events in such a way that it always adapts itself readily to what is feasible and is granted to it. For it attaches its preference to no specific material; rather it sets out to attain its primary objects, but not without reservation, and if it comes up against something else instead, it converts it into material for itself, much like a fire when it masters the things that fall into it. These would have extinguished a little lamp, but a blazing fire appropriates in an instant all that is heaped on to it, and devours it, making use of that very material to leap ever higher."

14. *Discourses* I.6.

15. *Enchiridion* 11.

16. *Enchiridion* 43.

17. *Enchiridion* 26.

18. Seneca, *Letter* 95.

19. *Discourses* II.4. See also I.23.

20. *Discourses* II.4.

21. *Discourses* I.11.

22. See *Discourses* II.10 and *Enchiridion* 30 for a detailed discussion of this idea.

23. See *Discourses* I.13, where, in response to a question about dealing with slaves, Epictetus explains, "My friend, it's a matter of bearing with your own brother, who has Zeus as his ancestor and is a son born of the same seed as yourself, with the same high lineage. . . . Remember that . . . they are kinsmen, brothers by nature, fellow descendents of Zeus."

24. *Discourses* II.10.

25. See also Cicero, *On Goals* 3.64: "They also hold that the cosmos is ruled by the will of the gods, that it is like a city shared by gods and men, and that each and every one of us is part of this cosmos. From which it follows that we put the

common advantage ahead of our own. For just as the laws put the well-being of all ahead of the well-being of individuals, so too the good and wise man, who is obedient to the laws and not unaware of his civic duty, looks out for the advantage of all more than for that of any one person or his own."

26. See *Discourses* II.8: "You . . . *are* a creature placed in charge, and a particle of God himself; there is a bit of God within you" (trans. Dobbin). The Stoics meant this quite literally: for them, God is a material that pervades the universe. Humans are self-reflective and capable of reason because we contain a fragment of that divine material.

5. ONE MUST IMAGINE DR. SEUSS HAPPY

1. Simone de Beauvoir, *The Ethics of Ambiguity*, trans. Bernard Frechtman (New York: Philosophical Library, 1948).

2. Bertrand Russell, *The Problems of Philosophy*, in *Philosophic Classics: From Plato to Derrida*, sixth edition, ed. Forrest Baird (Upper Saddle River, NJ: Prentice Hall, 2011), 1095.

3. For an exploration of this theme of the vulnerability of aging, take a look at another Dr. Seuss classic, *You're Only Old Once!*

4. Jean-Paul Sartre, "Existentialism Is a Humanism," in *Existentialism*, second edition, ed. Robert Solomon (Oxford: Oxford University Press, 2005), 207.

5. Jean-Paul Sartre, from a 1971 interview in *New Left Review*, in *Existentialism*, second edition, iii.

6. Sartre, "Existentialism Is a Humanism," 211.

7. Albert Camus, "The Myth of Sisyphus," in *Existentialism*, second edition, 191.

8. Camus, "The Myth of Sisyphus," 191.

9. Camus, "The Myth of Sisyphus," 198.

10. Camus, "The Myth of Sisyphus," 197.

6. YOUR ENDING IS WAITING

1. Edward Sorel, "Mind/Body/Health: The Shape That He's In," *New York Times*, March 23, 1986, accessed July 11, 2017, http://www.nytimes.com/1986/03/23/books/mind-body-health-the-shape-that-he-s-in.html.

2. Albert Camus, The Myth of Sisyphus and Other Essays , trans. Justin O'Brien (New York: Vintage Books, 1955), 75.

3. Camus, *The Myth of Sisyphus*, 121.

4. All references to Plato's works will use the marginal *Stephanus* pagination numbers, and the translation is from Plato, *Five Dialogues* (2nd ed.), trans. G. M. A. Grube (Indianapolis: Hackett, 2002).

5. Epicurus, *Letter to Menoeceus*, trans. Robert Drew Hicks, Internet Classics Archive, MIT, accessed July 30, 2017, http://classics.mit.edu/Epicuru/menoec.html.

6. See, D. Kahneman and A. Tversky, "Choices, Values, and Frames," *American Psychologist* 39, no. 4 (1984): 341–50.

7. DR. SEUSS AND ARISTOTLE ON THE MOST IMPORTANT FRIENDSHIP OF ALL

1. Donald E. Pease, *Theodor Seuss Geisel* (Oxford: Oxford University Press, 2010).

2. Aristotle, *Nicomachean Ethics*, book II, chapter 4, trans. W. D. Ross, http://classics.mit.edu/Aristotle/nicomachaen.html.

3. Aristotle, *Nicomachean Ethics*, book VIII, chapter 1.

4. Aristotle, *History of Animals: In Ten Books*, chapter 1, trans. Richard Cresswell (Henry G. Bohn, 1862), 6.

5. Aristotle, *Nicomachean Ethics*, book II, chapter 6.

6. Aristotle, *Nicomachean Ethics*, book VIII, chapter 3.

7. Attributed to Aristotle by Diogenes Laërtius, *The Lives and Opinions of Eminent Philosophers*. Literally translated by C. D. Yonge (Henry G. Bohn, 1853).

8. Aristotle, *Nicomachean Ethics*, book IX, chapter 4.

9. Aristotle, *Nicomachean Ethics*, book VIII, chapter 3.

10. As Mavis Biss puts it in "Aristotle on Friendship and Self Knowledge: The Friend beyond the Mirror," *History of Philosophy Quarterly* 28, no. 2 (April 2011).

8. IT SHOULD BE LIKE THAT!

1. Arthur Schopenhauer, *On the Basis of Morality*, trans. E. F. J. Payne (Providence, RI: Berghahn Books, 1995), 132.

2. Schopenhauer, *On the Basis of Morality*, 132.

3. *Selfish* would be a more accurate adjective to describe her, but that doesn't rhyme with *Mayzie*.

4. I am well aware that phrasing this scenario in this way makes this look like a perfect place to discuss abortion, or as if that argument is somehow to be inferred. It is not, nor will I digress into that matter here. But feel free to discuss among yourselves.

5. Schopenhauer, *On the Basis of Morality*, 134–35.

6. Schopenhauer, *On the Basis of Morality*, 129. I actually do begin my ethics class with this quote.

7. Schopenhauer, *On the Basis of Morality*, 131.

8. Schopenhauer, *On the Basis of Morality*, 134.

9. Schopenhauer, *On the Basis of Morality*, 139.

10. Schopenhauer, *On the Basis of Morality*, 140.

11. Schopenhauer, *On the Basis of Morality*, fn. 92.

12. David Fisher, *Morality and War: Can War Be Just in the Twenty-First Century?* (Oxford: Oxford University Press, 2011), 134.

13. Schopenhauer, *On the Basis of Morality*, 143.

14. John Kleinig, *On Loyalty and Loyalties: The Contours of a Problematic Virtue* (Oxford: Oxford University Press, 2014), 80.

15. J. G. Fichte, *Foundations of Natural Right: According to the Principles of the Wissenschaftslehre*, ed. Frederick Neuhouser, trans. Michael Baur (Cambridge: Cambridge University Press, 2000), 37–38.

16. Schopenhauer, *On the Basis of Morality*, fn. 92.

17. For a discussion of his virtue theory see David E. Cartwright, "Schopenhauer's Narrower Sense of Morality," in *The Cambridge Companion to Schopenhauer*, ed. Christopher Janaway (Cambridge: Cambridge University Press, 1999), 252–92.

18. Schopenhauer, *On the Basis of Morality*, 169.

19. Schopenhauer, *On the Basis of Morality*, 169.

20. Fantasy author Terry Pratchett (1948–2015) has one of his characters, Esmerelda "Granny" Weatherwax, voice this point when, in *Carpe Jugulum*, she says, "And sin . . . is when you treat people like things."

21. Arthur Schopenhauer, *The World as Will and Representation*, in two volumes: Volume I, translated by E. F. J. Payne (New York: Dover, 1969), 313.

9. FEELING AS, FEELING FOR, SEEING WHAT'S RIGHT, AND SO MUCH MORE

1. Among other scholarly articles cited here, see David Comer Kidd and Emanuele Castano's "Reading Literary Fiction Improves Theory of Mind," *ScienceExpress* (October 3, 2013), DOI 10.1126/science.1239918. Popular pieces consulted include Ceridwen Dovey's "Can Reading Make You Happier?"

New Yorker, June 9, 2015, or Pam Belluck's "For Better Social Skills, Scientists Recommend a Little Chekhov," *New York Times*, October 3, 2013.

2. See Claus Lamm and Jasminka Majdandzic's "The Role of Shared Neural Activations, Mirror Neurons, and Morality in Empathy—A Critical Comment," *Neuroscience Research* 90 (2015): 15–24. Here, the authors state, "we do not think that there is sufficient evidence to unequivocally decide" the role of mirror neurons in empathic response, particularly whether "mirror neuron responses serve action understanding or reflect action understanding" (17)—namely, whether they cause empathic response or are merely symptomatic of its occurrence.

3. See Matthew Jordan, Dorsa Amir, and Paul Bloom's "Are Empathy and Concern Psychologically Distinct?" *Emotion* 16, no. 8 (2016): 1107–16. Here, the authors note that in their empirical studies, "we find that concern, and not empathy, is the primary motivator of moral thoughts and actions" (1114). Lamm and Majdandzic agree, stating, "Increases in empathy do not necessarily make us behave more morally" (21). Janina Levin concurs in "Productive Dialogues across the Disciplines: Literature and Empathy Studies," stating, "Reading novels does not necessarily promote empathic behavior or altruism" (191). Levin's article appears in the *Journal of Modern Literature* 39, no. 4 (2014). Dan Johnson, Grace K. Cushman, Lauren A. Borden, and Madison S. McCune's "Potentiating Empathic Growth: Prosocial Behavior while Reading Fiction Increases Empathy and Prosocial Behavior," *Psychology of Aesthetics, Creativity and the Arts* 7, no. 3 (2013): 306–12, also addresses this issue.

4. See Marco Caracciolo and Thom Van Duuren's "Changed by Literature? A Critical Review of Psychological Research on the Effects of Reading Fiction," *Interdisciplinary Studies* 17, no. 4 (2015). Here, the authors discuss the tendency that studies have to focus on realist fiction (527), particularly short stories (526). They note that attention to other genres and forms of literature are warranted and speculate that it is "likely that longer, and perhaps therefore more complex narratives (e.g., novels) have a stronger effect" (526). See P. Matthijs Bal and Martijn Veltkamp's "How Does Fiction Reading Influence Empathy? An Experimental Investigation on the Role of Emotional Transportation," *Plos One* 8, no. 1 (January 2013). They echo Caracciolo and Van Duuren's point about full-length novels (10), and add that no reliable claims about the effects of fiction are tenable without longitudinal studies (1). Moreover, sources such as Cynthia Freeland's "Realist Horror," reprinted in *Aesthetics: The Big Questions*, ed. Carolyn Korsmeyer (Oxford: Blackwell Publishing, 1998), and Sally Markowitz's "Guilty Pleasures: Aesthetic Meta Response and Fiction," *Journal of Aesthetics and Art Criticism* 50, no. 4 (2001): 307–16, explore the potentially adverse impact of empathic identification. They suggest that works that foster empathic identification with immoral characters or arouse positive emotional responses to

actions or attitudes that are typically considered morally problematic can adversely influence readers' moral sensibility rather than improve it. I am grateful to Sidney Lewis for the conversations that she and I have had on this topic, conversations motivated by her enlightening thesis, "Missing Moral Compass: The Problem of Morally Ambiguous Young Adult Literature."

5. See Kevin Browne and Catherine Hamilton-Giachritsis's "The Influence of Violent Media on Children and Adolescents: A Public Health Approach," *Lancet* 365 (February 19, 2005). Here, the authors discuss the "urgent need to understand the short and long term effects" (708) of narrative, particularly narrative violence, on children and adolescents.

6. See Jordan et al. regarding the degree to which a clearly developed character promotes heightened empathic response (1113). Likewise, see Bal and Veltkamp for detailed discussion of the role of imagination, particularly imaginative immersion, and its impact on emotional engagement. Regarding different agents for empathic response, see Lamm and Majdandzic, who examine the differential impact of "abstract visual cues" (19) as compared to "pictorial presentation" (19).

7. See Lamm and Majdandzic, "The Role of Shared Neural Activations, Mirror Neurons, and Morality in Empathy," 20–21.

8. See Sigmund Freud's *The Uncanny* (New York: Penguin Classics, 2003), where he describes common means to elicit the experience of the uncanny, including animating that which is inanimate. Susan Bernstein also examines this phenomenon in her essay "It Walks: The Ambulatory Uncanny," *MLN* 118, no. 5, "Comparative Literature" (December 2003), 1111–39. http://www.jstor.org/stable/3251857.

9. Lamm and Majdandzic, "The Role of Shared Neural Activations, Mirror Neurons, and Morality in Empathy," 20.

10. Lamm and Majdandzic, "The Role of Shared Neural Activations, Mirror Neurons, and Morality in Empathy," 21.

11. Lamm and Majdandzic, "The Role of Shared Neural Activations, Mirror Neurons, and Morality in Empathy," 21.

12. Published in 1823, Moore's story is more commonly known by the title "'Twas the Night before Christmas."

13. Martha Nussbaum, *Love's Knowledge* (Oxford: Oxford University Press, 1990), 48.

14. Caracciolo and Van Duuren, "Changed by Literature?" 534.

15. Jordan et al., "Are Empathy and Concern Psychologically Distinct?" 1113.

16. Hung Chang Liao and Ya-Huei Wang, "The Application of Heterogeneous Cluster Grouping to Reflective Writing for Medical Humanities Literature

Study to Enhance Students' Empathy, Critical Thinking, and Reflective Writing," *BMC Education* 16 (2016): 234. DOI: 10.1186/s12909-016-0758-2.

17. Levin, "Productive Dialogues across the Disciplines," 189.

18. Bal and Veltkamp, "How Does Fiction Reading Influence Empathy?" 2; Johnson et al., "Potentiating Empathic Growth," 306; Kidd and Castano, "Reading Literary Fiction Improves Theory of Mind," 1.

19. Lamm and Majdandzic, "The Role of Shared Neural Activations, Mirror Neurons, and Morality in Empathy," 21.

20. Bal and Veltkamp, "How Does Fiction Reading Influence Empathy?" 2; Kidd and Castano, "Reading Literary Fiction Improves Theory of Mind," 1.

21. Bal and Veltkamp, "How Does Fiction Reading Influence Empathy?" 2.

22. Kidd and Castano, "Reading Literary Fiction Improves Theory of Mind," 1.

23. Bal and Veltkamp, "How Does Fiction Reading Influence Empathy?" 2.

24. Lamm and Majdandzic, "The Role of Shared Neural Activations, Mirror Neurons, and Morality in Empathy," 21.

25. Jordan et al., "Are Empathy and Concern Psychologically Distinct?" 1115.

26. Jordan et al., "Are Empathy and Concern Psychologically Distinct?" 1114.

27. Lamm and Majdandzic, "The Role of Shared Neural Activations, Mirror Neurons, and Morality in Empathy," 20.

28. Jordan et al., "Are Empathy and Concern Psychologically Distinct?" 1115.

29. Thomas Nagel, "What Is It Like to Be a Bat?" *Philosophical Review* LXXXIII, no. 4 (October 1974): 435–50. Accessed at http://members.aol.com/NeoNoetics/Nagel_Bat.html.

30. Lamm and Majdandzic, "The Role of Shared Neural Activations, Mirror Neurons, and Morality in Empathy," 16.

31. See, among others, Nussbaum's *Love's Knowledge*; David Novitz's *Knowledge, Fiction, Imagination* (Philadelphia: Temple University Press, 1987); Jenefer Robinson's "L'Educational Sentimentale," *Australian Journal of Philosophy* 73, no. 2 (1995): 212–26; and Susan Feagin's *Reading with Feeling* (Ithaca, NY: Cornell University Press, 1996).

32. Caracciolo and Van Duuren, "Changed by Literature?" 530.

33. Kidd and Castano, "Reading Literary Fiction Improves Theory of Mind," 1.

34. Belluck, "For Better Social Skills, Scientists Recommend a Little Chekhov," para. 15.

35. Kidd and Castano, "Reading Literary Fiction Improves Theory of Mind," 3.

36. Bal and Veltkamp, "How Does Fiction Reading Influence Empathy?" 2.

37. Claire Hooker, "Understanding Empathy: Why Phenomenology and Hermeneutics Can Help Medical Education and Practice," *Medical Health Care and Philosophy* 18 (2015): 541–52. DOI: 10.1007/s11019-015-9631-z.

10. HEARING WHOS AND MINDING OTHERS

1. Friedrich Schiller, *Sämtliche Werke* (Complete Works), ed. Gerhard Fricke and Herbert G. Göpfert (Munich: Hanser, 1962), 299. Translated by Janelle Pötzsch.

2. Immanel Kant, "Groundwork to the Metaphysics of Morals," in *Immanuel Kant: Practical Philosophy*, ed. Mary J. Gregor (Cambridge: Cambridge University Press, 2006), 94.

3. "Ethik ist in Wahrheit die leichteste aller Wissenschaften," see Arthur Schopenhauer, *Preisschrift über die Grundlage der Moral* (Prize Essay on the Basis of Morality), ed. Hans Ebeling (Hamburg: Meiner, 1979), 110. Translated by Janelle Pötzsch.

4. "[D]enn zu dieser [Menschenliebe, J.P.] ist der Anlaß meistens anschaulich und redet daher unmittelbar zum Mitleid, für welches die Weiber entschieden leichter empfänglich sind," Schopenhauer, *Prize Essay*, 112f. Translated by Janelle Pötzsch.

5. Carol Gilligan, *In a Different Voice: Psychological Theory and Women's Development* (Cambridge, MA: Harvard University Press, 1982).

6. Virginia Held, "The Ethics of Care," in *The Oxford Handbook of Ethical Theory*, ed. David Copp (Oxford: Oxford University Press, 2006), 537–66, 538.

7. Cf. Berenice Fisher and Joan Tronto, "Toward a Feminist Theory of Caring," in *Circles of Care*, ed. E. Abel and M. Nelson (Albany: State University of New York Press, 1990), 35–62.

8. Nel Noddings, *Caring: A Feminine Approach to Ethics and Moral Education* (Berkeley: University of California Press, 1984).

9. Michael Slote, *The Ethics of Care and Empathy* (New York: Routledge, 2007), 10.

10. Held, "Ethics of Care," 539.

11. Cf. Held, "Ethics of Care," 542.

12. Cf. Virginia Held, *Rights and Goods: Justifying Social Action* (New York: Free Press, 1984), chapter 5.

13. Held, "Ethics of Care," 543.

14. Cf. Noddings, *Caring*, 114, and the criticism in Claudia Card, "Caring and Evil," *Hypatia* 5, no. 1 (1990): 101–8.

15. Dietmut Bubeck, *Care, Gender, and Justice* (Oxford: Oxford University Press, 1995), 129.

16. To learn more about those troubling connections, check out the survey "Slavery Footprint" (http://www.slaveryfootprint.org). See "How many slaves work for you?"

17. In a similar vein, political philosopher Martha C. Nussbaum argues that the humanities are indispensable for raising competent democratic citizens, see Nussbaum, *Not for Profit: Why Democracy Needs the Humanities* (Princeton, NJ: Princeton University Press, 2010).

18. Held, "Ethics of Care," 544.

I I. NO KIND OF SNEETCH IS BEST

1. Søren Kierkegaard, *Works of Love* (New York: Harper Torchbooks, 1962), 97.

2. Po Bronson and Ashely Merryman, *Nurture Shock* (New York: Hachette Book Group, 2009).

3. You can see many of these cartoons compiled in Richard H. Minear, *Dr. Seuss Goes to War* (New York: New Press, 1999).

4. Judith Morgan and Neil Morgan, *Dr. Seuss and Mr. Geisel: A Biography* (New York: Random House, 1995), 144–45.

5. Minear, *Dr. Seuss Goes to War*, 264.

6. Erich Fromm, *Man for Himself: An Inquiry into the Psychology of Ethics* (New York: Henry Holt, 1947).

7. Gordon Allport, "The Nature of Hatred," in *Hatred, Bigotry, and Prejudice*, ed. Robert M. Baird and Stuart E. Rosenbaum (Amherst, NY: Prometheus Books, 1999), 92.

8. See, for example, R. Carter and J. Helms, "Racial Discrimination and Harassment: Race-Based Traumatic Stress," paper presented at the American College of Forensic Examiners Conference, Orlando, Florida; and L. Karumanchery, "The Colour of Trauma: New Perspectives on Racism, Politics, and Resistance," *Dissertation Abstracts International Section A: Humanities and Social Sciences* 64 (4–A).

9. Allport, "The Nature of Hatred," 92.

10. Edward Wilson, "Evolutionary Morality and Xenophobia," in *Hatred, Bigotry, and Prejudice* (Amherst, NY: Prometheus Books, 1999), 163.

11. Wilson, "Evolutionary Morality and Xenophobia," 163.

12. Wilson, "Evolutionary Morality and Xenophobia," 163.

13. Allport, "The Nature of Hatred," 93.

14. David Livingstone Smith, *Less Than Human: Why We Demean, Enslave, and Exterminate Others* (New York: St. Martin's Press, 2011), 18–19.

15. Richard Delgado, "Words That Wound: A Tort Action for Racial Insults, Epithets, and Name-Calling," *Harvard Civil Rights-Civil Liberties Law Review* 17 (1982): 133–81, at 135–36.

16. Kristin Myers and Passion Williamson, "Race Talk: The Perpetuation of Racism through Private Discourse," *Race and Society* 4, no. 1 (2001): 3–26, at 11.

17. Nick Haslam, "Dehumanization: An Integrative Review," *Personality and Social Psychology Review* 10, no. 3 (2006): 252–64, at 255.

18. Allport, "The Nature of Hatred," 91–92.

19. Smith, *Less Than Human*, 16.

20. Smith, *Less Than Human*, 17.

21. Smith, *Less Than Human*, 15.

22. Ralph Ellison, *Invisible Man* (New York: Vintage Books, 1947), 29.

23. See Michelle Malkin, *In Defense of Internment: The Case for "Racial Profiling" in World War II and the War on Terror* (New York: Regnery Publishing, 2004).

24. Kierkegaard, *Works of Love*, 63.

25. Kierkegaard, *Works of Love*, 97.

26. Emmanuel Levinas, *Totality and Infinity: An Essay on the Exteriority* (Netherlands: Kluwer Academic Publishers, 1969), 66 and 198.

27. Minear, *Dr. Seuss Goes to War*, 263.

28. Kierkegaard, *Works of Love*, 37.

29. Levinas, *Totality and Infinity*, 201.

30. Minear, *Dr. Seuss Goes to War*, 121.

31. Elliot Aronson, "Causes of Prejudice," in *Hatred, Bigotry, and Prejudice* (Amherst, NY: Prometheus Books, 1999), 135.

32. Smith, *Less Than Human*, 11.

12. THE *OTHER* SNEETCHES

1. I have fond memories of taking graduate classes with John Portelli many years ago. In one class on democracy and education, John read *The Sneetches*, and then led a dialogue on the ideas and questions within the story. I always looked forward to John's classes, and without those experiences this chapter wouldn't exist.

2. Michel Foucault, *Discipline and Punish: The Birth of the Prison*, trans. Alan Sheridan (New York: Random House, 1977/1995), 184.

3. The story was originally published in the July 1953 issue of *Redbook*. It was included in a collection in 1961 and then adapted as a cartoon for the 1973 special *Dr. Seuss on the Loose: The Sneetches, The Zax, Green Eggs and Ham*.

4. See Jonathan Cott, *Pipers at the Gates of Dawn: The Wisdom of Children's Literature* (New York: Random House, 1983). See also Thomas Fensch, *Of Sneetches and Whos and the Good Dr. Seuss: Essays on the Writings and Life of Theodor Geisel* (Jefferson, NC: McFarland, 1997/2005).

5. Martha Minow, *Making All the Difference: Inclusion, Exclusion, and American Law* (Ithaca, NY: Cornell University Press, 1990), 3–4.

6. To read about the hidden curriculum, see Henry A. Giroux, *Theory and Resistance in Education: Towards a Pedagogy for the Opposition*, revised and expanded edition (Westport, CT: Bergin & Garvey, 2001), 42–71.

7. To read about Bourdieu's view of social-cultural capital, see, Pierre Bourdieu, "The Forms of Capital" (241–58), in *Handbook of Theory and Research for Sociology in Education*, ed. John G. Richardson (New York: Greenwood, 1985). Bourdieu's work has been debated and interpreted in a variety of ways over the years. An interesting discussion on social-cultural capital theory may be found in a paper by Alejandro Portes, "Social Capital: Its Origins and Applications in Modern Society," *Annual Review of Sociology* 24 (1998): 1–24.

8. Giroux, *Theory and Resistance in Education*, 39.

9. The Toronto District School Board (TDSB), for instance, has developed documents outlining an *Equity Foundation Statement, Human Rights Policy and Procedures*, as well as *Guidelines and Procedures for Religious Accommodations*. These documents may be found by visiting the TDSB website at http://www.tdsb.on.ca/HighSchool/Equityinclusion/Guidelinespolicies.aspx. A newspaper article on the topic of religious accommodations and exemptions appeared in Toronto's *Globe and Mail* at the start of the 2016 school year. See Caroline Alphonso, "Toronto-Area Schools to Allow Religion-Based Class Exemptions," *Globe and Mail*, September 6, 2016. The article may be found on the newspaper's website: https://www.theglobeandmail.com/news/national/education/toronto-schools-to-allow-religion-based-class-exemptions/article31731974/. In a matter of days, the article accumulated nearly two hundred comments from readers, many of whom were clearly angry. A perusal of those comments indicates that some champion conformity and vehemently disagree with the notion of making accommodations for families with differing faith customs. So, while some believe that accommodations/exemptions should not be made, others feel that providing them is a viable solution. A third view holds that fuelling a need for accommodations is problematic because it perpetuates a system with a dominant center point and social othering.

10. See Michael Warner, *The Trouble with Normal: Sex, Politics, and the Ethics of Queer Life* (Cambridge, MA: Harvard University Press, 1999/2000).

11. Paulo Freire discusses these ideas in his classic work *Pedagogy of the Oppressed*, trans. Donaldo Macedo (New York: Bloomsbury, 1970/2000). To read about *banking education*, see 72–86; for *problem posing*, see 79–86; and to peruse Freire's view of *dialogue*, see 87–96.

12. There are a rich variety of books that delve into issues of discrimination in the United States and Canada, and I will list a few here. For older works, see Samuel Bowles and Herbert Gintis, *Schooling in Capitalist America: Educational Reform and the Contradictions of Economic Life* (New York: Basic Books, 1976), as well as bell hooks, *Teaching to Transgress: Education as the Practice of Freedom* (New York: Routledge, 1994). See also Gail Collins, *America's Women: 400 Years of Dolls, Drudges, Helpmates, and Heroines* (New York: HarperCollins, 2003). For more recent texts, see Michelle Alexander, *The New Jim Crow: Mass Incarceration in the Age of Colorblindness* (New York: New Press, 2010), as well as Eduardo Bonilla-Silva, *Racism without Racists: Color-Blind Racism and the Persistence of Racial Inequality in America* (Lanham, MD: Rowman & Littlefield, 2013). See also Ira Robinson, *A History of Antisemitism in Canada* (Waterloo: Wilfred Laurier University Press, 2015), as well as Truth and Reconciliation Commission of Canada, *Canada's Residential Schools: Missing Children and Unmarked Burials: The Final Report of the Truth and Reconciliation Commission of Canada, Volume 4* (McGill-Queen's Native and Northern Series) (Montreal: McGill-Queen's University Press, 2015).

13. See Freire, *Pedagogy of the Oppressed*. See also Mary Ellen Stratthaus, "Flaw in the Jewel: Housing Discrimination against Jews in La Jolla, California," *American Jewish Quarterly* 84, no. 3 (1996): 189–219.

14. Freire, *Pedagogy of the Oppressed*; Stratthaus, "Flaw in the Jewel."

13. OH, THE MISTAKES YOU'LL MAKE WHEN YOU'RE FREE

1. F. A. Hayek, *The Constitution of Liberty* (Chicago: University of Chicago Press, 2011), 81.

2. Hayek, *The Constitution of Liberty*, 79.

3. Hayek, *The Constitution of Liberty*, 199.

4. Hayek, *The Constitution of Liberty*, 200.

5. Hayek, *The Constitution of Liberty*, 71.

6. Hayek, *The Constitution of Liberty*, 202.

7. Hayek, *The Constitution of Liberty*, 203.

8. Hayek, *The Constitution of Liberty*, 203.

9. Hayek, *The Constitution of Liberty*, 204.

10. Hayek, *The Constitution of Liberty*, 200.

11. F. A. Hayek, *The Road to Serfdom: Texts and Documents*, the definitive edition (Chicago: University of Chicago Press, 2007), 134ff.

12. Hayek, *The Constitution of Liberty*, 226.

13. Hayek, *The Constitution of Liberty*, 207.

14. Hayek, *The Constitution of Liberty*, 150.

15. Hayek, *The Constitution of Liberty*, 148ff.

16. Hayek, *The Constitution of Liberty*, 60.

17. Hayek, *The Constitution of Liberty*, 204.

18. Puns are an acquired taste. Enjoy!

19. Hayek, *The Constitution of Liberty*, 341.

20. Hayek, *The Constitution of Liberty*, 151.

21. Hayek, *The Constitution of Liberty*, 149–50.

22. Hayek, *The Road to Serfdom*, 110.

23. Hayek, *The Constitution of Liberty*, 193.

24. Hayek, *The Constitution of Liberty*, 151.

25. Hayek, *The Constitution of Liberty*, 193.

26. Hayek, *The Constitution of Liberty*, 195.

27. Thomas Jefferson, *Notes on the State of Virginia*.

28. Hayek, *The Constitution of Liberty*, 214.

29. Hayek, *The Constitution of Liberty*, 225.

30. Hayek, *The Constitution of Liberty*, 221.

31. Hayek, *The Constitution of Liberty*, 223.

32. Hayek, *The Constitution of Liberty*, 173.

33. Hayek, *The Constitution of Liberty*, 167.

34. Hayek, *The Constitution of Liberty*, 167.

35. Hayek, *The Constitution of Liberty*, 323.

36. Hayek, *The Constitution of Liberty*, 71.

37. Hayek, *The Constitution of Liberty*, 87.

38. Hayek, *The Constitution of Liberty*, 208n14.

39. Hayek, *The Constitution of Liberty*, 78.

40. Hayek, *The Constitution of Liberty*, 74.

41. Hayek, *The Constitution of Liberty*, 75, quoting L. White.

42. F. A. Hayek, "The Uses of Knowledge in Society," *American Economic Review* XXXV, no. 4 (1945): 522.

43. Hayek, *The Road to Serfdom*, 100ff.

44. Hayek, *The Road to Serfdom*, 102.

45. Hayek, *The Constitution of Liberty*, 80.

14. STATE POWER AND INDIVIDUAL
RIGHTS IN DR. SEUSS

1. John Locke, *Second Treatise of Government*, ed. C. B Macpherson (Indianapolis: Hackett, 1980), 14.

2. John Locke, *Two Treatises of Government*, ed. Peter Laslett (Cambridge: Cambridge University Press, 1960).

3. Thomas Jefferson, *Declaration of Independence* (1776).

4. Plato, *Statesman*, trans. Christopher Rowe (Indianapolis: Hackett, 1999).

5. See, e.g., David Ricardo, *On the Principles of Political Economy and Taxation*, in *The Works and Correspondence of David Ricardo*, ed. Piero Sraffa and M. H. Dobb (Cambridge: Cambridge University Press, 1951–1973).

6. Thomas Hobbes, *Leviathan*, ed. Richard Tuck (Cambridge: Cambridge University Press, 1991).

7. I discuss this at length in "Thidwick the Big-Hearted Bearer of Property Rights" in *Dr. Seuss and Philosophy*, ed. Jacob M. Held (Lanham, MD: Rowman & Littlefield, 2011), 159–65.

15. THE FAILURES OF KINGS DERWIN
AND YERTLE

1. Joseph Raz, *The Authority of Law: Essays on Law and Morality*, second edition (Oxford: Oxford University Press, 2009), 7.

2. Raz, *The Authority of Law*, 12.

3. See Raz, *The Authority of Law*, 52.

4. John Rawls, *A Theory of Justice*, revised edition (Cambridge, MA: Belknap Press, 1999), 207.

5. Rawls, *A Theory of Justice*, 211.

6. John Finnis, *Natural Law & Natural Rights*, second edition (Oxford: Oxford University Press, 2011), 250.

7. Finnis, *Natural Law & Natural Rights*, 263.

8. F. A. Hayek, *The Constitution of Liberty*, the definitive edition, ed. Ronald Hamowy (Chicago: University of Chicago Press, 2011), 288.

9. Raz, *The Authority of Law*, 214.

10. Finnis, *Natural Law & Natural Rights*, 273.

11. John Gardner, *Law as Leap of Faith: Essays on Law in General* (Oxford: Oxford University Press, 2012), 213.

12. H. L. A. Hart as quoted in Gardner, *Law as Leap of Faith: Essays on Law in General*, 231.

13. Finnis, *Natural Law & Natural Rights*, 270–71.

14. For the full account, see Lon L. Fuller, *The Morality of Law*, revised edition (New Haven, CT: Yale University Press, 1969), chapter 2.

15. Fuller, *The Morality of Law*, 39.

16. Gardner, *Law as Leap of Faith: Essays on Law in General*, 215.

17. Hayek, *The Constitution of Liberty*, 310.

18. See Gardner, *Law as Leap of Faith: Essays on Law in General*, chapter 2.

19. Cicero, "On the Laws," in *On the Commonwealth and On the Laws*, ed. James E. G. Zetzel (Cambridge: Cambridge University Press, 2008), 120–21.

20. I'm wary of using classifications such as these since they often obscure subtleties among thinkers and within traditions. But they can be useful shorthand for quickly orienting a reader.

21. Saint Thomas Aquinas, "Selections from *On Law, Morality, and Politics*," in *Philosophy of Law*, eighth edition, ed. Joel Feinberg and Jules Coleman (Belmont, CA: Thomson Wadsworth, 2008), 10. Aquinas covers this topic in *Summa Theologiae* I–II. Q 90. A 2.

22. Finnis, *Natural Law & Natural Rights*, 69–70.

23. Finnis, *Natural Law & Natural Rights*, 73.

24. Consider for a moment the practice of judicial review and the power/authority of the Supreme Court of the United States.

25. Finnis, *Natural Law & Natural Rights*, 155.

26. Finnis, *Natural Law & Natural Rights*, 351.

27. Fuller, *The Morality of Law*, 96.

28. Fuller, *The Morality of Law*, 162.

29. Fuller, *The Morality of Law*, 205.

30. Noted in both Finnis, *Natural Law & Natural Rights*, chapter 7, and Fuller, *The Morality of Law*, chapter 1.

31. Finnis, *Natural Law & Natural Rights*, 351.

32. See David A. Reidy, *On the Philosophy of Law* (Belmont, CA: Thomson Wadsworth, 2007), chapter 6.

33. Finnis, *Natural Law & Natural Rights*, 363.

34. For a discussion see Finnis, *Natural Law & Natural Rights*, chapter 12, section 2.

35. William of Ockham, "An Excerpt from *Eight Questions on The Power of the Pope*," in *Readings in Medieval Philosophy*, ed. Andrew B. Schoedinger (Oxford: Oxford University Press, 1996), 420–21.

36. Finnis, *Natural Law & Natural Rights*, 359–60.

37. See John Rawls, "The Justification of Civil Disobedience," in *Collected Papers*, ed. Samuel Freeman (Cambridge, MA: Harvard University Press, 1999), 183–86.

16. THE SNEETCHES, THE ZAX, AND
TOO MANY DAVES

1. Iris Marion Young, *Justice and the Politics of Difference* (Princeton, NJ: Princeton University Press, 1990), 227.

2. Young, *Justice and the Politics of Difference*, 48.

3. Iris Marion Young, *Inclusion and Democracy* (Oxford: Oxford University Press, 2000), 114.

4. Young, *Justice and the Politics of Difference*, 106.

5. Young, *Inclusion and Democracy*, 119.

6. Young, *Inclusion and Democracy*, 57.

7. Young, *Inclusion and Democracy*, 61.

8. Young, *Inclusion and Democracy*, 69.

9. Young, *Inclusion and Democracy*, 76.

10. Young, *Inclusion and Democracy*, 117.

17. YOOKS AND ZOOKS

1. Cited in *The Ethics of War: Classic and Contemporary Readings*, ed. Gregory M. Reichberg, Henrik Syse, and Endre Begby (Malden, MA: Wiley Publishing, 2006), 339.

2. David Luban, "War Crimes: The Law of Hell," in *War: Essays in Political Philosophy*, ed. Larry May with the assistance of Emily Crookston (Cambridge: Cambridge University Press, 2008), 268.

3. Michael Walzer, *Just and Unjust Wars: A Moral Argument with Historical Illustrations*, fourth edition (New York: Basic Books, 2006), 20.

4. See David Fisher, *Morality and War: Can War Be Just in the Twenty-first Century?* (Oxford: Oxford University Press, 2011), 27.

5. James P. Sterba, "Reconciling Pacifists and Just War Theorists," in *Doing Ethics: Moral Reasoning and Contemporary Issues*, second edition, ed. Lewis Vaughn (New York: W. W. Norton, 2010), 629.

6. For a good, succinct, standard account of *jus ad bellum* and *jus in bello*, see William V. O'Brien, *The Conduct of Just and Limited War* (New York: Praeger, 1981), especially chapters 2 and 3.

7. For a good account of defensive wars, see Gregory M. Reichberg, "Jus ad Bellum," in *War: Essays in Political Philosophy*, ed. Larry May with the assistance of Emily Crookston (Cambridge: Cambridge University Press, 2008).

8. Nicholas Rengger, "Jus in Bello in Historical and Philosophical Perspective," in *War: Essays in Political Philosophy*, ed. Larry May with the assistance of Emily Crookston (Cambridge: Cambridge University Press, 2008), 38.

9. In response to modern, asymmetrical conflicts, such as the "war on terror," some now talk about degrees of participation and liability instead of simple classifications like combatant and noncombatant. See Michael Gross, *Moral Dilemmas of Modern War: Torture, Assassination, and Blackmail in an Age of Asymmetric Conflict* (Cambridge: Cambridge University Press, 2010), especially chapter 2.

10. This idea is known in the literature as the principle or doctrine of double effect.

11. Fisher, *Morality and War*, 87.

12. Walzer, *Just and Unjust Wars*, 276.

13. Larry May, "The Principle of Just Cause," in *War: Essays in Political Philosophy*, ed. Larry May with the assistance of Emily Crookston (Cambridge: Cambridge University Press, 2008), 61.

14. May, "The Principle of Just Cause," in *War: Essays in Political Philosophy*, 65.

15. Sarcasm doesn't always translate well on a page. I'm being sarcastic.

16. Douglas P. Lackey, "Pacifism," in *Social and Personal Ethics*, seventh edition, ed. William H. Shaw (Boston: Wadsworth, Cengage Learning, 2011), 322.

17. Lackey, "Pacifism," 322.

18. For a discussion of this idea, see Larry May, "The Principle of Just Cause," in *War: Essays in Political Philosophy*.

19. For an expression of this idea, see Thomas Hurka, "Proportionality and Necessity," in *War: Essays in Political Philosophy*, ed. Larry May with the assistance of Emily Crookston (Cambridge: Cambridge University Press, 2008), 142.

20. Hurka, "Proportionality and Necessity," 143.

EPILOGUE

1. See *Dr. Seuss and Philosophy: Oh, the Thinks You Can Think!* ed. Jacob M. Held (Lanham, MD: Rowman & Littlefield, 2011).

2. This is a reference to Saint Anselm, who famously said, "I do not understand so that I may believe; but I believe so that I may understand," a position described as "faith seeking understanding." See Anselm of Canterbury, "Proslogion," in *The Major Works including Monologion, Proslogion, and Why God*

Became Man, eds. Brian Davies and G. R. Evans (Oxford: Oxford University Press, 2008), 87.

3. This is a reference to Kant's famous three questions: What can I know? What ought I to do? What may I hope? See his *Critique of Pure Reason*, The Canon of Pure Reason, Section 2 (A805/B833).

4. In the interest of transparency, I should mention that this rhyme was inspired after my last viewing of Monty Python's *The Meaning of Life*, where at the end of the film the meaning of life is declared to be the following: "Try and be nice to people, avoid eating fat, read a good book every now and then, get some walking in, and try and live together in peace and harmony with people of all creeds and nations."

INDEX

AUTHOR BIOGRAPHIES

Elizabeth Butterfield is an associate professor of philosophy at Georgia Southern University, where she teaches courses in existentialism, ethics, and philosophy of religion. Lately she's particularly interested in the philosophy of happiness. She has contributed to other volumes on pop culture and philosophy as well, with articles on James Bond, *The Devil's Advocate*, and Roald Dahl's *Matilda*. Along with her husband and two children, Elizabeth makes a point of laughing a great Sisyphean laugh every chance she gets, and in this way she remembers to be grateful that she doesn't have troubles—well, very few.

Cam Cobb is an associate professor in the faculty of education at the University of Windsor. His research focuses on such topics as social justice in special education, narrative pedagogy, and coteaching in adult learning contexts. Over the past few years his work has been published in a variety of journals, including *Per la Filosofia, Cinema: Journal of Philosophy and the Moving Image, F. Scott Fitzgerald Review, British Journal of Special Education, International Journal of Bilingual Education and Bilingualism*, and *International Journal of Inclusive Education.* His book, *What's Big and Purple and Lives in the Ocean? The Moby Grape Story*, will be published in April 2018.

Timothy M. Dale is an associate professor of political science at the University of Wisconsin–La Crosse and chair of the department of political science and public administration. He teaches in the area of political philosophy, and his research interests include democratic theory, civil society, and the scholarship of teaching and learning. He is coeditor of several books on popular culture and politics, including *Jim Henson and Philosophy: Imagination and the Magic of Mayhem* (2015), *Homer Simpson Ponders Politics: Popular Culture as Political Theory* (2013), and *Homer Simpson Marches on Washington: Dissent through American Popular Culture* (2010), and he is coauthor of *Political Thinking, Political Theory, and Civil Society* (2009).

Joseph J. Foy is an associate professor of political science and serves as the associate vice chancellor for academic affairs for the University of Wisconsin Colleges. He is the editor of *Homer Simpson Goes to Washington: American Politics through Popular Culture* and *SpongeBob SquarePants and Philosophy*. Foy is also the coeditor of *Homer Simpson Marches on Washington: Dissent through American Popular Culture*, *Homer Simpson Ponders Politics: Popular Culture as Political Theory*, and *Jim Henson and Philosophy*.

Kevin Guilfoy is associate professor of philosophy at Carroll University in Wisconsin, where he is director of the philosophy, politics, and economics program. He has written several articles on medieval philosophy, ethics, and philosophy in popular culture.

Jacob M. Held is associate professor of philosophy at the University of Central Arkansas in Conway. His other edited books include *Dr. Seuss and Philosophy: Oh, the Thinks You Can Think!* (2011), *Roald Dahl and Philosophy: A Little Nonsense Now and Then* (2014), and *Stephen King and Philosophy* (2016). In addition, he's coeditor of *The Philosophy of Pornography: Contemporary Perspectives* (2014) and *The Philosophy of Sex: Contemporary Readings*, seventh edition (2017), all with Rowman & Littlefield. Since finishing this book, he's decided to only write philosophy in rhyme.

Glenn Jellenik is assistant professor of English at the University of Central Arkansas. His research explores textual adaptation from a historical perspective—specifically, long eighteenth-century adaptation and the productive intersections and tensions that exist between literature and mass culture. He spends most days encouraging his students (and himself!) to push on beyond zebra.

Sharon Kaye is a professor of philosophy at John Carroll University in Cleveland, Ohio. She loves to write, she loves to race, and she found Jake in the Waiting Place.

Dennis Knepp and his wife, Jennifer McCarthy, raised two kids on a steady diet of Dr. Seuss in the desert of Moses Lake, Washington, where it is rarely too rainy to go out to play. Dennis teaches philosophy and religious studies, and Jen teaches French and German at Big Bend Community College. Family favorites include *Hop on Pop*, *There's a Wocket in My Pocket*, and the tongue twisters of *Fox in Socks*. Dennis has adopted as a family motto the line from *The Cat in the Hat*: "It is fun to have fun, but you have to know how!"

Robert Main is assistant professor of philosophy at West Chester University of Pennsylvania, where he is frequently mistaken for a student. He has written and presented on American pragmatism, aesthetics, and the philosophy of language. He regularly teaches classes on the intersection of philosophy and pop culture, including *The Simpsons*, *South Park*, and *Watchmen*. His current research explores the philosophy of culture and counterculture, focusing on thinkers who, like Dr. Seuss, are "subversive as hell."

Bertha Alvarez Manninen received her PhD from Purdue University and is currently associate professor of philosophy at Arizona State University's West campus. Her main areas of research and teaching are applied ethics, philosophy of religion, social/political philosophy, and philosophy and film. During her spare time with her husband, Tuomas, she is the parent of two little girls who love to read Dr. Seuss books, though they won't try green eggs and ham. She also has a dog named Max, who does not help her steal Christmas, and Potter, who loves all persons no matter how small. Additionally, she shares her house with five cats, none of whom wear hats and all of whom cause havoc.

Jennifer L. McMahon is professor of philosophy and English at East Central University in Ada, Oklahoma. She has expertise in existentialism, aesthetics, and comparative philosophy. She has published numerous essays on philosophy and popular culture, most recently in *The Philosophy of Documentary Film* (2016), *Buddhism and American Cinema* (2014), and *Death in Classic and Contemporary Cinema* (2013). She has edited collections including *The Philosophy of Tim Burton* (2014) and *The Philosophy of the Western* (2010).

> When it comes to Seuss stories McMahon has long been a fan,
> Of Sneetches on beaches and green pants that ran,
> She reexperienced Seuss's works when her children were small,
> And now celebrates another return to their call,
> To these works that have taught us without us knowing,
> And kept each generation of their readers growing.

Matthew Pierlott is associate professor of philosophy at West Chester University of Pennsylvania. He largely avoids having to face the big questions about the meaning of life by teaching classes that force his students to face them. He has contributed to other philosophy and pop culture editions, including *Dr. Seuss and Philosophy: Oh, the Thinks You Can Think!* and *Stephen Colbert and Philosophy: I Am Philosophy (And So Can You!)*. His areas of teaching and research include ethical theory and applied ethics, the intersection of science and religion, social justice, and other fun stuff. He plays too many games and eats too much chocolate. His heart grows three sizes when he thinks about his wife and three children. And they all love their dog, Ziggy, a real zigzag zoomer when she is not a lazy mayzie.

Janelle Pötzsch is a researcher at the Institute for Advanced Studies in the Humanities in Essen, Germany, where she works on the ethics of immigration. She earned a PhD in philosophy at Ruhr-Universität Bochum, Germany, on the ethics of sweatshop labor. Apart from business ethics and political philosophy, she takes a keen interest in the history of ideas and likes to explore philosophical themes in literature, which is why she has contributed papers to *Jane Austen and Philosophy* and *Frankenstein and Philosophy*, among others; she also recently edited *Jonathan Swift and Philosophy*. After pondering the pros and cons of keeping a Houyhnhnm, she sometimes wonders whether an elephant-bird wouldn't make a better pet.

Benjamin Rider is associate professor of philosophy at the University of Central Arkansas, specializing in ancient philosophies of life. He practices Stoic techniques in order to accept and take a better perspective on the deficiencies in his tennis game.

Aeon J. Skoble is professor of philosophy and co-coordinator of the program in philosophy, politics, and economics at Bridgewater State University. Skoble is the author of *Deleting the State: An Argument about Government* (2008), editor of *Reading Rasmussen and Den Uyl: Critical Essays on Norms of Liberty* (2008), and coeditor of *Political Philosophy: Essential Selections* (1999) and *Reality, Reason, and Rights* (2011). In addition, he has frequently lectured and written for the Institute for Humane Studies and the Foundation for Economic Education, and he is a senior fellow at the Fraser Institute. His main research includes theories of rights, the nature and justification of authority, and virtue ethics. He also writes widely on the intersection of philosophy and popular culture, among other things coediting the best-selling *The Simpsons and Philosophy* (2000) and three other books on film and television.